DAVI... .... published to great acclaim in 1...., and ... ., ...ness of Sisters, published in 2002, is a groundbreaking work of romantic biography. In 2005 the highly acclaimed *Scott of the Antarctic* was ....hed, followed by *Men of War*, a collection of nineteenth-........ry naval biographies, in 2009. *Empires of the Dead* was .....listed for the 2013 Samuel Johnson Prize for Non-Fiction. Cr... ...e lives in north-west Scotland.

F.... m the reviews of *Empires of the Dead*:

.....tstanding . . . Crane shows how extraordinary a physical, ...tical and administrative feat it was to bury or commemorate ....e than half a million dead in individual graves. And he reveals ....this Herculean task was accomplished largely due to the ....rts of one man: Fabian Ware'   *Independent on Sunday*

....vid and thought-provoking . . . David Crane writes exuberant, ...al prose. He is acutely aware of the ambiguities and nuances ....ounding the issues of war and death, and that makes this a ....and troubling book, as well as a riveting read' *Literary Review*

....trikes at the heart of the current debate about what we are ....memorating, celebrating or deploring in the flood of cere-mo....y, debate and literary rows about the meaning of the First World War today. Crane succeeds in doing so by looking at the achievement of Fabian Ware, who to this day is almost an ....nown in the pantheon of heroes or villains associated with th.. conflict'   *Evening Standard*

Also by David Crane

*Men of War: The Changing Face of Heroism
in the 19th Century Navy*

*Scott of the Antarctic: A Life of Courage and Tragedy
in the Extreme South*

*The Kindness of Sisters: Annabella Milbanke and the Destruction
of the Byrons*

Lord Byron's Jackal: A Life of Trelawny

EMPIRES OF THE DEAD

*How One Man's Vision Led to the
Creation of WWI's War Graves*

DAVID CRANE

WILLIAM
COLLINS

William Collins
An imprint of HarperCollins*Publishers*
77–85 Fulham Palace Road
Hammersmith, London W6 8JB
WilliamCollinsBooks.com

This William Collins paperback edition published 2014

1

First published in Great Britain by William Collins in 2013

Copyright © David Crane 2013

David Crane asserts the moral right to
be identified as the author of this work

A catalogue record for this book
is available from the British Library

ISBN 978-0-00-745668-0

Set in Adobe Garamond by Palimpsest Book Production Limited,
Falkirk, Stirlingshire

Printed and bound in Great Britain by
Clays Ltd, St Ives plc

MIX
Paper from
responsible sources
FSC™ C007454

FSC™ is a non-profit international organisation established to promote
the responsible management of the world's forests. Products carrying the
FSC label are independently certified to assure consumers that they come
from forests that are managed to meet the social, economic and
ecological needs of present and future generations,
and other controlled sources.

Find out more about HarperCollins and the environment at
www.harpercollins.co.uk/green

CONTENTS

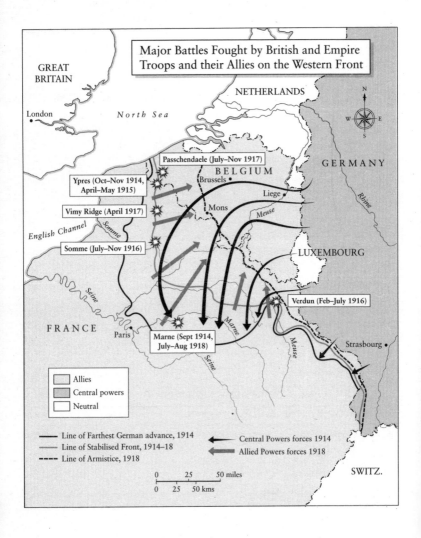

Major Battles Fought by British and Empire Troops and their Allies on the Western Front

GREAT BRITAIN

London

North Sea

NETHERLANDS

GERMANY

Passchendaele (July–Nov 1917)

Ypres (Oct–Nov 1914, April–May 1915)

BELGIUM

Brussels

Liege

Vimy Ridge (April 1917)

Mons

Meuse

English Channel

Somme

Somme (July–Nov 1916)

LUXEMBOURG

Seine

Verdun (Feb–July 1916)

FRANCE

Paris

Marne

Marne (Sept 1914, July–Aug 1918)

Seine

Meuse

Strasbourg

Allies
Central powers
Neutral

——— Line of Farthest German advance, 1914
——— Line of Stabilised Front, 1914–18
-------- Line of Armistice, 1918

◀ Central Powers forces 1914
◀ Allied Powers forces 1918

0   25   50 miles
0   25   50 kms

SWITZ.

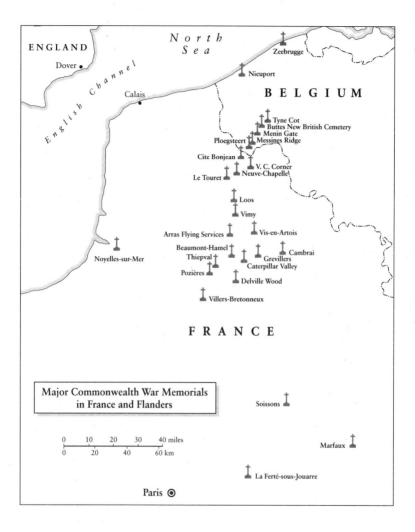

ENGLAND

*North
Sea*

Dover ●

English Channel

Calais ●

BELGIUM

Zeebrugge

Nieuport

Tyne Cot
Buttes New British Cemetery
Menin Gate
Ploegsteert   Messines Ridge
Cite Bonjean

V. C. Corner
Neuve-Chapelle
Le Touret

Loos

Vimy

Arras Flying Services   Vis-en-Artois

Beaumont-Hamel   Cambrai
Thiepval   Grevillers
Caterpillar Valley
Pozières
Delville Wood

Noyelles-sur-Mer

Villers-Bretonneux

F R A N C E

Major Commonwealth War Memorials
in France and Flanders

| 0 | 10 | 20 | 30 | 40 miles |
| 0 | 20 | 40 | | 60 km |

Soissons

Marfaux

La Ferté-sous-Jouarre

Paris ◉

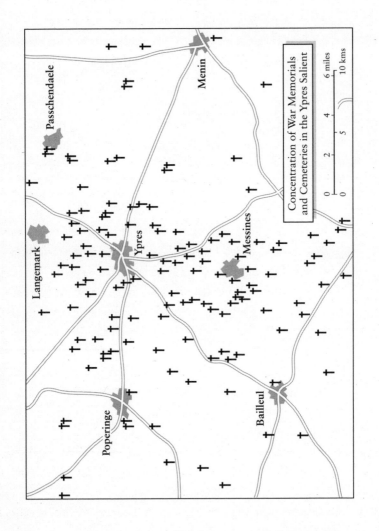

Concentration of War Memorials
and Cemeteries in the Ypres Salient

Passchendaele

Menin

Langemark

Ypres

Messines

Poperinge

Bailleul

| 0 | | 2 | | 4 | | 6 miles |
| 0 | 5 | | | | 10 kms |

LIST OF ILLUSTRATIONS

7. Charles Holden by Francis Dodd, oil on canvas (© *The Art Workers' Guild Trustees Limited, London, UK / The Bridgeman Art Library*)

8. The main entrance to the Serre Road Cemetery, No. 2, France (© *Maurice Savage / Alamy*)

9. Serre Road Cemetery, No. 2, France (© *Maurice Savage / Alamy*)

10. Etaples Cemetery, France (*courtesy Honor Clerk*)

11. 'The Cemetery, Etaples, 1919' by Sir John Lavery, 1919, oil on canvas

12. The Thiepval Memorial to the Missing of the Somme, France, *c*.1935 (© *Hulton Archive / Getty Images*)

13. Stonemason hand-engraving a Canadian headstone destined for a cemetery in France (*courtesy Commonwealth War Graves Commission*)

14. Ypres, Belgium in ruins, 1919 (*Photo by W. L. King*)

15. 'Menin Gate at Midnight' by Will Longstaff, 1927, oil on canvas (*courtesy Australian War Memorial*)

16. Reginald Blomfield by James Jebusa Shannon, 1915, oil on canvas (*courtesy RIBA Library Drawings & Archives Collections*)

17. Inscription of names at the Menin Gate, Belgium (© *Tim Bekaert*)

18. Lone Pine Cemetery, Turkey (© *Universal Images Group / DeAgostini / Alamy*)

19. Funeral of a St John's Ambulance Brigade nursing sister, Annie Bain, at Etaples (© *Popperfoto / Getty Images*)

20. Headstone of nursing sister A. W. Bain (*courtesy Honor Clerk*)

21. 'Mourning Parents' sculpture by Käthe Kollwitz at Vladslo Cemetery, Germany (© *David Crossland / Alamy*)

22. Verdun Cemetery, France (© *Jean-Pol Grandmont*)

23. Tyne Cot Cemetery, Belgium (*Photograph by Brian Harris for the Commonwealth War Graves Commission © 2006*)

24. Funeral of the Unknown Warrior, 11 November 1920 (© *Topical Press Agency / Hulton Archive / Getty Images*)

25. A sketch of the proposed design for the Cenotaph with explanatory notes by Edwin Lutyens (© *The Artist's Estate; image © Imperial War Museum, Art.IWM ART 16377 3*)

26. Unveiling of the Cenotaph, 11 November 1920 (© *Imperial War Museum, Q 31513*)

27. 'The Resurrection of the Soldiers', wall painting at Sandham Memorial Chapel by Stanley Spencer, 1923–7 (© *The Estate of Stanley Spencer 2013. All rights reserved DACS; image © National Trust Photographic Library / A C Cooper / The Bridgeman Art Library*)

While every effort has been made to trace the owners of copyright material reproduced herein, the publishers would like to apologise for any omissions and would be pleased to incorporate missing acknowledgements in future editions.

PROLOGUE

They throw in Drummer Hodge, to rest
Uncoffined – just as found:
His landmark is a kopje-crest
That breaks the veldt around:
And foreign constellations west
Each night above his mound.

'Drummer Hodge', THOMAS HARDY

High on the north wall of Florence's Duomo can be seen one of the most arresting images of the early Italian Renaissance. Against a deep red background a knight sits on horseback, a spectral figure painted in a cadaverous *terra verde* that emerges out of the cathedral gloom like some menacing cross between the great equestrian bronze of Marcus Aurelius and Mozart's avenging Commendatore.

The fresco is the work of Paolo Uccello, and in it Renaissance and Middle Ages meet. The eyes are sightless, the lips drawn back, but astride his ghostly green charger – off-fore raised, neck curved in a gracefully submissive arc – Uccello's rider still grasps firmly on to his baton of earthly command. Here, simultaneously, is a celebration of life and *memento mori*, a portrait of power and dissolution, of individual glory and universal mortality, the creation of an age that understood war and death and had seen more than its fair share of both. Pride, fame, blood-guilt, atonement, hope, gratitude – all those complex feelings that lie behind every war memorial – they are all here, and so too is the universal fact of mortality that unites subject and viewer in one common fate. '*Ioannes Acutus Eques Britannicus*' reads the inscription beneath, '*Dux Aetatis Suae Cautissimus Et Rei Militaris Pertissimus Habitus Est*' – 'This is John Hawkwood, British knight, esteemed the most cautious and expert general of his age.'

It seems a perverse irony that the first – and for a very long time only – memorial raised on European soil to an English soldier by a grateful government is Florence's tribute to the great fourteenth-century mercenary and *diavolo incarnato*, Sir John Hawkwood. Over the centuries that followed Hawkwood's death, British armies fought and died across the length and breadth of the continent, and yet anyone walking Europe's battlefields now in search of some trace of their existence would have about as much chance of finding it as they would the snow off the boots of mythical Russian soldiers marching through the north of England in 1914.

A thin scattering of British graves across Europe does survive – three at Elvas in Portugal, another cluster on the rocky Atlantic-facing slopes above San Sebastián, three from 1813 in the mayoral garden at Biarritz, a few tablets preserved by Napoleon III from the Battle of Toulouse, Bayonne, a tiny clutch on the slopes of the Alma, sixteen in Brussels – but these are almost all the product of family or regimental piety and closer in their air of melancholy to forgotten pet cemeteries than to national monuments.[1]

These are virtually all officers' graves; the 'Die-hards' who fell where they stood at Albuera or the 'scum of the earth' who won Waterloo could never expect anything more than a rapidly dug pit and a mass burial. In the immediate aftermath of battle the danger of disease naturally dictated haste, and yet it is hard not to wonder at the failure of imagination or humanity that separated the age which built All Souls, Oxford in memory of the dead of the Hundred Years War, or raised a chantry chapel on the field of Shrewsbury from that which could sanction the post-battle horrors of Waterloo. 'The countrymen told us, that so great were the number of the slain, that it was impossible entirely to consume them,' wrote Charlotte Eaton, who had picked her way through the human skulls and fleshless hands jutting out of the earth of Waterloo a month after the battle. 'Pits had been dug, into which they had been thrown, but they were obliged to be raised far above the surface of the ground. These dreadful heaps were covered with piles of wood, which were set on fire, so that underneath the ashes lay numbers of human bodies unconsumed.'

---

1 In Brussels, there is a Waterloo Monument over the graves of fifteen officers and a warrant officer, but these bodies had been moved there from abandoned cemeteries, and it was unveiled seventy-five years after the battle. High on the ramparts above Corunna, the tomb of Sir John Moore also comes closer to expectations, but even this – the grave of the man who did as much as anyone to drag the British Army out of the morass of its late eighteenth-century condition – owed more to Spanish punctilio than it did to the gratitude of a parliament more interested in making politics of his death than honouring his memory in the field.

A complex interplay of social, cultural and religious factors divides the medieval mindset from Waterloo, but a simpler reason is that it took a long time for Britain to overcome a deep-rooted suspicion of its armies. In the course of the nineteenth century something like a rapprochement did occur, but for great tracts of its early modern history, Britain's European wars were widely seen as 'ministers' wars', or 'Hanover's wars', or 'Tory wars', and her armies either instruments of oppression or costly pawns in dynastic coalition struggles that had more to do with an imported monarchy's German interests than they had with those of a resentful John Bull.

It was not simply a matter of politics, though, because the drunk, the thief, the debtor, the gullible and the unemployed who stocked Britain's regiments between Cromwell's God-infused soldiers of Naseby and the citizen armies of the twentieth century, were not easy men to love. Dr Johnson might insist that every man thought the less of himself for not having been a soldier, but one would be hard pressed, as Charles Carrington who served his military apprenticeship in the trenches of the Western Front pointed out, to find much between Shakespeare's *Henry V* and Kipling that offered anything like a sympathetic vision of the common soldier.

The sense of alienation was largely mutual and if there were clearly men fired by patriotism – or at least a consistent contempt for foreigners that did just as well – the loyalties that made the British Army so formidable a fighting force were to friends, comrades, regiment and then, just sometimes, their officers. There was a good deal made in recruiting posters of the opportunities for glory in the service of the Queen or King, and yet when all is said, these were men – especially the Irish and Scots – fighting for a society that had found no room for them before they enlisted and from which, when they finished their service, they could expect nothing in return.

From the long perspective of the twenty-first century, when within living memory two world wars have forged a covenant of army and nation, it is hard to grasp how little the armies and great victories of the coalition Wars of Austrian or Spanish Succession, for example, belonged to the nation as a whole. In an age of battlefield tourism, those conflicts are probably now better known and recorded than they have ever been, but generations of British travellers and Grand Tourists, who would happily cross Europe to gaze upon the 'holy, haunted ground' of Marathon and Thermopylae, would no more have dreamed of visiting Ramillies or Malplaquet than the young Byron – the first major poet of modern warfare, after all – could bother to make the small detour from his Peninsula travels in 1808 to see where Vimeiro had just been fought and won by Wellington's men.

This lack of connection did not stop the Votes of Thanks in Parliament, the busts and statues in Westminster Abbey and St Paul's, the building of Blenheim Palace, the patriotic odes or the sporadic outbursts of national triumphalism, but there was no genuine sense of national identification. In the early phases of the struggle against Napoleon, the fear of invasion created something like a national consensus, and yet even Waterloo – the first British battlefield to become a shrine for tourists – was fought against a rainbow opposition of Whig, mercantile and radical opinion that left a great swathe of the country deeply resentful of the 'abuse' of British power in the service of a bloated Catholic despot like Louis XVIII.

In the age of the Peterloo Massacre and the 'Piccadilly Butchers' – that mini-ice age when the military were used as an instrument of civil power – it is not surprising that the old historic dislike of a standing army persisted, but Waterloo still represents a watershed. It is impossible to put a date to anything so gradual as a shift of public consciousness, and yet in the diaries and travel journals of English men and women in the years after 1815 it is possible to trace a change in that triangular relationship of government, army and people that begins with Waterloo and victory over Napoleon, and is still played out in the press over every defence cut or equipment deficiency that might threaten soldiers' lives overseas.

This healing process that began with Waterloo – and was finally, and permanently, sealed by the fighting courage and stoic heroism of the common soldier in the Crimea – was in its turn part of a wider social change that affected the Army as much as it did every other aspect of British life. The list of the dead and wounded in Wellington's Waterloo despatch might just as well have been torn out of Debrett's, but the heroes of the Crimea and Indian Mutiny were made of different stuff, men such as William Peel and Henry Havelock or Captain Hedley Vicars, who were closer in their high-minded earnestness and Bible-carrying piety to the new middle classes of England from which they sprang than to their Godless predecessors of Badajoz and San Sebastián.

This convergence of identities was important for changing attitudes to the Army, because it coincided with that growing sense of national prestige and providential 'destiny' that was to become such a feature of British attitudes during its imperial heyday. Since the time of the Reformation, a profoundly Protestant belief in a divinely appointed national 'election' had entered into the English psyche, and as the country emerged from the Napoleonic Wars as the world's pre-eminent power, this growing sense of predestined mission helped turn her armies from the tools of arbitrary government to place them and the Empire they were creating squarely in the vanguard of Christ's Second Coming.

Gone were the days when Byron could sneer that 'after Troy and Marathon' the field of Waterloo was 'not much'; gone the Lilliputian embarrassment of Hazlitt when he compared moderns and ancients; gone the sense that Benjamin West's painting of the death of General Wolfe was an act of blatant *lèse majesté*. For the eighteenth-century artist, the proper business of history painting might have been the classical past, but to West's successors of the nineteenth century the natural subject matter of art was not so much the doings of Regulus or Agrippina as the defence of the Coldstream colours at Sandbank Battery, or the Thin Red Line, or the bald-headed heroics of the Marquis of Granby.

Along with this burgeoning sense of pride went a deepening sense of responsibility to the country's army and the country's dead. 'Would it have been possible, think you, to have concealed and slurred over our failures?' demanded W. H. Russell, the great *Times* war correspondent who brought home the incompetence of the High Command in the Crimea to a British public demanding aristocratic heads; 'No: the very dead on Cathcart's Hill would be wronged as they lay mute in their bloody shrouds, and calumny and falsehood would insult that warrior race, which is not less than Roman, because it too has known a Trebisand and a Thrasymene.'

With the desolating Retreat from Kabul behind them, and the horrors of the Indian Mutiny only months ahead of them, Victorian England was getting used to extracting what comfort it could out of defeat. Here, however, is a note that would not have been heard even forty years earlier. Through the summer of 1815 there had certainly been collections and subscriptions the length of Britain for the widows and orphans of Waterloo, but the sense of responsibility and debt that Russell articulates, the recognition that the dead of the Crimea had their claim on the life of the nation was something very different in the relationship of Britain and her army.

It was one thing to talk like this, one thing for the Americans to hallow the soil of Gettysburg – it was American soil and American dead on both sides – but it was another to turn a distant piece of Russia or Turkey or any other bit of Europe into a little piece of England. At the end of the Crimean War in 1856 there had been 139 cemeteries of varying sizes scattered on the heights around Sevastopol and the Alma, but within twenty years this number had shrunk to eleven and then to one, as a hostile world of nomadic grave-robbers, winter frosts, earthquakes, vandals and grazing cattle took its random revenge on the men who had humiliated Mother Russia and reduced Sevastopol to ruins.

Perhaps the only surprise is not that there are so few surviving graves from Britain's eighteenth- and nineteenth-century European wars, but that there are any at all. For those who cheerfully suffered the miseries of a Crimean winter, the work of the British Army in the Crimea was manifestly Christ's work, but for all those countries that Britain fought against or even with, for Islamic Turkey or Orthodox Russia, for its Soviet successors who found themselves the custodians of Lord Raglan's viscera, or Spanish nationalists recalling the sack of San Sebastián, the graves of Britain's soldiers were not the sacred places of a burgeoning British mythology, but symbols of national humiliation, exploitation and desecration.

And then, out of nowhere, all that changed. In 1914 the number of surviving British war graves from Portugal to the Ionian Isles could be counted in their handfuls. Four years later they numbered in their hundreds of thousands. A war that had been fought on a hitherto unimaginable, industrial scale had been commemorated in kind. Something like a million British and Empire soldiers, sailors and airmen had been killed and on gravestones, memorials and monuments across the battlefields of the Western Front, Palestine, Mesopotamia, East Africa, Greece and Italy the task had begun of ensuring that their names would not be forgotten. 'Imagine them moving in one long continuous column, four abreast,' an early commentator at the Cenotaph Armistice Day service once said, giving graphic visual meaning to the sheer scale of the task that Britain had taken on,

as the head of that column reaches the Cenotaph the last four men would be at Durham. In Canada that column would stretch across the land from Quebec to Ottawa; in Australia from Melbourne to Canberra; in South Africa from Bloemfontein to Pretoria; in New Zealand from

Christchurch to Wellington; in Newfoundland from coast to coast of the Island, and in India from Lahore to Delhi. It would take these million men eighty-four hours, or three and a half days, to march past the Cenotaph in London.

It is hard to know what is more extraordinary, the success of the attempt or the seismic shift of sensibility that brought it about in the first place. A 'corner of a foreign field' that for centuries had been no more than a scattered collection of neglected graves could now only be bound by walls fifty miles in length. How was it that nations and governments that had squandered lives in such obscene profusion could suddenly become so protective of their memory? How was it that a post-war Britain marked by class division and mutual suspicion could achieve its most democratic expression in the celebration of its dead? How did a country and empire that was historically so inimical to militarism and regulation, find its most potent expression of 'Britishness' in the straight lines, regularity, and enforced conformity of its war cemeteries? What, ultimately, lies behind these cemeteries and memorials? Grief? Pride? Gratitude? Guilt? Atonement? Reparation? Political acumen? Which was it? Catharsis, or 'the old lie' – '*Dulce et Decorum est*' – that the poet Wilfred Owen, killed in the last week of the war, wrote of?

The fact that these questions are not more often asked is a tribute to the remarkable success with which the process of commemoration was carried out. Success carries with it a sense of its own inevitability and the images of Britain's war cemeteries – the immaculate rows of graves, the memorials, the flowers and Crosses of Sacrifice, the biblical inscriptions – are so visually and imaginatively compelling that it is hard to realise that there was nothing preordained or self-evident about them. Nor, either, were they once the sacred cows that they now are. They did not appear without a struggle. They were as much the product of debate and argument as they were an expression of national unity, and they brought about divisions that were bitter and lasting. This is now largely, and perhaps properly, forgotten but it would have been surprising if it had been any other way. A traumatised society was dealing with death, grief, pride and anger on an unprecedented scale and it had little to guide it. A nation characterised by a deep and self-conscious class awareness was forced to cope with a war that was as indiscriminate in its killing as the plague. Where, in the twentieth century, was it to find the equivalent of that universality of understanding that raised Battle Abbey, or lies behind the Uccello memorial? How was it to balance the claims of the individual and of the nation? How does a Christian society remember its Muslim, Hindu or Jewish dead? How does it juggle the just claims of victory and the dictates of a wider, healing vision? How, even before you have begun to address these cultural questions, do you begin the vast task of commemorating the million casualties of a war that obliterated every vestige of human identity in the way that the great battles of the Western Front had done?

That answers were found and took the form they did is largely the work of one man. They came at the end of a century that had seen a gradual but profound change of attitude to its armies. They came too just a year after the centenary of the Battle of Leipzig and the fiftieth anniversary of Gettysburg had raised the Western world's consciousness of its historical debts. And they emerged, of course, from long cultural traditions, from the country's Christian roots, and from a human piety that is older even than those. But if history can ever be said to belong to the individual, then it is the history of Britain's war cemeteries and the process by which they came into being. Along with the trenches – their mirror image and polar antithesis – they are how most of us now see the First World War. And yet the identity of the man responsible for them is largely forgotten. Almost everyone, asked for the name of the commander responsible for the slaughter of the Western Front, would, fairly or not, come up with Haig. Most, asked for the architect of the Cenotaph, could make a stab at Lutyens. But the man who mediated between them, who made it possible for a country to come to terms with the slaughter and unbearable debt it owed its dead, is scarcely better known now than the unidentified thousands whose graves only bear the inscription 'Known unto God'. His name was Fabian Ware.

ONE

The Making of a Visionary

'Now, God be thanked Who has matched us with His hour,'

RUPERT BROOKE

On the afternoon of Saturday 19 September 1914, a spare, dark-haired man in his mid-forties arrived at Lille in northern France to take command of the motley collection of vehicles and drivers that made up the British Red Cross's 'flying unit'. For the past four years he had been largely out of the public eye, but if there were few in the unit who would have recognised the face, they would undoubtedly have known the name of the man who for five turbulent years had been the erratically brilliant, 'warmongering' editor of the right-wing, imperialist *Morning Post*.

If they imagined that this was all that was to be said about him they would not have been entirely wrong – he did not idolise Napoleon for nothing – but it was by no means the most interesting thing about him. There were certainly men at the *Morning Post* who had only ever seen the bully in him, but Fabian Ware was a dreamer as much as a doer, as much a scholar and visionary as a bruising newspaperman, and which side of 'this Rupert of the pen and sword' had brought him to France would be hard to say.

It is very possible that he did not know himself, but if ever a man was made for France and what lay ahead, it was Fabian Ware. There are natural warriors who only come fully alive in battle, and then there is another, more alarming kind of man altogether: the romantic idealist and patriot who can glimpse among the horrors of war spiritual absolutes that the shabbier and greyer realities of peace deny; who can find in the call to sacrifice and suffering, in the democracy of death and the comradeship of war, not just a realisation of nation-hood, but a healing balm for all the divisions, inequalities, subterfuges, and selfishness of ordinary political life.

For the best part of a decade Ware had been warning the country against the German menace, but then his whole adult life had been lived under the shadow of Britain's decline. The generation before his that had grown up in the rich afterglow of Waterloo could reasonably expect to live and die in undisturbed possession of the world. It was Ware's luck to take his place in public life at a moment when an era of expansive confidence and optimism gave way to that endlessly contradictory, paranoid, self-assertive and self-questioning Edwardian age, which would only finally come to an end with Jutland and the Somme.

It was an age of political paralysis at home and the naval race abroad, of gross inequalities and bitter industrial unrest, of national shame in South Africa and looming civil war in Ireland. But if these were the crises that shaped Ware's politics something else is needed to explain the man. This is the history of an idea and not the biography of an individual, and yet when that idea so clearly bears the stamp of one man's personality and moral convictions, we need at least some sense of what it was that would enable a middle-aged man to transform the random command of a small, volunteer ambulance force into an empire that would change the way a whole country would see and commemorate itself.

Fabian Arthur Goulstone Ware was born at Glendower House in Clifton, Bristol, on 17 June 1869, the third son of the second marriage of a prosperous member of Bristol's Plymouth Brethren community and his schoolteacher wife. There is as little known of these early Clifton years as there is of his own married life, but if one was looking for a single clue to Ware's character and development, one influence that, above all, made him the zealot and idealist he was, it probably lies in a childhood steeped in the Millenarian visions and theological rancour of Victorian England's most combative, divisive and embattled Calvinist sect. It would be many years before Ware escaped the intellectual straitjacket of this world – years before he even 'dared question what he had been taught to regard as the only conceivable premise for all thoughts and all actions' – and in critical ways he remained the child of the Brethren he had always been. In adult life he seems to have achieved an amused and tolerant detachment from his Bethesda roots and yet, like many another Victorian apostate, his whole life remained a constant search for a faith or dream – Culture, Bloomsbury, Socialism, Industry, Philanthropy, Empire, Sex, Crusading Journalism, Women's Rights, the alternatives were endless – that would provide a secular substitute for the religious certitudes and deep seriousness of the faith he had intellectually abandoned.

It was a powerful and energising legacy, and if the passion for battle, the conviction of righteousness, the love of autocracy also left their mark, these were only the reverse of that spirit of independence that is the great birthright of all Protestant dissent. In the most obvious sense, Ware's whole life became a violent rejection of a sect that had turned its back against the world, but even when his work took him to the heart of the British establishment, he never sold out, never lost that critical power of detachment or sense of distance that, in the struggles ahead, would prove the most creative and important inheritance of his Brethren upbringing.

Even if Ware had wanted to 'belong' to that establishment world, his formative years and education inevitably reinforced a sense of apartness. In the late nineteenth century, the public schools and universities offered a well-trodden path to public service, but while his contemporaries were filling the reformed civil service and dying on Majuba Hill, soldiering with Stalky on the North West Frontier, or running the Empire, Ware was trudging down an obscure road that took him from a private tutor at home in Clifton to a struggling career as an indigent and ill-qualified schoolteacher. 'My academic qualifications are not worth counting,' he confessed in 1911, forced by the abortive hope of a post at Sheffield University to rehearse the long and dusty route that had brought him, at the age of forty-three, to the life of an unemployed ex-newspaperman working in Paris on a book no one was ever likely to read:

First class tutors up to eighteen (my people were Plymouth Brethren & took me away from a Preparatory School when I was twelve because I had been made captain of a cricket XI. I was never allowed to go back to school); then my father died & I had to earn my own living by teaching in private schools – I could only afford to work for a London degree – after having passed two of the three examinations I chucked it as I was getting no teaching, & saved up to come to Paris & took my Baccalaureate in science . . . Returning from Paris I was for several years assistant master in the Bradford Grammar School, then I reported to Sadler on foreign educational systems (Germany), was British Educational Representative at the Paris exhibition in 1900 and, when I came out . . . in 1901, was inspecting secondary schools for the Board of Education and was to be made a permanent inspector as soon as the inspectorate was established . . . All this counts for nothing among English academic people who smile at it all as they would smile at my Paris pinkish-mauve hood & cap of the same colour which is a cross between a coster's headdress & a biretta!!

For an ambitious, sensitive and highly gifted idealist, there must have been endless frustrations, although in the long run this education opened up a richer and more varied experience than a conventional and insular English public school could ever have done. In the last decades of the nineteenth century, the life of a secondary schoolmaster was as miserable as it has ever been, but it crucially gave Ware the experience and right – a right he would claim in the pages of the *Morning Post* and again in France – to speak for that other Britain which, in the years ahead, would make up the Pals' battalions and fight and die in their anonymous thousands in the mud of Flanders and the Somme.

If it was the years of educational drudgery and poverty that made an egalitarian and social reformer of Ware, it was the next phase of his career that hardened 'pity and indignation' into the kind of vision and ideal that was so crucial to a lapsed child of the Brethren. In 1900 he had published the first of two books on educational reform, and on the back of a growing reputation he went out to South Africa the following year to oversee the post-war reconstruction of education in the Transvaal alongside that famous 'Kindergarten' of talented and devoted young imperialists that the High Commissioner, Lord Milner, had gathered around him.

The figure of Viscount Milner has receded so far into the background of history that it is hard now to remember how large he once loomed over the Edwardian political landscape. Alfred Milner was born in Giessen, Hesse in 1854 of Anglo-German stock and received his early education at a Gymnasium in Tübingen. On the death of his mother in 1869, the fifteen-year-old Milner returned to England, and in 1872 won a scholarship to Benjamin Jowett's Balliol, where a brilliant undergraduate career and a fistful of university prizes was rounded off with a First in Classics and a fellowship to New College.

This was the Oxford of Ruskinian high-mindedness and social intervention, of Arnold Toynbee and H. H. Asquith, of the Canadian imperialist George Parkin, and Cecil Rhodes – and it was the dominant influence on Milner's life. 'As an undergraduate at Oxford,' he later wrote,

I was first stirred by a new vision of the British Empire. In that vision it appeared no longer as a number of infant or dependent communities revolving around this ancient kingdom but as a world encircling group of related nations, some of them destined to outgrow the mother country, united in a bond of equality and partnership, and united . . . by moral and spiritual bonds.

At the heart of Milner's 'New Imperialism' was a quasi-religious belief in the innate superiority of the English 'race' and an unshakeable conviction of its civilising destiny, and one of the great tragedies of British history is that he found himself in a position to implement it. On leaving Oxford he had gained a formidable reputation as an administrator and public servant, and after a formative colonial apprenticeship in Egypt under Lord Cromer, he went with the blessings of all parties to 'Southern Africa' as High Commissioner and Governor of the Cape Colony at a time when the Jameson Raid and President Kruger's treatment of British *Uitlanders* in the Transvaal had forced South Africa to the front of the political agenda.

It was a disastrous appointment – a crisis that called for cool pragmatism and the government had sent an imperial visionary, negotiations that demanded compromise and tact and they had sent the one man in England as obdurate as Kruger – and Britain reaped what it had sown. It is very possible that nobody could have dealt with Kruger and his dismal combination of 'hatred' and 'invincible ignorance', but Milner had never any intention of trying to find a peaceful answer to the problems of the Transvaal. When negotiations finally broke down in the summer of 1899 he had the war with the Afrikaner republics that he had wanted.

The Second Boer War was known as 'Milner's War' for good reason. Milner was not a man to shy away from the personal or public opprobrium brought about by a brutal and ugly conflict. In the spring of 1901 he had returned to England to face down a storm of Liberal criticism from his old allies, but within the year he was back again with a peerage and the support of a Conservative government to tighten the final terms of the Boer surrender and begin the vast post-war task of reconstructing a united, reformed and anglicised South Africa along the imperial lines he had always dreamt of.

It was as part of this work of political, legal, economic and educational reconstruction that Fabian Ware went out to join the Kindergarten of zealous young administrators: men like Geoffrey Dawson, the future editor of *The Times*; Philip Kerr, Britain's Ambassador to the United States at the outbreak of the Second World War; the novelist and future Governor General of Canada, John Buchan; the future Governor General of South Africa, Patrick Gordon; Lionel Curtis, the driving force of the 'Round Table', who shared Milner's vision and would carry the Milner torch deep into the twentieth century.

For the first time in his adult career, Ware had the man and the faith he needed, and the substitution of the *religio Milneriana* for his father's Millenarianism marks the great 'conversion experience' of his life. Under the influence of Milner's 'race patriotism' he learned his sense of Britain's global destiny, under Milner he honed his doctrine in the subordination of the individual to the collective, under Milner he gave political shape to his social conscience, and under Milner – cold, austere and 'Germanic' in public, generous and warm in private – he learned the virtue of public service that would be his own lodestar. 'For you your job was your mistress, and was no step-mother to those who worked under you,' Ware addressed him on the eve of the First World War in an open letter that is as close to a personal manifesto as he ever came,

> You taught them to regard their own success as dependent on and inseparably associated with the success of their job. They rose, as it were, on the work which they built up, you, the supreme architect, from your lofty outlook warning off those evil fellows . . . who would have taken advantage of their absorption in their daily task to climb up, unnoticed on the growing structures and supplant them.

It was under Milner too that Ware got his first chance to show his own remarkable abilities as an administrator. The early months in South Africa produced a series of frictions that provide an interesting 'taster' of the battles ahead, but from the day he established his independence he was in his element, doubling within four years the number of children in education in the Transvaal, addressing the technical mining and agricultural needs of the newly annexed state, breathing in the heady fumes of imperialism, and battling – and no one loved a battle like Ware – with a Boer clergy so bigoted and intransigently hostile to reform or reason that even the Brethren could have learned a lesson from them.

'I was working late last night,' he would write to his old 'chief' from Paris in 1911, the memories of the Transvaal and their imperial venture as fresh and intoxicating after six years as if it had all been only yesterday,

> & watched the sunrise – behind the Pantheon & the Bibliothèque Ste Genevieve – and whenever I see it, it reminds me of S. Africa & takes one by the throat as the French say . . . What a time it was & how we worked – & always when we were conscious of having done rather more than our hardest hoping that it would please *you:* I suppose I was a fool not to stay on doing your work. But as you say, it is no good regretting.

Ware might have been a fool not to have stayed, but as an ambitious man in his mid-thirties he would have been a bigger fool not to have left when, in 1905, he was offered the editorship of the *Morning Post*. The offer must have come as much of a surprise to him as it did to everyone else in journalism, but as the newspaper world soon found out, he was a born editor, the ideal man to take a hopelessly moribund Tory newspaper like the *Morning Post* and kick and bully and charm it into becoming the most influential and combative paper of its day.

The paper had no library or reference support for its journalists, no salaried leader-writers, no proper offices at this time, even, nothing but temporary wooden sheds near the Aldwych, and 'a regular mythology of minor deities created by the old traditions'. 'It is magnificent but it is not business,' Ware wrote to the paper's owner, Lord Glenesk, as he began the Augean task of modernisation,

I will take an example. The Art Critic is, I believe, actually bedridden. At any rate I have never seen him. He draws his salary and farms out the work. He does this with discrimination . . . But he breaks the first condition which should attach to such service and that is regular attendance at the office.

There was something else that he had learned under Milner that stood him in good stead in these early days at the *Morning Post*, and that was how to make use of that informal network of connections that held the British establishment together. The group of young zealots who had made up Milner's Kindergarten had nearly all been Oxford men, and one of Ware's first acts as editor was to write off to the Master of Balliol – Milner's old college – to scout for talent. When the answer came back in the shape of 'an ugly mannered but honest, self devoted young reformer of the practical kind called William Beveridge', Ware took it and him in his stride. He asked me 'to come on the staff completely to undertake all the articles and leaders on social questions!' an astonished Beveridge – the future architect of the modern Welfare State – later wrote of their interview,

I told him of course that in party politics I was certainly not a Conservative and that in speculative politics I was a bit of a Socialist. He rather liked that than the reverse. I told him I wasn't a journalist; he said there was no such thing as a journalist, that it was all practice. It was a flattering approach. I went about feeling like a beggar-boy who had just been proposed to by a Queen.

The change of regime was seldom as smooth or happy a transformation as this suggests, however, and if Lord Glenesk knew what he wanted when he appointed Ware, it is less certain that he knew what he had got. He had brought in an outsider to put an ailing business back on its feet, and over the next five 'erratic but brilliant' years he found that he had not so much bought himself a 'new broom' as a high-jacker, an unruly Milnerian cuckoo in the comfortable old Tory nest, an imperial zealot, Tariff Reformer, and universal conscript-monger, hell-bent on readying Britain and the Empire for a war with Germany that he half feared and half wanted. 'At the time of the Delcassé incident' – the first 'Moroccan Crisis' of 1905 – he later told Spenser Wilkinson, his influential military correspondent,

> we threw the whole weight of the *Morning Post* against war with Germany. I am ashamed that I did not understand what we were doing at the time. I now believe that England ought to have fought them then – at any rate she is every month becoming less prepared relatively to Germany to fight her than she was then . . . It [the *Morning Post*] should boldly point to the German danger and use the lesson of present events to rub in the immediate necessity of universal military service and the reorganizing of naval matters.

Ware was perfectly genuine in his campaigning hatred of social injustice and sweated labour – it was all part of the Milnerian imperial package to improve the 'race' – but as international crisis followed crisis it was the German threat and thought of an opportunity lost for 'urging compulsory service' that left him awake and 'miserable' at night. Wilkinson 'has been wanting to write saying that there are no causes for misunderstanding between England and Germany at the present', he complained to Lady Bathurst, Glenesk's daughter and successor as proprietor, as the gap between Ware and his military correspondent widened to open warfare, 'but I *won't* let him: to allay fears of Germany is to throw away our *only* chance of getting the people to bestir themselves'.

There were genuine strategic differences at stake: Wilkinson thought Ware's obsessions with imperial defence and conscription woefully inadequate to the real nature of Britain's military and naval deficiencies, but it was essentially a battle of wills between two men equally determined to get their way. Ware had already shown what a generous and imaginative boss he could be with a young man like Beveridge, but line him up against a leader-writer who had been publishing on defence issues while Ware was still a Bradford schoolteacher and the iron entered his soul. He could not bear to share authority. The *Morning Post* must speak with one voice and that voice was his. He had fought with Glenesk, he had battled his manager, and he was not going to give in to Wilkinson. What he wanted, when it came to issues of Empire and defence, was not an independent thinker of stature but a 'party hack'.

'I am to take the views that he thinks right,' Wilkinson complained to Lady Bathurst, 'and he even explained to me what my views, which he thinks he knows better than I do, really are.' It was a dangerous omniscience to insist on. This time he won his battle (Wilkinson could not even bring himself to mention

Ware's name when he wrote his memoirs) but Ware's own days at the *Morning Post* were numbered. In the bitter infighting within the Conservative Party over Tariff Reform he had alienated some powerful interests, and when in 1910 a fundraising appeal, sponsored by the *Morning Post*, to buy the nation an airship to counter the 'Zeppelin menace' ended in chaos, farce and serious financial embarrassment for Lady Bathurst, Ware was forced to go.

It was a grubby end to a brilliant, maverick, error-strewn age for the *Morning Post* and left Ware in a limbo that was both new and familiar to him. The terms of his severance gave him a measure of financial independence for the immediate future, but for a man who had been at the heart of the country's political life for a decade – a man, moreover, with not just a wife, Anna, now but two small children and no more obvious prospects than he had when living in student poverty almost twenty years before – dismissal was a psychological blow from which it would take a war to help him recover.

In his open 'letter' to Milner, written in France as a preface in 1912 to his last book, *The Worker and His Country*, Ware bravely trumpeted the blessing of his new-found 'freedom', but it was the Cassandra cry of a prophet without honour in his own country. 'The existence of the United Kingdom to-day as a first-class Power is indissolubly bound up in the integrity of the British Empire,' Ware warned from his 'old student quarters' in Paris, as he contemplated a France on the brink of civil war, a Britain torn apart by strikes, political atrophy and civil unrest, Ireland on the edge of disintegration and international relations stumbling from crisis to crisis,

The gravity of the responsibilities thus incurred needs no emphasising; they will be accepted calmly by a race which has brought so large a portion of the earth within its rule . . . So long as patriotism is the controlling force, dominating all classes, the supreme instinct in the hour of crisis, no renunciation and no sacrifice will be too great in the cause of unity.

It was only too horribly prophetic. For Ware, though, even if he could never have admitted it, the imminent prospect of war carried its own dark consolations. Spenser Wilkinson had once accused him of being a warmonger and he was only half wrong. If it seemed to Ware, in his gloomier moments, a mere toss-up whether civil strife or a European conflagration would come first, at least part of him saw the latter as the solution to the former. If the country could not heal its divisions in peace, perhaps it could in war. If 'Milnerism', the dream of a united, federated, white empire spanning the globe, was already unravelling in Ireland and South Africa then perhaps war – the great purging, unifying engine of change – might redeem it.

He had dreamed and preached of the individual absorbed in the family, the family in the nation and the nation in that 'highest attainment of human collectivity that the world has yet seen, the British Empire', and just when it seemed that history had left that dream behind, war had come to give sacrificial patriotism a last, bloody chance. In the final summer of peace, the headmaster of Uppingham School had told his departing sixth form that unless they could serve their country they would be better dead, and for a heady moment in that autumn of 1914 it was as if the whole country had been listening – not just that headmaster's 'country', not the country of Wykehamists and Etonians desperate to get to France before it was all over, but the 300,000 men who volunteered in August, the 450,000 in September, the 137,000 in October, forerunners of the five million who, in one way or another, would find themselves in uniform before the war's end to bear out Kipling's prophecy that it would be the 'third-class carriages' that would save the country.

It was the same too on the broader scale, where all those dreams of imperial preference and closer union had seemed the vision of a departing age. The First World War would only hasten the centrifugal forces at work within the Empire, but before it did that it would prove a macabre theatre for the realisation of Ware's dream. The parliaments of the Empire had no more say in the declaration of war than did the Imperial Parliament at Westminster, but as the Viceroy in India and each governor general issued the King's proclamation, the same enthusiasm that had fired Britain brought the Dominion troops in their tens of thousands to sacrifice their lives – 65,000 Canadians, 60,000 Australians, 18,000 New Zealanders, more than 9,000 South Africans – in a war that only sentiment, historical ties and a shared linguistic and cultural heritage, can remotely have suggested was theirs.

As Fabian Ware made his way across to France to take up his new post as commander of the Mobile Ambulance Unit, he at least knew what he wanted out of this war. Milner had found him a consultancy with Rio Tinto, but that was now forgotten. In October 1914 he had no idea, of course, where his Red Cross work would ultimately take him, but no one could have been better equipped to recognise and fill the need when it came. He had arrived with all the qualifications for the task – ambition, connections, intelligence, energy, diplomatic skills, charm, iron will, fluent French – but at the core of everything he would do was a belief in the rightness of the cause: belief in the Empire, belief in France, and a belief in a patriotic sacrifice. Fifteen years earlier he had written that the purpose of education was to produce the citizen 'ready to perform, to the utmost of his ability, those duties which his country demands of him', and war had only changed the nature of that call. 'So long as . . . patriotism is the controlling force . . . no sacrifice will be thought too great in the cause of unity,' he had concluded his political credo, and he was not going to shy away from the consequences now. Only at the moment of birth and death, he had written just two years earlier, can men be truly equal. Desperate and shameful poverty in England might have given the lie to the first part of that proposition, but, from now on, his life's work would be to make sure that the second half of it, at least, would come true.

TWO

The Mobile Unit

At the distance of a hundred years, the First World War and the attritional fighting of the Somme or Passchendaele have become so synonymous in the public mind that it is hard to remember that it was not always so. For any soldier going to France between the spring of 1915 and the end of 1917 this might well have been the one experience of war he would ever know, but for the men of the British Expeditionary Force (BEF) in August 1914, or their conscript heirs of 1918 who arrived in time to face the last German offensives and the final Advance to Victory, the Great War was a war not of entrenchment but of mobility, retreat and advance.

It was this initial, highly fluid phase – defined for the British by their first, brilliant action at Mons on 23 August and by the death knell of the Old Army at the first battle of Ypres in early November – that had brought Ware and his Mobile Ambulance Unit into the conflict. In these early weeks of the war, before security fears dictated a stricter regime, it was easy enough for civilians to get over to France, and few things so beautifully capture the bizarre mix of amateurishness and high professionalism with which Britain went into battle in 1914 as the advertisement that Ware had seen in *The Times* on the day after the declaration of war: 'The Royal Automobile Club,' it announced over the name of the Hon. A. Stanley, the philanthropic chairman of the RAC who had just been brought in to try to make the Red Cross and St John Ambulance work together after more than thirty years of institutional bickering, 'will be glad to receive the names of members and associates who will offer the services of their cars or their services with their cars either for home or foreign service, in case of need.'

There was a certain scepticism from the Army over civilian involvement, but in the days when the nation still believed in Kitchener, Kitchener's pronouncement in September that he could see 'no objection to parties with Motor Ambulances searching villages that are not in occupation by the Germans for wounded and to obtain particulars of the missing and to convey them to hospital', was all that was needed. On the Sunday morning following it, the first vehicles and owners embarked at Folkestone for France, and by the end of the month twenty-five vehicles had made the crossing, the vanguard of over two hundred cars that were collected by road and rail from across the country by engineers before being converted into ambulances and shipped out under the aegis of the Red Cross to Le Havre.

Among the first of these arrivals was the collection of owners and cars – a Hudson, Vauxhall, Morris Oxford, Sunbeam, Daimler – that made up the unit that Fabian Ware had come out to command. The Mobile Unit was not the only Red Cross team operating in northern France during these opening weeks, but from the first, Ware's was unusual in being a quasi-autonomous command, enjoying a jealously guarded independence owing something to its original remit, but still more to Ware's iron determination to run his own show in France as he had done in South Africa or at the *Morning Post*.

He was lucky in his bosses – lucky they were for the most part on the other side of the Channel, lucky they were the kind of men they were – and Arthur Stanley, in particular, had never been a man to see a committee as anything but a rubber stamp. Over the next months there would be various challenges to the unit's independence, but the Joint Finance Committee of the Red Cross and St John Ambulance was always ready to back him, sanctioning his local initiatives and giving him his own budget – £2,000 for these first three months, £3,000 for the second – perfectly happy to believe what he told them and bask in the reflected glory of the work that the unit carried out.

It was a necessary latitude because for all that it was a hand-to-mouth existence in these early weeks – petrol to be begged, hotel rooms and office space to be found, cars to be mended, jurisdictional niceties to be negotiated, rivals to be seen off, Uhlans to be avoided – Ware had arrived at a moment when events were rapidly outstripping the unit's original modest remit. 'The Mobile Unit was organised under the command of Mr Fabian Ware, shortly after the Battle of the Marne,' Ware himself – always perfectly at ease talking of himself in the third person – reported back to the Red Cross in London on the first steps in its evolution into something a world away from anything Kitchener had had in mind when he first sanctioned their searches,

32

and the original object of the Unit was to search for British wounded and missing in the district which had been overrun by the Germans during the retreat from Mons, and to convey them back to the British lines or to a British base. Fighting was still proceeding in some of these districts, and the French authorities invited the help of ambulance care for the conveyance of the wounded.

That 'invitation' had come at Amiens in early October at a time when the town of Albert was under heavy bombardment and for the next six months the Mobile Unit worked increasingly with the wounded and dying of the French army. By the middle of the month Ware had added a mobile light hospital and medical staff to his growing fleet of ambulances, and before the unit was finally disbanded it had dealt with more than twelve thousand casualties, ferrying and treating the wounded from Amiens to Ypres as the rival armies began their crab-like 'race for the sea' and stalemate.

After the years of frustration and disappointment, Ware was in his element, crisscrossing north-western France, liaising one day in Paris and the next in London, putting down his marker here, warning off a potential rival there, his energy and optimism seemingly inexhaustible. 'October 29th', his diary reads – a typical, and gloriously White Rabbit-ish entry, sent off to London to explain why he had no time to send the Joint War Committee the full report he owed them,

Left Doullens 6.10 a.m., where I had arrived the night before (in order to confer with Colonel Barry and to define sphere).

Breakfasted at St Pol 6.50. Met and despatched from here one of our sections at 7 a.m. (This had come to me by appointment at Headin.) Arrived Houdain Station at 7.30 a.m. Met a party in charge of Dr Kelly which I had sent out the night before in order to determine the site of our light hospital. Arrived at Bethune 8.55 a.m. Consulted with the director of the RAMC there. Left Bethune at 9.45 a.m. . . . Arrived Noeux les Nines at 10.5 a.m. . . . Arrived Merville 11.45 a.m. Arranged with the General commanding the 1st Corps of French Cavalry to place our light hospital at Merville for the use of both French and British. Left Merville 2 p.m.

There was, too, in these early fluid days, real danger, and the unit's work could often bring them under direct enemy fire. 'To be fair to them, and heap coals of fire on their heads,' Ware wrote to Sir Arthur Lawley, another Milner appointee in the Transvaal and a staunch support at the Red Cross, after a second abortive attempt to rescue a wounded girl from among the ruins of Albert had brought the German artillery down on their defenceless convoy,

I think it possible that they may not have distinguished the Red Cross at that distance . . . I have never been in such a scene of desolation – it was like nothing on earth but the pictures one saw in one's childhood of the Last Day. The place was so ruined that they couldn't recognise the streets and there was a minute when I thought that we should go round and round and never find our way. All the time we were going *towards* the guns! . . . We stopped at the remains of a corner to ask a man the way, but he wouldn't stay long enough to do more than point down a street and then run off . . . We found the house, and a woman with two dear little children came up from the cellar, and crying her heart out told us the girl was dead.

Ware was no more immune to the frisson of danger than his men – 'the thought that [the shells] were meant for oneself brought rather a sporting element in to the thing', he reported – but as an old newspaperman he also knew good copy when he saw it and was not going to be slow to pass it on. 'The strong and able had been able to quit long before,' he wrote of another rescue from among the shattered ruins of a nursing convent, proffering it with the suggestion that the Red Cross might think about exploiting the story for fundraising purposes,

and these poor helpless, old souls, cared for so kindly by the Sisters of the Convent, alone remained perforce. Could any request to members of our Society be more fitting? Would not every member at once go forward and rejoice at having this opportunity?

The utter desolation and destruction baffles description; let it suffice to explain that below were over fifty women of ages varying from 70 to 95 years – many bedridden for years and others too infirm to help themselves . . .

Five dead were removed from this awful debris, others it was impossible to extricate. Of those who lived some had limbs shattered by the cruel missiles of a heartless enemy . . . all bearing an expression of awful terror, such a scene only seen on the field of war . . .

It was 4 p.m. when we had finished our work at Ypres, but what cared members of the Red Cross for the incessant cannonading or for the constant and deafening explosion of bursting shells. We knew we were carrying out the work of some of those generous subscribers at home by making such use of their ambulances, and if any of them could have seen and understood the expressions of relief and gratitude in the faces of those we saved he would indeed have felt that his money had been well spent.

A streak of genial cynicism in Ware and an unashamed gift for self-promotion make it easy to forget that they were only the accidental trappings of a deeply romantic attachment to France and her people. In the letters and memoirs of the British soldier one glimpses a very different world, but in the Panglossian France that Ware inhabited – a France in which everything was for the best even in the worst of all possible worlds – nothing is ever allowed to darken the sunlit landscape or shake the faith and love of his Paris youth.

There are no defeatists in Ware's France, no meanness, no ugliness, no deep-rooted suspicions, no resentment of Albion, no offending calvaries, no truculent farmers, no haggling women, no syphilis, none of the stock French characters with their 'monkey' language and monkey habits and monkey morals who fill the British Tommy's memories of this time, but only a country of devoted doctors and tireless curés, of debonair cavalry generals and saintly bishops, of grateful faces, 'delightful camaraderie' and stoic courage in which none but the Hun is vile.

The remarkable thing about Ware, though, was that he was

one of the few men connected with the BEF in France with the charm and the language to turn this dream of France into something approaching reality. There is no reason to believe that the reports he sent home offer anything more than a highly subjective truth, but in these early months with the Mobile Unit, the only cloud on his horizon was one that had bubbled up on the other side of the Channel. 'It *is* good work out here,' he insisted in a letter to his old chief, Lord Milner, on 13 October,

> Of course we can be crabbed for working for the *French* only, but everybody so far who has come to crab has ended by begging to be allowed to join us and the search for the missing is going on.
>
> If only I had time to write a letter to *The Times* on this:- an extraordinarily fine French priest who I have met once or twice with the wounded & become friends with put his hands on my shoulder the other day as I was [showing] an English paper to one of my men for its prominent account of a football match, & said in an inexpressibly pained but friendly way '*mais, mon commandant, ce n'est past le moment pour le football*'. If only people at home could have seen the surroundings in which that was said, wounded & dying all around us, they would at least stop *reporting* their damned football.

God protect us from 'all the muddle and mischief which Satan finds for idle hands in England', he complained again to Milner, and in letter after letter he returned to the same theme. 'The

British Red Cross has been directly or indirectly responsible for men working among the French, whose presence among them has I think done positive harm to the Allied cause,' he lectured Lawley,

> Therefore it is absolutely essential that they should be carefully selected. Men of the proper sort are, as you know, extremely rare, and there are very few men who we could think really qualified to go off alone with a few cars uncontrolled and in a position to make their own arrangements and conduct negotiations with the French. Of the men who are not competent two extreme types have come under my notice . . . One, the man who speaking a little French complains of the food the French provide, and the French ways – and two, the man who speaks no more French, but adopts a patronising air towards the French and attempts to organise everything for them.

It was all the more important for Ware to scotch these Little Englander attitudes because the unit's searches were leading to another line of work for which the co-operation of the French was vital. In the first days of the war the Red Cross had set up a Wounded and Missing Department under Lord Robert Cecil, but with only a handful of volunteers to handle enquiries, no adequate database to cope with the soaring casualty figures and, as yet, no one like the archaeologist, traveller, alpinist and Middle East expert, Gertrude Bell to impose some system on the mounting chaos of letters, casualty lists and hospital returns, the oblivion that had been the historical fate of the dead British soldier in all previous wars looked well on the way to repeating itself.

The casualties had been unimaginable in their scale – 16,200 officers and men killed by the end of 1914, 47,707 wounded, 16,746 missing or captured (by comparison, Wellington's losses at Waterloo were 3,500) – and behind each of those numbers lay a personal history and a personal loss. 'I shall never forget the scene at Boulogne,' recalled Sir Lionel Earle, a future colleague and sparring partner of Ware's, in France searching for news of his brother, a Grenadier officer last seen beside the Menin Road near Ypres, lying on the ground with a bullet through his head and one eye lying on his cheek. 'Scores of Indian troops, sitting patiently along the wharf with bandages on their heads, arms, legs, and bodies, some soaked with blood, waiting for some hospital ship to take them away. Scores and scores of ambulance wagons, full of wounded, kept on entering the town . . .'

There would be rumours one day that Earle's brother was dead in Frankfurt, counter-rumours the next that he was 'lying on the straw' with a mass of German wounded in the Town Hall at Courtrai, and then 'nothing more for some weeks', continued Earle, all the bitterness and hatred as fresh after twenty-one years as if it had all happened the day before,

when one day my sister-in-law received a letter unsigned, asking if she would go to a certain tabernacle in the East End at a certain hour and day, as there was news waiting her there. She came to consult me as to whether she ought to go or not, and I advised her to go, as it might be news about her husband.

She went, and found this little tabernacle empty, when suddenly she saw a man, who looked like a foreign clergyman. She went up to him, and he handed her a note. This was a line from my brother, saying he was in hospital and suffering terribly in his head. This clergyman was a Swiss, and was walking one day in Brussels with a small grip in his hand, when a girl came up to him and asked if he was going home on a journey. 'Yes,' he replied, 'to England.' Upon which she slipped a note into his hand, addressed to my sister-in-law.

My brother's wounds were more severe, even than we had thought, as after the bullet had gone clean through his head, the regimental doctor was binding up his head, when the Germans surrounded them, blew the brains of the doctor, although unarmed and covered with Red Cross, all over my brother's face, and the orderly was killed at close range by a rifle bullet, which after passing through the poor man's stomach, passed all down the leg of my brother, infecting the whole leg with *Bacillus coli*. I expect my brother was spared, as probably the Germans thought that a colonel of the Guards might be of value as regards exchange of prisoners at some future date.

Lionel Earle was lucky – as ultimately was his brother, if eight operations, gangrene, 'the studied malevolence' of his German doctors, stone deafness and partial blindness counts as lucky – because he could at least call in favours from Embassy officials and pre-war connections, but it would have been another story again for that orderly killed at his brother's side. In these early months of the war, the Red Cross office had at least created card indexes of the officers admitted to base hospitals, but for the relatives of missing rank and file, obstructed on all sides by an army determined to hide actual casualty figures and keep Red Cross personnel away from the field hospitals, there was nothing but an interminable wait and the grim sense that nothing had changed in the century since the British Army had last fought in the Low Countries.

It was partly in response to this growing crisis that Ware's Mobile Unit first became involved in the work that would eventually lead to the creation of the Imperial War Graves Commission (IWGC). From the early weeks of September his men had been searching the line of the British retreat from Mons and Le Cateau to the Marne, and it was a short step from sharing information with Cecil that might transform a 'missing' into a 'wounded' or 'killed' on the Red Cross lists, to a protective interest in the graves themselves. 'The experience gained in the search for British wounded has helped the Unit in taking up another most useful piece of work,' Ware wrote back to London – as ever, reporting to his masters after the event, 'viz: the identification of places in which British killed have been hastily buried, and the placing of crosses on the spots thus identified, with inscriptions designed to preserve the rough records which in many cases are already in danger of becoming obliterated.'

The arbitrary and ad hoc nature of this work assumed a more formal shape after a meeting with a Lieutenant Colonel Stewart, who was inspecting the Mobile Unit on behalf of the Red Cross. 'It was while . . . visiting Bethune Cemetery,' Ware recalled an encounter that has since become part of Imperial War Graves Commission lore, that [Stewart] informed me that the B.R.C.S. were prepared to provide funds necessary for replacing the rough, and often only pencilled, inscriptions on the crosses erected over graves with inscriptions of a more durable kind. Beginning in Bethune cemetery I immediately gave instructions for the inscriptions to be painted on the crosses over the graves there; but finding that, notwithstanding the best intentions, the local people employed frequently made mistakes we next secured stencils and my officers and men devoted their spare time when not engaged in the work of carrying wounded to stencilling the inscriptions themselves to certain crosses which were procured. The work rapidly developed, and the stencils were replaced by stamping machines providing inscriptions on metal tapes.

In the area around the Aisne and Marne, the southernmost point of the Allied retreat in 1914, Cecil's deputy Ian Malcolm was already carrying out similar searches, but it was Ware's unit that made the decisive difference to the way that Britain's dead were recorded. The overwhelming burden of its work still lay with the French army and ambulance duties, but whenever enemy movements allowed it, his handful of men would be out in the field, liaising with local civic and medical authorities, collecting identification plaques, painstakingly patching together scraps of information or ploughing through the mud after children eager to display some isolated grave.

Sometimes the trail would lead to a single grave, sometimes a cluster or a mass burial and sometimes – it was odd what a different perspective grave-hunting gave a man – to disappointment.

'I may add that we are not always rewarded for our muddy tramp,' one of Ware's team recalled in December, 'as on more than one occasion, I have found at the end of it the grave of a German soldier and then I have felt inclined to box the wretched child's ears until I notice that the cross has been erected by British troops as the inscription is in English.'

The same element of uncertainty entered into the process of identification, where often only some chance initiative or faintly pencilled inscription on a roughly made cross stood between the dead and oblivion. 'Another and very ingenious method of recording the names of fallen soldiers,' the same searcher, a volunteer called Broadley recorded, 'is by writing their names on a piece of paper and placing this in a bottle. I came across a bottle only a day or two ago with a list of thirty names of men of the Royal Scots killed in action, with a note of the name of the Chaplain (Revd. Gibbs) stating that he had officiated at the burial.'

For a volunteer like Broadley, 'the proud satisfaction of knowing that I had done some slight honour to one brave man who has died for his country' was reward enough, but as Ware was always keen to point out, it could never have begun without the sympathy of a population that had already adopted the British dead as their own. 'I feel sure that the graves in these back gardens will always be treated . . . as sacred property,' Broadley reported after one hunt had taken him to a site newly planted with London Pride,

> This brings to mind an incident when I called at a farm near Meteren and a farmer showed me the graves of two nameless heroes of the Seaforth Highlanders which were in

a field. He explained that he had the greatest difficulty in keeping the cows away and added with tears in his eyes that he would give all the money in the world if these brave fellows could have been buried in his back garden instead of a field close by.

One of the enduring themes, in fact, running through the origins of the Imperial War Graves Commission is the generosity of the French state and people, and Ware was determined that nothing was going to threaten this. 'With very few exceptions the graves which we have seen up to the present are beautifully made and kept,' he reported again back to the chairman of the Joint War Committee, Arthur Stanley, anxious to make sure that no ingratitude was shown to a population 'that have been so ready to take upon themselves the pious care' of British burial plots.

The personal interest will cause many relatives to hesitate after the war before removing them. In many cases the exact circumstances of death were witnessed by the villagers and are engraved on their memories. Here a woman will relate how she saw a dragoon, whose grave is in her orchard, step under a tree to pick an apple and how while he was in the act a shell took his head off; there a woman will tell you how she watched a lancer, buried close by, kneeling on the bridge and firing on the Germans until he fell.

The other thing that sustained his searchers in their harrowing and often dangerous work – and another important thread in the IWGC's history – was the evidence of what it meant to the fighting soldier. 'I was endeavouring to erect a cross in a field,' Broadley wrote, when the bitter cold of early December 1914 had made the earth 'as hard as iron,

> and my work was not progressing very rapidly. Some 'Tommies' who were marching down the road . . . obtained leave to fall out and help me. With their assistance the cross was speedily placed in position and then, without a word they all sprang to attention and solemnly saluted the grave of their dead comrade-in-arms. It was a most impressive and touching sight.

There is something in this vignette – something in its air of reverence, of innocence almost – that movingly evokes a world that was disappearing even as Broadley described it. In the last two weeks of November 1914, he alone had located some three hundred graves in an area from Laventie to Steenvoorde, and yet this was still war and death on a scale that left room for all those human pieties and sensibilities that would sink in the mud and horror of the trenches.

These would never entirely disappear – on the eve of the Somme, Sir Lionel Earle reassured *The Weekly Dispatch*'s readers that 'our soldiers in the shell swept zones never tire of making reverent pilgrimages to the cemeteries where their dead comrades lie' – but never again would the mores and social baggage of the pre-war world seem so real to men at the front.

This was partly because those men were different, but it was also because the British Army itself had changed. In the first months of the fighting it was a far smaller and tighter entity than it later became, and even in 1915 a territorial like Captain Ian Mackay of the Cameron Highlanders, coming out to France for the first time, could hardly move behind the lines without stumbling into someone with whom he had been at school or danced an eightsome at the Northern Meeting.

To officers like Mackay, the dead were not anonymous strangers but friends and estate workers with names and families: 'Beauly and Portree boys' with whom the Mackays had always historically gone to war; men called 'Gray Buchanan a great Fettes pal of Ian Innes', and Ian Innes himself; their graves places to visit, their funerals snatched moments of shared humanity in the din of war. 'We had one poor fellow killed when walking along a road with a message some distance behind the front line,' Mackay wrote home from Busnes in the winter of 1915,

> We sent for our padre . . . and I went to the funeral in a little British cemetery near a ruined farm not far from our firing line. It was a regular Sir John Moore burial as our guns were thundering at the time and while we were at the grave the Germans sent over several shrapnel and high explosives . . . which burst unpleasantly near.

There were regiments, of course, who never relaxed their pre-war standards – Duff Cooper might have found himself in an unusually dangerous bit of Mayfair when he arrived at the front in 1918 for all the difference war made to his social life – but the old hierarchies were never so unashamedly honoured as in these early days. 'Dear Miss F. Robertson,' one former servant, now 'Private Young, 4 Company, Divisional wiring, c/o

Head Qrs', wrote back in pencil from Ypres to his previous employer's family,

> Yesterday I visited the Town Major's office for the purpose of locating Mr. Lewis's grave, the plans of the city were handed to me and with the address you gave me the exact spot was easy to find. After making my way through the ruins of the convent I came to the grounds which are badly damaged by shell fire. I cannot express to you how glad I was to find the grave in perfect order, except for weeds, brick and various other articles lying around, the bottom of the cross is damaged by shrapnel, however I will get to work right away, and make a new cross, which can stand behind the old one, also rearrange things and clear all rubbish away. While I am here you can depend on me to see that the grave is kept in good order. I have ample time on hand and can spare an hour or more work every day it is no trouble to me whatever I am only too glad, that the little service I hoped for, for months, has at last been fulfilled. If there is any plans you would like me to carry out, just mention them, I will be only to [sic] delighted to be of what little service that is possible for me to do. Must conclude in haste, I am quite fit and happy. Sincerely yours, D. Young.

The arrival of the first Territorial battalions in November 1914, Sir Nevil Macready, the Adjutant General in France, recognised, had made this sense of 'family', with its attendant psychological complications, all the stronger too. Among the old regulars the response to a death might be no more than a few 'words of rough regret' and 'a determination to get their own back', but for the closely knit Territorials, bound together by every social tie of peacetime life, the brutal shock of seeing 'hundreds of their comrades . . . swept away' in battle would cause 'a great wave of grief and depression' which would take days to overcome.

It was a pointer to the future, and to the damage that whole communities would suffer when the Pals' battalions went into action, and in such a climate the work of the Mobile Ambulance Unit took on a significance that probably caught even Ware by surprise. From the first he had issued instructions against the taking of undue risks, but he knew as well as his men that nothing added more to the prestige of the unit than the fact that they shared the dangers of the front-line troops. 'It is fully recognised that the work of the organisation is of purely sentimental value, and that it does not directly contribute to the successful termination of the war,' General Haig wrote to the War Office in March 1915, blithely unconscious of just how big a butcher's bill he would finally be presenting to the nation,

It has, however, an extraordinary moral value to the troops in the field as well as to the relatives and friends of the dead at home. The mere fact that these officers visit day after day the cemeteries close behind the trenches, fully exposed to shell and rifle fire, accurately to record not only the names of the dead but also the exact place of burial, has a symbolic value to the men that it would be difficult to exaggerate. Further, it should be borne in mind that on the termination of hostilities the nation will demand an account from the Government as to the steps which have been taken to mark and classify the burial places of the dead, steps which can only be effectively taken at, or soon after, burial.

If Haig's letter is a sure sign of the impact Ware's unit had made it seems all the more extraordinary that it had been eight months in coming. In many ways the BEF had been the most professional army the country had ever sent abroad but when it came to the question of its dead and the accurate registration of burials, it might as well have been back in the Peninsula for all the planning or provisions that had been made.

There were excuses – Treasury reluctance to spend money on anything that did not directly contribute to victory – but it was not as if the men in command had no first-hand experience of the distress and confusion that previous failures had caused. In the aftermath of the Boer War, the Loyal Women's Guild had done its 'admirable' but 'unsatisfactory' best to fill the gap, but 'a lot of trouble over soldiers' graves', Sir Nevil Macready, another old South Africa hand, later told a War Office committee, 'would have been avoidable had a proper organisation been created to meet the need at the commencement of the war'.

In the failure of the authorities to provide their own organisation, however, Ware saw his opportunity and it could not have come at a better moment. In the first months of the war he had been determined to keep the Army at arm's length, but his men in the field had always found the absence of military rank a disadvantage and with the scale of work expanding all the time

– by May 1915, 4,300 graves would be registered – and Ian Malcolm and the Paris office of the International Red Cross still operating to the south in the Marne and Aisne areas, the point had been reached at which Ware's independence could best be preserved from within the Army rather than from without.

The Army needed no persuasion of the value of his work – distressed relatives' letters in the newspapers at home were reminders that there would come a reckoning if they continued to do nothing – but what Ware wanted was a *monopoly* of it and in late February he secured himself an appointment with the Adjutant General to make his case. 'Into the old-fashioned French bedroom which served as my office came a spare, dark individual, dressed in the uniform of the French Croix-Rouge,' Nevil Macready recalled,

He explained that he had been working with the French, and was at that moment with General Conneau's cavalry, but wished, if there was an opening, to give his services to his own countrymen. We chatted for some time, and I found that he had considerable administrative experience and was a fluent French scholar. His memory was better than mine, and it transpired that some forty years before, when we were both small boys, he had been present at a meeting house of the Plymouth Brethren, to which I had been taken by an aunt, and when I got into some difficulties over the ritual, an episode which had evidently impressed him. Before he left my room I had booked him to create an organisation to [find] and record the names of our soldiers.

There can have been few First World War generals who had been bounced on Dickens's knee as a child, but then a son of the great Victorian actor-manager Charles Macready and the great-grandson of the artist Sir William Beechey, Nevil Macready was hardly typical in the first place. As a young boy growing up in Cheltenham he would have preferred the stage to the Army, but his father was having none of it and after Sandhurst, and a brief and bloody baptism at Tel-el-Kebir in Egypt, he had gravitated into staff work as if born to it, rising quietly and seamlessly from an appointment with the military police in Alexandria to be Assistant Adjutant General and Chief Staff Officer for Cape Colony at the end of the Boer War. If the thespian in the fastidiously elegant Macready never entirely died – it is no surprise that he was the first to take off his moustache when he lifted the injunction against clean-shaven officers in the Army – the role he always played best was that of the brusquely efficient administrator. During the South African war he had seen more than his fair share of fighting at Ladysmith, but his real métier remained the staff and it was back at the War Office with responsibility for the deployment of troops in aid of the civil power that his talents came fully into their own.

The years immediately before the war were not good ones for soldiers, years of widespread industrial violence and looming civil war in Ireland that drew the British Army into a policing role, but Macready was one of the few men to come out of them with his reputation enhanced. In 1910 he had taken command of operations in South Wales during the bitter miners' strikes, and the name he made for himself there marked him for the top at a time when his qualities of judgment, firmness, and political impartiality had never been at a higher premium.

With their Plymouth Brethren connections, Milner's South Africa and even political sympathies in common – Ware, a social radical in conservative clothing, Macready, by military standards at least, the next thing to a Bolshevik in uniform – the two men might have been made for each other. The result was the creation of a Graves Registration Commission (GRC) with Ware at the helm. 'At the beginning of the present war,' Macready later told a War Office Committee, smoothly glossing over the turf wars and bloodletting that lay behind its birth, he had,

> talked over the matter with the . . . Chief Engineer, BEF, and decided to create an organisation to deal with the graves question. Certain members of the Red Cross Society at the time were in a spasmodic way interesting themselves in the matter and expending their energies in different directions. But there was no control and, to cut a long story short, [I] obtained the services of . . . Ware, and put him in charge.

Although in some ways the new GRC remained a curiously hybrid, semi-detached sort of unit – the Red Cross continued to supply men and vehicles, while Ware was given the local rank of major (with two captains and seven lieutenants under him) and the Army took on the costs of crosses, rations and fuel – the crucial thing for Ware was that the GRC had the monopoly he had wanted. In the first months of the war he been obliged to share power with the Red Cross's Paris office, and with Macready now behind him, he moved swiftly and ruthlessly to take control of the work being done in the Aisne/Marne district by Ian Malcolm and bring it under a single unified command.

He was right to do what he did – unauthorised individuals had become involved, vital identification evidence removed, questionable exhumations carried out – but it was unmistakably the old Ware of South Africa and *Morning Post* days who had ruthlessly squeezed out Spenser Wilkinson. In the earliest days in France he had often found the Red Cross were actually ahead of him in their work, and yet if Malcolm imagined now that that would count for anything he was in for a sad awakening. 'There is not, of course, much in the *personal* point,' Malcolm pleaded with Lawley,

> though I am bound to say I feel rather aggrieved at being completely passed over and superseded in my own area where I have worked so hard for five months [but on public grounds, to avoid replication]. Would it not, therefore, be well if the A.G., or Fabian Ware . . . could entrust me with their official programme? Can you not help to arrange this?

'It would be a matter of the greatest disappointment to me if all this were suddenly taken from out of my hands,' he wrote in the same plaintive vein to Ware on 11 March, 'and I should feel sure that it would be far from your wish that it should be so.'

He did not know his man, and within the week all his maps, lists and cemetery concessions were on the new director's desk, as Ware began the business of putting their old grave work on a more organised footing. At the outset Ware still had all the problems of a volunteer workforce and a War Office that 'neither cares nor understands', but by the middle of August 1915 plans had already assumed a 'definite' enough shape for him to be able to describe the organisation in a report to Macready that shows just why he had been the right choice for the job.

Ware had divided the Commission into two parts, with seven distinct sections to carry out the field work and a headquarters responsible for the compilation and update of two registers. The first of these was a registration of graves with the names of officers and men listed by regiment, with details of any existing cross or inscriptions where the sites were accessible, and a note of who had reported them where they could no longer be reached, along with a record of any outstanding enquiries.

The second, complementing the regimental lists, was a geographical register. 'By means of this,' Ware explained, with all the breezy confidence of a man who still did not know what lay ahead,

it is possible to state at once how many burial grounds are in existence, how many graves are in each, and in what units they belong. The register also enables crosses destroyed by shell fire or otherwise to be replaced, and it is practically impossible for any grave once located to be lost sight of.

All enquiries, half of them from France, half from home, were also dealt with at their chateau headquarters at Lillers, but the real spade-work, as it were, was carried out by the sections. In the first reorganisation Ware had envisaged that there would be four of these, but by the August of 1915 those four had swelled to seven – 'A' and 'G' at Bethune for instance, 'D' at Aisne and

Marne – with the officer in charge of each district responsible for marking and reporting burials to headquarters, tracking down and verifying old graves, collating daily returns from chaplains, units and hospitals, and finally preparing and erecting wooden crosses with their machine-punched metal identification plates.

In tandem with this work, often carried out under conditions of great risk, as Haig noted, went a growing number of local enquiries, and the first rudimentary improvements to the appearance of cemeteries sparked off by a torrent of requests for photographs from families back in Britain. Macready had already exempted the Graves Registration Commission from the prohibition against photography, and with funds from the Joint War Committee of the Red Cross and St John Ambulance a separate department was set up and three 'first-class' professional photographers put to work over the summer months to begin the task of photographing all the graves.

Six thousand graves photographed, 800 photographs despatched to families in England, 18,173 graves registered, it was an extraordinary workload that had been completed by the middle of August. However there was a limit to what even Ware could do. In the first days of the GRC he had wanted the old Mobile Unit to continue its ambulance duties, but with his resources stretched to the limit by the expanding GRC work it was probably as well that a rare breakdown in his relations, and an even rarer show of offended dignity from Ware, forced his hand.

It was a sad end to a fertile partnership, but it cleared the way for Ware to concentrate on his graves work. It also foreshadowed another equally inevitable development in the story of the GRC. Macready and the Old Army – with memories of the chaos in

South Africa – had never been entirely comfortable co-operating with the Red Cross and a change of status was needed. With the volume of work growing by the day, and a volunteer manpower inadequate to the task, the existing compromise made no sense. 'I saw the AG the other day,' Sir Arthur Lawley wrote in mock outrage to Ware at the end of August,

> who hinted at an act of Piracy so audacious that I am still dumb with horror at the mere suggestion.
>
> He proposes to swallow at one gulp the GRC and all its merry men.
>
> Could you ever endure to be torn from the sheltering arms of the Red Cross?
>
> 'Now!' I hear you say.
>
> I will do all I can to save you.

Within weeks it was a *faint accompli*. On 6 September, Macready recommended to the War Office that the GRC should 'be placed on a proper footing as part of His Majesty's forces', and a month later its old hybrid existence came to an end. It marked the end of the first phase of Ware's life work. The enduring, impressive and controversial aspects of that work – the questions of repatriation, commemoration, permanence, uniformity, imperial involvement and authority – still lay ahead but without the Mobile Ambulance Unit none of it could have happened.

'I am sorry and at the same time glad that it should be so,' Lawley wrote again at the end of October, after the Army's 'piracy' had become official, sorry of course that we can no longer look upon your achievements as 'our' work and claim a share in its reflected glory; glad on the other hand that the excellent quality of your work and its value has received the flattering recognition which is manifested by the Army's absorption of your entire organisation.

It was a rightly generous tribute to the work that had been done, and a sober recognition of what lay ahead. The war had changed and the Army with it. By the end of 1914, the four infantry divisions and the one cavalry division of the BEF that had crossed the Channel in August had almost trebled in size to a force of two armies and a cavalry corps of more than 270,000 men. By the spring of 1916 this would rise to a million and a peak in the summer of 1917 of 1,721,056 men. Already a newly arrived officer like Cameron Highlander Ian Mackay, who only reached France in the spring of 1915, could look back with a sense of awe on the achievements of the BEF at Mons and its aftermath as if they belonged to a wholly different conflict. They had been 'marvellous', he told his mother – the perfect answer 'to the crokers who lamented the decadence of the race. No troops in the world could have done what they have done.'

Mackay's war, until it ended in an unmarked grave in 1917, would be very different. The romance, the pride, the glamour, the professional elan of the early days had died with the Old Army and all that was left to their successors was to endure. From the Channel coast to the Swiss border, an unbroken line of earthworks, stretching for 475 miles, marked the front line. This line would define Mackay's experience of France as it still largely shapes the collective memory of what the war was like. It would also be the phase of the fighting that projected the work of Ware and his men on to a scale that makes the world of orchards, farms and solitary and scattered graves that Broadley and his colleagues searched in late 1914 seem to belong to an unimaginably remote past.

THREE
With an Eye to the Future

There were possibly any number of administrators who could have put the work of the Graves Registration Commission on an efficient footing in 1915, but how many could also have dealt with the political complexities and negotiation that went with it is a very different matter. In the early spring of 1915, Ware had begun talks in Paris with the French government on the status of British war graves, and over the next weeks and months he was in constant contact with the different government departments involved, assuaging cultural differences and repairing real or imagined slights with the finesse of a born diplomat and the political savvy of an old newspaperman.

There were the usual 'us and them' gripes – the War Office were 'blighters', he told Milner, and their clerks should be shipped over to the trenches for a week – but as 'the *sole* intermediary between the British Army in the Field and the French military and civil authorities on all matters relating to graves' he had the complete authority he wanted. In the earliest days with the Mobile Ambulance Unit his work had inevitably been essentially reactive, but here, for the first time, was a chance to think and plan for the future on a scale appropriate to his energy and vision and to the growing magnitude of the Allies' sacrifice.

It is impossible to do much more than guess what the Army had in mind when it placed Ware in charge of the negotiations. They knew that in Ware they had found a man with the experience and tact to smooth over difficulties, but if they imagined that they were taking on a kind of glorified Undertaker General to the Forces to put an acceptable face on Death for the benefit of a disturbed public back at home, then they had hopelessly underestimated their man.

He would certainly do that for them – no one in the history of warfare has transformed the horrors and suffering of a battlefield into oases of peace like Ware – but from early in their alliance he and the Army had different objectives in view. There was nothing stupid or blinkered about a man like Nevil Macready, but where he saw a problem Ware saw an opportunity; where the soldier and administrator simply recognised a failure in procedures that would come back to haunt the Army, the visionary saw the glimmer of an answer to all those pre-war dreams of unity and equality he had preached. One of the most intriguing questions that the history of the war graves poses, in fact, is when Ware first realised precisely what he was *doing* in France. There is an element of self-congratulation in the traditional accounts of the War Graves Commission that makes it all sound inevitable from the start, but if there is certainly a retrospective logic to its history that links the Mobile Ambulance Unit and its various reincarnations to the Commonwealth War Graves Commission of today, it owed as much to chance and opportunism as it did to vision or principle.

Ware was without question a visionary and idealist, but the real quality that enabled him to achieve things was an eye for the main chance, a politician's instinct for popular movement, an intuitive sense of the zeitgeist, and at no time was that more obvious than in the summer of 1915. Over the late spring and early summer of that year there would be two decisions taken in France that were absolutely seminal to the future of Britain's war graves, but if anyone other than Ware so much as glimpsed the implications of them or the social and political transformation they foreshadowed, then he kept very quiet about it.

Ware could not possibly have seen the future or even the full consequences of all the decisions he was taking, but then who in 1915 could be sure that there would be a future? In the popular consciousness the year forms a muted intermezzo between the high hopes of 1914 and the horrors of the Somme, but for those who lived through it this was the year of Neuve-Chapelle, German gas and Loos, of the naval and military disasters of Gallipoli, the year in which even the sinking of the *Lusitania* and the Armenian Massacres failed to shake Woodrow Wilson's high-minded neutrality – the year that ended for Britain with the silent evacuation of one beaten army from the beaches of Turkey, the hopeless and disease-ravaged rump of another besieged in the Iraqi city of Kut, and any hopes of an Allied breakthrough on the Western Front looking more delusory than ever.

For Vera Brittain, for Rudyard Kipling and his wife Carrie, for the relatives of the 11,500 dead of Aubers Ridge who had died for nothing, of the 16,500 of Festubert who at least had their thousand yards to show for it, of the 43,000 lost at Loos, the greatest battle yet fought by a British army – it was the year that the world stopped and for the volunteers of 1914 it was their welcome to Erich Remarque's universal enemy, Death. 'The dug-outs have been nearly all blown in,' Roland Leighton, Vera Brittain's fiancé and one of the brightest of those golden youths who had sat listening to Uppingham's headmaster only a year before, wrote bitterly home,

> and in among the chaos of twisted iron and splintered timber and shapeless earth are the fleshless, blackened bones of simple men who poured out their red, sweet wine of youth unknowing, for nothing more tangible than Honour or their Country's Glory or another Lust of Power. Let him who thinks War is a glorious, golden thing, who loves to roll forth stirring words of exhortation, invoking Honour and Praise and Valour and Love of Country with as thoughtless and fervid faith as inspired the priests of Baal to call on their own slumbering deity, let him but look at a little pile of sodden grey rags that cover half a skull and a shin bone and what might have been his ribs, or at this skeleton lying on its side, resting, half crouching, as it fell, perfect but that it is headless . . . and let him think how grand and glorious a thing it is to have distilled all Youth and Joy and Life into a foetid heap of hideous putrescence!

Leighton himself would be dead by Christmas, shot through the stomach, but if this year of disillusionment and rising casualties brought home the grim paradox at the heart of Ware's steady rise up the military ladder, that only made him the more resolved to 'stick to it'. 'I told you in my last letter I regarded things then as on the knees of the Gods,' he wrote to Milner at the end of April, just a week after the first gas attacks against French and French African troops north of Ypres.[2] 'Well the work is going well (touching wood, very well). Macready is very pleased . . . I am absolutely *persuaded of the importance* of the work out here.'

There were any number of sensitive and potentially divisive issues that fell within his new remit – cremations, exhumations, the proliferation of unauthorised private memorials – but at the centre of Ware's negotiations was the key question of land expropriation for the burial of the Allied dead. Initially it had been possible to deal with these matters at local level, but as the cemeteries and churchyards immediately behind the front line filled, the problem of acquiring new land and establishing rights over old burial grounds had become a matter for the state and not the municipality. The kindness and gratitude of the

2   'Talking about Gods,' Ware flippantly added for his old chief's benefit, 'when the Turcos saw the yellow fumes slowly advancing towards them they thought it was a Gin and legged it!' This was the crisis that was redeemed in large part by the heroics of the 1st Canadian Division in a series of desperate actions commemorated by Frederick Chapman Clemesha's St Julien Memorial at 'Vancouver Corner', north-east of Ypres, an 11-metre-high single shaft of Vosges granite surmounted by a 'Brooding Soldier', head bowed, reversed arms. It bears the inscription: THIS COLUMN MARKS THE BATTLEFIELD WHERE 18,000 CANADIANS ON THE BRITISH LEFT WITHSTOOD THE FIRST GERMAN GAS ATTACKS THE 22nd – 24th OF APRIL. 2,000 FELL AND HERE LIE BURIED. 'The Canadians paid heavily for their sacrifice,' Marshal Foch declared at the unveiling ceremony in 1923, 'and the corner of earth on which this Memorial of gratitude and piety rises has been bathed in their blood. They wrote here the first page in that Book of Glory which is the history of their participation in the war.'

French people had been a constant theme of Ware's early letters and reports, and in the crisis summer of 1915 their government followed suit with an inimitably Gallic elan, claiming for France not just the duty but the *right* 'to adopt as her child and to honour . . . every soldier who has fallen on her soil for justice and the freedom of the nations'. It would be the best part of a year before Ware's negotiations finally bore legislative fruit in an 'expropriation bill', but in all the complex and often fractious wartime dealings of the Allies, it would be hard to find a more signal act of friendship and imagination than France's response to the British dead.

There would be difficulties and frustrations ahead, delays and amendments in the bill's committee stage, rumblings in the Senate, legal questions and unease over the effective appropriation of French land by a foreign government, but Ware was at least determined to make sure that his own side did not make things worse. 'I have warned the Press to tell their correspondents to be on the lookout for M. Millerand's speech,' he wrote to his deputy Captain Messer at a crucial stage at the end of June, when the French Minister of War was ready to move the bill, convinced, as ever, that if he did not tell people what to say and when to say it, then no one – not the Army, the Paris Embassy, the politicians at home, the newspapers, not even the Royal Family – could be trusted to do or say the right thing at the right time, 'and I have also been privately promised that the Prime Minister will make a suitable reply in the House of Commons to M. Millerand.'

Could the Adjutant General put some pressure on the Embassy to be a little more gracious? Could a telegram of thanks from the King be sent at the right time? Could Britain not be more generous with her decorations to French civilians? It was the old Ware of the *Morning Post* again, prodding and cajoling, dropping a 'hint' to the *Times* editor here, soothing a minister's vanity there, and if there was a touch of megalomania in it all, it clearly worked. By September, Millerand's bill had been carried through the Chamber of Deputies on the back of an emotional appeal from the Rapporteur, and in December at last became law in a form that enshrined all the most disinterested intentions of the original bill with the addition of one crucial clause that would give Britain control over the future upkeep of its war graves.

Ware never did anything more important in his life and that last clause had a lot to do with it. 'The law of 29 December' was all and more than he could have hoped for – 'perpetuity of sepulture' for Britain and her Empire's dead, the cost of all lands to be borne on the French budget, but it was this last provision for a single 'properly constituted' British authority to supervise and finance the maintenance of the cemeteries that proved the key to their enduring character.

It would be hard to exaggerate the importance of this provision and difficult to imagine what Britain's war cemeteries would have looked like without it, because in relieving France of the financial burden of their maintenance, Ware had secured control over every detail of their future. At this stage of the conflict it remained a largely theoretical concern of course, but the concession guaranteed that when the time came there could be no conflicts of authority over decisions that up until this point had been matters of chance and private initiative.

It would be hard to say who Ware saw as the principal danger to this future – British units who seemed bent on turning France into a giant memorial park or French advocates of giant ossuaries – but another issue had already underlined how vital that control was. In the early months of 1915 the rising numbers of unidentified dead had presented the French authorities with an almost insuperable problem, and in the middle of June, a scientific committee set up to explore alternatives to burial, had released a report that had sent Ware scuttling around the Ministries of the Interior, War and Hygiene in panic.

The solution proposed by the committee was for a continuous chain of *plein air* crematoria, a hundred metres square in size, and sited between the front line and the artillery parks at ten-kilometre intervals along the whole length of the front. Around the perimeter of each area the committee had recommended that a portable canvas screen two metres high should be erected, and at the centre of the field a large pit dug in the shape of an inverted and truncated pyramid that could be layered for cremations – 'in the simple manner of Indians', the report adds with an engagingly Rousseau-ian note – with successive strata of wood and naked bodies. Fifty crematoria in all, petrol or tar to expedite the process, ready access to wood and transport, twenty-five gravediggers to each site, twenty woodsmen, twenty carriers, one doctor, one engineer officer, several NCOs, one priest and, 'if possible', one rabbi 'to provide for the satisfaction of every religious sentiment': death on an industrial scale met death as *gloire* in a final exhortation that blended French swank, Enlightenment rationalism and a proto-Nazi thoroughness in a way peculiarly designed to disquiet John Bull.

'In all ages from the earliest times up to our own day cremation has been practised in time of war,' the report had declared,

> The hot weather is approaching. It is in the spring that epidemics develop with the greatest vigour . . . Myriads of worms swarm in the corpses . . . myriads of flies will alike sow those germs of death sprung from the dead . . . Great evils need great remedies. We have only just time to act . . .
>
> Soldiers sacrificed their lives without hesitation. They behaved like heroes. But with the sacrifice of their lives let them and their relatives sacrifice their bodies also. Let us honour them as the ancients honoured their heroes by burning their bodies and thus rendering their cinders imperishable. The whole of the country will be their tomb. Let us free ourselves from the prejudice of the old customs which under existing conditions may be fatal . . . Let us not shrink from any sacrifice for those who fight.

It was a proposal that in the end died of its own technocratic afflatus, but Ware's negotiations had crucially guaranteed that no similar threat hung over the future of Britain's war cemeteries. The liberality of the French authorities had made some kind of settlement a formality from the start, but it was Ware who had created a treaty that would be a model for every subsequent agreement, Ware who had picked his way through the legal obstacles, Ware who had the tact and journalistic nous to mobilise establishment opinion, Ware who protected France from an uncontrolled rash of British monuments and – above all – Ware who had the foresight to recognise cultural differences in attitudes to the dead that all the Francophilia in the world was never going to bridge.

If the law of 29 December shows one side of Ware, however, the second seminal development that makes 1915 the crucial year in the history of Britain's war graves shows the other, opportunistic side of his character. In the early months of the war a number of private exhumations had been carried out by families who wanted their son's or husband's bodies home, but at Ware's prompting the Adjutant General, Macready, had written to Ian Malcolm at the end of February spelling out a new stance for the BEF. 'As regards the question in general,' Macready told him,

> of exhuming bodies either for the purpose of identification or for removal to England, the Commander in Chief has issued instructions that this shall not be done, and it is never allowed in the British area . . . if it is carried out it must be distinctly understood that it is not done with the approval of Sir John French.

There was no abiding principle involved in this, no sense that the embargo would stretch beyond the duration of the war, and when two weeks later General Joffre issued a proclamation banning all exhumations on French soil, that too was done on health grounds. In late 1914, Malcolm had carried out the exhumation of a mass grave that revealed more than sixty identifications, but while Ware had never been happy about this, it was not until the death of one particular officer more than a month after Macready's letter that unease hardened into a principle that would become one of the battle cries of the Imperial War Graves Commission.

The officer in question was a twenty-nine-year-old lieutenant in the Royal Welsh Fusiliers who had only been at the front a matter of days when he was killed. He had sailed over to France on 15 March, and after a week at base camp at Le Havre had joined his battalion in the Ypres Salient on the twenty-first. Two days later he had his first experience of German shells. 'The noise is just like the tearing of calico,' he wrote home to his mother, the enclosed, feminine world of his childhood still lingering comfortingly on among the miseries of the Salient. 'It grew louder and louder,' he went on, 'until the explosion ends the rending sound.'

From there his story unfolds with a poignant inevitability that makes it a minor classic of its kind. He had never wanted to fight – 'Heaven knows, so far from having the least inclination for military service, I dread it and dislike it intensely,' he had written on volunteering – but oddly now that he was with his battalion he seems to have felt no fear at all. 'I am very glad and proud to have got to the front,' he wrote again, Christian faith and sense of duty girding him against what he seems to have known from the first was going to happen. 'It is not the length of existence that counts, but what is achieved during that existence, however short.' And short it was. 'We have been definitely informed that we go into the trenches tomorrow night,' he wrote again on 10 April, 'I rather dread the work, because I am so unfamiliar with it, and one will omit things through innocence which are essential to the safety of one's men . . . but I am delighted to get at the real thing at last.'

He was as inept a soldier as he feared. On the night of the eleventh he was welcomed to the front trenches by the 'whistle of stray bullets' from the German line 'about the length of the terrace away', and had his first, brief experience of a subaltern's night duties. 'I thoroughly enjoyed it,' he wrote reassuringly the next day,

> scrambled out over the parapet to my two groups, fell prostrate over the barbed wire, was duly found by the now thoroughly awake listening post – nearly stepped into an old deep trench full of water, and eventually got to sleep at 2.20 – only to be awoken at 4 A.M. by the order to stand to, i.e. ready for an attack at dawn – everything was cold and miserable, and after such a short sleep one did not feel whether one was on one's head or feet – (I must now break off for a purpose, which I will tell you about tomorrow).

For William Glynne Charles Gladstone MP, the twenty-nine-year-old grandson of W. E. Gladstone, master of Hawarden Castle and Lord Lieutenant of Flintshire, there would be no tomorrow. Across the bottom of this letter is a note in his mother's hand. 'This unfinished letter was his last to me,' she wrote. 'I found it in his writing-pad among his things returned to me from the front.' Genetic inheritance, in a fatal combination of physical and moral attributes, had claimed another victim. A strong, family sense of duty had brought him to France and his mother's Blantyre genes finished him off. Like his maternal grandfather, the 12th Lord, William Gladstone was very tall, and he had been shot by a sniper while standing, head exposed, behind a collapsed section of parapet that he had been detailed to repair on his first arrival at the front. He had been warned by his company commander 'to be careful', his uncle was later told,

but Will said he could not always be crouching, his men would think he was funking . . . All his men loved him [and] thinking that Will had a chance of life, and it being impossible to get him along the twisting trench, the doctor called for volunteers to get out of the trench and run the risk of taking him back across the open – the distance at that spot between the German and British lines being only one hundred yards.

If he had made little mark on the Army alive, his death was another matter. By the time Gladstone was killed the Joffre ban on exhumations had been in force for almost a month, but the news had no sooner reached Hawarden than the social and political cogs began to turn. 'It was the earnest wish of his mother that the body should be brought home,' Will's uncle blandly recalled,

and Henry [another uncle] took prompt and effective action. He communicated with the Prime Minister, and by permission of the King, the War Office gave the necessary instructions for the 'King's Lieutenant' to be brought home . . . Henry received every assistance from the military authorities, and in the early morning of 22nd April, arrived with Will at Hawarden. The body was placed in the Temple of Peace. The funeral on the following day showed how deeply and widely Will's loss was felt . . . With full military honours, Will was laid to rest by the side of his father in the quiet churchyard of Hawarden.[3]

'I notice Gladstone's body has been sent home,' Robert Cecil wrote wearily to Ware four days later, 'and I understand that this was done in obedience to pressure from a very high quarter. It is from the point of view of administration perhaps a little unfortunate.'

It might have seemed unfortunate to Cecil, it was anything but to Ware. He had never been happy about exhumations, though it was probably quite enough that it was Ian Malcolm who was carrying them out, and he saw in this Old World exercise of privilege the 'cause' he had been looking for. In Kitchener's New Army what place was there for this kind of social discrimination? In a war where men of every class were giving up their lives in their thousands why should only the rich be able to bring their dead home? And if Will Gladstone was everything that the politician and old dissenter in Ware disliked – anti-Milnerian and pro-free trade, anti-war and pro-United Ireland, socially conservative and High Church – then so much the better. 'CONFIDENTIAL', he wrote back to Cecil on 5 May, scenting blood,

There is possible trouble ahead about some exhumations at

3　Robert Graves, inevitably, had a rather different take on it. According to Graves, Gladstone had only volunteered in the first place because those same mourning tenants threatened to chuck him in the duck pond if he didn't.

Poperinghe. I entirely agree with your remark about Gladstone's body. Incidentally, the exhumation was carried out by British soldiers under fire. Fortunately (?or unfortunately) nobody was hit. The impression it has created among the soldiers out here is to be regretted. The one point of view overlooked in this matter is that of the officers themselves, who in ninety-nine cases out of a hundred will tell you that if they are killed would wish to be among their men.

The death and repatriation of Gladstone had highlighted a conflict between freedom and equality that would define the battleground of Ware's life for years to come. On the face of it the abstract proposition that all should be treated equally seems unarguable; however if the death of Will Gladstone underlines anything it is that there was nothing 'abstract' about Ware's work. Gladstone was not a statistic in the GRC's swelling register – another 27,000 names over the summer months of 1915 – but an individual with all the rights, ties, obligations and history that the word implies. And where did the body of William Gladstone belong if not in a grave next to his father in their own parish church? How could the proper resting place of so reluctant and inept a soldier – a man to whom the whole idea of war was 'detestable . . . alien from his mind and soul . . . repugnant to his whole moral fibre' – be the mud of Flanders? By what order of precedence should the fleeting camaraderie of the trenches take precedence over the deeply felt and shared community of Hawarden? Who else but his mother and sisters should say where and how he should be commemorated? By what moral or legal right beyond the question of hygiene could or should any organisation override those wishes? By what overweening extension of state power or political will should the country presume to claim the dead as its own?

These were all questions that Ware would eventually have to address, but in the short term the fortunes of war had delivered him a trump card in the shape of the Eton and Oxford Gladstone. The only privilege that an Etonian could claim at the front was the high probability of dying, but the intervention of the King and the suggestion of political influence enabled Ware to recast as an issue of privilege what was at bottom a matter of individual freedoms that held as true for a private in a Pals' battalion as for a lord lieutenant.

It also disguised – for the moment at least – a contradiction that lay at the heart of Ware's grave work. The impetus that drove men like Broadley to hunt down every grave they could find in the first weeks of the war was one of simple piety. They wanted to record and honour each individual who had died and preserve that individuality. Their loyalties, unarticulated but strong, were to the families whose dead they were recording. How, though, could that be squared with death on the unimaginable scale that the war was now unfolding? How could it be balanced against a new and democratic demand for equality of treatment? Were individualism and equality any more compatible beyond the grave than they were this side of it?

These were no longer questions that could be ducked. Ware's successful negotiations for the permanent sepulture of Britain's dead on French soil meant that the future had to be considered. Already, private speculation was rushing in to fill the official vacuum. 'Here the Germans are almost on three sides of us,' one young officer, Douglas Gillespie, whose brother Thomas, a Gold medal-winning Olympic oarsman, had already been culled in 1914, wrote home in June 1915, just four months before his own death,

> and the dead have been buried just where they fell, behind the trenches. There are graves scattered up and down, some with crosses and names on them, some nameless and unmarked – as I think my brother's grave must be, for they have been fighting round about the village where he was killed all through these last eight months. That doesn't trouble me much . . . but still, these fields are sacred in a sense, and I wish that when peace comes, our Government might combine with the French Government to make one long avenue between the lines from the Vosges to the sea, or if that is too much, at any rate from La Bassée to Ypres . . . I would make a fine broad road in the No Man's Land between the lines, with paths for pilgrims on foot, and plant trees for shade, and fruit trees, so that the soil should not be altogether wasted. Some of the shattered farms and houses might be left as evidence, and the regiments might put up their records beside the trenches which they held all through the winter. Then I would like to send every man, woman and child in Western Europe on pilgrimage along that *Via Sacra,* so that they might think and learn what war means from the silent witnesses on either side.

The makeshift solutions of 1914 were no longer acceptable. There was 'much to be desired' in the state of the cemeteries, Sir

Arthur Lawley told Ware in July, offering Red Cross funds for a rudimentary programme of gardening to make them 'less miserable and unsightly'. From the Dominions, too, letters were coming in asking what was being done to particularise the graves of the Empire's dead. 'I believe that you occupy the lugubrious post of controller of all graves in France and Flanders,' the Secretary of the Overseas Club wrote to Ware over the suggestion that maples should be planted around Canadian graves, 'and I should like to get your views on the subject. Judging by the manner in which the idea has been taken up in Canada, I believe it would appeal to Canadian sentiment extraordinarily if we could manage to do this.'

This was music to Ware's imperialist ears. It is never easy to be sure where he is responding to public opinion and where he is shaping it, but he and the zeitgeist were one. Public opinion across the Empire demanded action and he had in place the legal structure, organisation and experience to respond. The work in France and the other theatres of war required not just an undertaker but a leader and an overriding philosophy. And in a field where the interests of the individual and the community needed to be weighed, who better than a man who had spent the last pre-war years of political 'exile' attempting to square that particular circle?

FOUR

Consolidation

If ever a man's philosophy emerged out of the needs of his own idiosyncratic personality it was Fabian Ware's. As a young boy growing up in Clifton he had been imbued with both the autocracy and the idealism of the Brethren, and his whole life was, in one shape or another, an attempt to resolve the tensions between his own unbending individualism and the communitarian dream.

Ware was a profound believer in individual and political freedoms – both for the person and, within the organic structure of the Empire, the separate nations that made it up – but he was at heart a collectivist. 'Collectivist, individualist, collectivist, individualist,' he had written in his 1912 'manifesto', describing the organic ascent of the individual to an ever wider and deeper sense of community life that would subordinate the interests of the individual to a higher collective 'good':

such is the life of man. Throughout, each tendency struggles for supremacy; and in the flower of his age they balance one another, producing that equilibrium which is perfection and which, because it is perfection, may not, until freed

77

from the laws of nature endure. At this stage, when his powers have reached their zenith, the individual is merged in the family . . . the family in the nation . . . And so the nation, in mature consideration of its individuality [in] the highest attainment of human collectivity which the world has yet seen . . . the empire.

Everything that Ware did with the Imperial War Graves Commission flowed out of this larger faith. For most of those who worked for him their focus remained the graves, and yet for Ware the work was a means to a political end, with every detail of it subordinated to this overarching imperial vision. 'To Fabian Ware,' Violet Markham, an educational reformer and imperialist in the Ware mould, wrote in 1924 as they looked back together over his war graves work, 'it had been a great opportunity no less than a great mission . . . "Think [he told her] what this organisation of ours means as a model of what Imperial co-operation might be".'

Like many another good communitarian, like his old boss, Milner, in fact, Ware's idea of co-operation was the rest of the community doing what he wanted it to do, but that did not make his vision any less compelling. There would always remain a streak of Pope's 'Atticus' about him – a determination 'to bear, like the Turk, no rival near the throne' – but for those who shared or responded to his idealism, energy, and sheer personal magnetism he was an irresistible force.

The thing that had most struck the Red Cross's Colonel Stewart, when he visited Ware's men in the autumn of 1914, was the 'keenness of all the Unit and their loyalty to their chief', and that would remain a constant of Ware's working life. 'Vitalisers are few and far between in the drab world,' Violet Markham wrote admiringly after seeing Ware for the first time since the heady days of the *Morning Post* more than a decade earlier,

> and Fabian Ware had, I remembered, a gift all his own of raising any subject on to a plane where the dross falls away and only gold remains . . .
>
> Here was . . . a man without illusions, who saw the chaos, but whose vision of ultimate realities remained serene and unclouded . . . The fine head – gay, humorous, sensitive – had lost none of its quality. We create in a large measure what we will and desire, and in this Rupert of the pen and sword, teacher, administrator, editor, [soldier] the spirit of high adventure shone forth unquenched. To sit by such a fire was to relight the candles of one's own doubting spirit.

The loyalty and enthusiasm Ware could inspire in those who worked for him was vital, because as 1915 drew to its grim conclusion and Millerand's land expropriation bill finally became law, Ware was freed to concentrate on the larger picture. The law of 29 December had given the British everything they could want, but in providing for the creation of a 'legally constituted body' with sole responsibility for everything to do with the graves, Ware had potentially allowed a rival cuckoo in the uncompromising shape of the formidable Sir Alfred Mond, industrialist, financier and First Commissioner at the Office of Works, within his jealously guarded nest.

The problem was that in the past the Office of Works had

been responsible for the upkeep of British cemeteries abroad, notably the Crimean, and Mond was no more than Ware a man to give up power willingly. The scale of the work facing the GRC in France and the Middle East clearly required a new organisation, but what Ware wanted was an arrangement that would simultaneously reflect the growing national and imperial importance of his task and squeeze Mond and his faceless government department out of any share in the real power.

It was a turf war that would rumble on for years to come (they would still be at it in the thirties) and in the battle of the mastodons Ware got his way, with the old GRC fully integrated into the Army as the Directorate of Graves Registration and Enquiries (DGR&E), retaining responsibility for the duration of the war, and a 'sleeper' committee set up to plan for the future. 'With such examples [the Office of Works' Crimean cemeteries] as a warning,' Ware recalled two years later, as deft as ever at invoking the mood of the nation when it happened to coincide with his own,

the Army towards the end of 1915 proposed to the Government the appointment of a National Committee for the Care of Soldiers' Graves, which would take over the work of the Directorate after the War. It was felt that the nation would expect that the government should undertake the care of the last resting places of those who had fallen, but at the same time that relatives would consider that work of so intimate a nature should be entrusted to a specially appointed body rather than to any existing Government department . . . As a result a Committee was appointed by the Prime Minister in January, 1916, and His Royal Highness the Prince of Wales was graciously pleased to accept the presidency.

The National Committee for the Care of Soldiers' Graves was every bit as dormant as Ware intended, and as the legally recognised association required by the French law of 29 December it forms another link in the evolution of the Imperial War Graves Commission. It would be difficult to point to anything it actually *did* during its short and harmless life, but its mere existence under royal patronage was the final imprimatur on the work that had begun so modestly and almost accidentally in the autumn of 1914 among the orchards and farms of northern France.

From the first meeting the membership of the committee reflected this new status, with the Directorate of Graves Registration and Enquiries, the French, the British Army and all the relevant government departments represented. However it was only when Empire representatives were added in September 1916 that Ware had the body he wanted. The Dominions had come into the conflict automatically on the King's declaration of war in 1914, and by 1916 there was not a theatre of war from the Pacific to Ypres and from Mesopotamia to East Africa where British cemeteries were not already full of the Empire's dead.

Almost nine thousand Australians and three thousand New Zealanders at Gallipoli alone, heavy Canadian casualties at Ypres during the first gas attacks, the Newfoundlanders virtually wiped out in a savage hour at Beaumont-Hamel, Delville Wood engraved on the South African psyche, the Indians at Neuve-Chapelle

– even before Vimy Ridge was added to the Empire's battle honours – new narratives of nationhood were being forged and it was clear to Ware that any new body must reflect this imperial reality. 'He had heard rumours of a Committee being formed in Canada,' Macready, as ever singing from the same song sheet, told a meeting that for the first time included representatives of the Dominions and the government of India, 'and we were anxious to see whether we could not come to a modus operandi by which the wishes of the Dominions and Colonies would all come up for discussion in the Central Committee which would then speak with the voice of Empire.'

It is possible that after the tragedy of Gallipoli, where Australian losses gave birth to a new sense of identity that was from the first conceived in opposition to a 'class-bound and incompetent' Britain, the Empire would never speak with a single voice, but no one was better equipped by his natural sympathies to reconcile a central authority with the legitimate and diverging aspirations of the Empire than Ware. Over the previous summer he had kept in close touch with Dominion forces in the field, and he had come to this first meeting armed with cemetery plans, photographs and planting schemes to show what was already being done to meet the different national sensitivities.

For Macready this was simply a matter of practicalities, but for Ware himself, the significance of the meeting was as much political and symbolic as it was narrowly about his graves work. For most of his adult life he had argued and campaigned for closer imperial unity, and here at last, at a meeting in the War Office of government and Empire representatives with their own varying concerns and agendas, was a chance to realise the dream of an un-federated Empire of Equals that had, in one form or another, inspired him since his South African days.

The stamp of royal approval, the support of the Treasury, the backing of the Army, 'the voice of Empire' speaking as one, a largely dormant committee – it was Ware's idea of heaven. And if all that was not enough, a letter to an old friend, Philippe Millet, shows how little in practice had changed. 'I am sending you confidentially,' he wrote to him at the beginning of July 1916, one week into the Battle of the Somme and almost six months after Millerand's bill had become law,

(1) A copy of a letter I have written to the French mission and (2) a copy of a letter that the Foreign Office has sent to our ambassador in Paris. My object in doing so is that you should see that at last I have got our lazy people to acknowledge in something like fitting terms (as I am responsible for the draft I cannot say more!) the action of the French Nation in providing land for the burial of British Soldiers . . .

While one does not want to say that the Prince of Wales is *responsible* in any way (we have to shield our Royalties from all responsibility in this democratic country!) he does take a very great interest in the matter . . . and very deeply appreciated the sympathy which has been shown by the French Nation in this matter.

The new, imperial status of Ware's organisation was most obviously reflected in his decision, in May 1916, to move the

Directorate's headquarters from France to St James's Square in London, but the focus and model for all its work remained the Western Front. The French government had laid down the legal framework for the burial of British and Belgian soldiers in 1915, and within days of its final ratification Macready had issued in General Routine Orders his instructions for how this was to be carried out on the ground. Most of these regulations were of a purely administrative nature – the role of 'A Branch' in choosing sites, the number of burial plots to each corps, the consultation process with the Directorate officers, additional grounds for casualty clearing and field ambulance centres, map scales, registration procedures, legal formalities, the precise dimensions and spacing of graves ('9" to 12" apart and a path not exceeding 3' in width . . . between the rows of graves') – but shining through the thick fog of acronyms and echelons and duplicates and interminable forms is the old 'fieldcraft' of Ware's Mobile Ambulance Unit days. '(4) At the time of burial, "Instructions to Chaplains",' read:

> The grave must be marked in such a way as to ensure identification. Chaplains are responsible that, even in cases when the unit proposes to erect a cross, a grave is properly marked by other means until this is done. Pegs with labels attached are supplied by the Graves Registration Units for the purpose.

The lessons of the early days had been well learned. Particulars were to be written on the label in 'hard-black lead' and not with indelible pencil, the pegs were to be placed at forty-five degrees

IOANNES·ACVTVS·EQVES·BRITANNICVS·DVX·AETATIS·S
VAE·CAVTISSIMVS·ET·REI·MILITARIS·PERITISSIMVS·HABITVS·EST

·PAVLI·VGIELLI·OPVS·

Previous page: *Il Diavolo Incarnato.* Paolo Uccello's equestrian memorial to Sir John Hawkwood, the notorious fourteenth-century English mercenary and scourge of Italy commemorated by a grateful city in Florence's Duom

ve: *Gallipoli*. A soldier salutes at the grave prepared for the remains of New Zealand dead, killed in the savage
ing for Chunuk Bair on 8 August 1915. After a gap of five years identification was often impossible, but the bones
been arranged in a forlorn attempt to give an individual integrity to each burial.

Above: *Thiepval, 1 August 1932.* Fabian Ware – 'The Great Commemorator' and moving spirit of the Imperial War Graves Commission – with the Prince of Wales at the unveiling of Lutyens's Memorial to the Missing of the Somme. Lutyens can be seen in the background on the left.

Right: *Vendresse Cemetery, south of Laon in the Department of the Aisne, France.* In its utter simplicity and pastoral quiet, perhaps the archetypal Commission cemetery. It contains the graves of more than seven hundred men killed, principally, in the fighting of 1914 and 1918, of whom only 327 have names.

Left: *'Have you news of my boy Jack?'*. Rudyard Kipling and his son John, killed at the age of eighteen at the Battle of Loos in 1915. As both the Poet of Empire and bereaved father who never recovered from his son's loss, Kipling enjoyed an immense influence as the Imperial War Graves Commission's first literary advisor.

Top: *Armed for battle.* William Nicholls's caricature of the Commission architects Edwin Lutyens and Herbert Baker, who had badly fallen out over the building of New Delhi and brought their differences with them to France.

Bottom: The official war artist Francis Dodd's portrait of his friend Charles Holden, the most austere of the Principal Architects in charge of the cemeteries along the old Western Front.

Above: *Sir Edwin Lutyens's Serre Road Cemetery, No. 2.* Just one of the seemingly interminable line of cemeteries t̶ mark the Battle of the Somme in 1916, and the 1918 German spring advance over the same bitterly won ground. cemetery was begun in 1917 and enlarged after the war as the process of concentration began. Almost 5,000 of th 7,127 burials are unidentified.

to the grave, the labels on the underside protected from the weather. 'In special cases where the eventual erection of crosses may be difficult or delayed,'

> a record written with hard-black lead pencil is, in addition, to be placed in a tin or bottle (neck downwards) half-buried in the ground. Where one tin or bottle is necessarily used to mark several graves, the record enclosed must be so marked as to ensure the proper identification of each grave . . .
>
> In authorised cemeteries, numbered pegs are now being placed to show where graves are to be dug. These numbers should be shown on the burial returns as graves are used.
>
> Under no circumstances are crosses erected or registered by the Graves Registration Units to be removed or altered without authority from the DGR&E.

It was, however, in matters of general policy and philosophy that Ware's influence was most clearly needed because this was not just a European but a global war. It was already clear from that first meeting with imperial representatives that even the largely white and Christian Dominions had their own aspirations, but what of the Indian forces in the field? What of their Muslim troops? Or Sikh? Or Indian Christians? Or Egyptian Copts? Or the Chinese Labour Corps? Or the South African native troops? Or the men of the British West Indies?

They had 'experts' to call on for advice – though the history of the British Empire would not suggest that was an infallible assistance – but if there is anything in the slow evolution of the old Mobile Unit into the Commonwealth War Graves Commission that chimes with modern sensibilities it is the way in which Ware answered these questions. There is the occasional use of language that highlights the inevitable gulf that separates his world from ours, and yet it is difficult to imagine that anyone operating within the cultural assumptions of the age could have come up with policies that offered so few hostages to the future: 'On no account should [Egyptian] Mohammedans be buried in Christian consecrated ground' . . . 'Mohammedan' graves were to be 'at least 6 feet deep' . . .; their burial grounds, wherever possible, should be 'dug by Egyptian labour' . . .; a small stone either end of the grave to be allowed, but no writing . . . Copts should be placed in coffins in Christian burial grounds and a modified service read at the chaplain's direction . . . Jewish graves were to be marked with a double triangle on a stake. 'Under no circumstances should a cross be erected over an Indian Grave . . .'

Within the all-embracing ambition that graves should be sited 'facing the enemy' to the east – a stipulation that conveniently satisfied religious as well as military sensibilities – the permutations were daunting and the punctilio and desire to respect difference faultless. 'The ideal site to secure repose and drive away evil spirits,' Ware's revised 1918 instructions for the burial of Chinese dead, explains,

> is on sloping ground with a stream below, or gully down which water always or occasionally passes. The grave should not be parallel to the north, south, east or west. This is especially important to Chinese Mohammedans. It should

be about 4ft deep, with the head towards the hill and the feet towards the water. A mound of earth about 2ft high is piled over the grave . . . Whenever possible the friends of the deceased should be allowed access to the corpse, and should be allowed to handle it, as they like to dress it and show marks of respect.

There were limits to cultural sympathies – a strict ban, for instance, on firing parties or European troops at the burials of South African natives – and a wartime speech from General Smuts offers a sobering reminder of the realities that lay behind even the most inclusive vision of Empire. 'We were not aware of the great military value of the natives until this war,' the old Boer poacher turned imperial gamekeeper told a meeting at London's Savoy that was chaired by Lord Selborne, Milner's successor in South Africa,

This war has been an eye-opener in many new directions. It will be a serious question for the statesmen of the Empire and Europe whether they are going to allow a state of affairs like that to be possible, and to become a menace not just to Africa, but perhaps to Europe itself. I hope that one of the results of this war will be some arrangement or convention among the nations interested in Central Africa by which the military training of natives in that area will be prevented, as we have prevented it in South Africa. It can well be foreseen that armies may be trained there, which under proper leadership might prove a danger to civilisation itself.

There was also the problem of dealing with a professional army that was finding its practices and assumptions coming under the sustained scrutiny of a civilian world. 'In April, 1916, I was appointed by the War Cabinet to be a member of an International War Graves Committee,' Sir Lionel Earle later wrote, recalling an inspection visit of the cemeteries near Albert,[4]

> In some of the cemeteries I noticed two or three isolated graves with wooden crosses with nothing on them. I asked what they were, and whether they were German soldiers; I was told not to ask any questions. I insisted on knowing, and was informed that they were graves of men who had paid the penalty for cowardice in the field. This segregation of graves worried me, as I felt that the men had paid the penalty for their weakness, which may be largely physical, and that it was absolutely wrong to brand them for all time, inflicting pain on their relatives.
>
> I do not think my views were accepted by our military companions, so I submitted a minute on the subject to the War Cabinet, and they endorsed my view, so this custom was abolished and the graves merged with the others.

The Army was not going to fade away tamely – the inscription on the graves of executed men was to be marked 'DIED' instead

4 This was the same Earle whose brother had been reported killed in 1914. His own personal experience of the war was improbably enhanced in 1918 when a fragment of an anti-aircraft shell landed on him in St James's Park.

of 'KILLED IN ACTION' or 'DIED OF WOUNDS' – but the old order was inevitably changing and the face of the cemeteries changing with it. In 1915 the Red Cross had offered funds for some simple gardening work to begin, and in the early part of 1916, Arthur Hill, the assistant director of the Royal Botanic Gardens at Kew, went on a tour of the Western Front cemeteries at Ware's request to advise on a systematic programme of planting.

As the work of the Directorate expanded to other theatres – Palestine, Egypt, Mesopotamia, Salonika, Gallipoli, Italy – the challenges would only grow more acute and various; even within the area defined by the British-held sector of the Western Front there were issues enough. The pressure from the Dominions for native plants remained Hill's principal concern, but in the cold climate of northern France, with loam on top of chalk and the thin topsoil often buried under the impact of exploding shells, there was a limit to what could be done. 'South Africa,' Hill later lamented, 'except for annuals, can have no permanent commemorative plant; nor alas! can we show our respect, by any floral emblem, to our West Indian, West African, Malayan and other Colonial soldiers who have fought and died in France.'

There were also interminable French regulations governing the distance of trees and hedges from cemetery borders and the size of paths and grave plots to curb Hill's ambitions, but with maple seeds from Canada, Tasmanian Eucalyptus and New Zealand shrubs arriving at Kew the first real progress was made. In his original tour of France, Arthur Hill had inspected thirty-seven different cemeteries, and over the next two years this number swelled to almost two hundred with four nurseries and an

expanding staff of officers, gardeners and the Women's Army
Auxiliary Corps volunteers to service them.

It was all very well issuing detailed instructions to gravediggers to
reserve the topsoil, or talk of planting wattle[5] among the whitening
bones at Gallipoli, though, because the horrors of 1916 can have
left no one in doubt that the real work would have to wait. By
the beginning of that summer Ware's men had already registered
more than 50,000 graves, but from that first misty July morning on
the Somme, when the opening waves of Kitchener's raw, un-blooded
New Army went over the top for the first (and for 20,000 of them,
the last) time, that figure would come to seem almost nothing.

There were 58,000 British casualties on that first day – 415,000
killed, wounded or missing over the next four and a half months,
one and a quarter million Allied and enemy in all. It was not
just the scale of death, but the nature of it that seemed to make
a mockery of everything Ware's organisation stood for. 'Beyond
the area called on the map Thiepval,' the poet Edmund Blunden,
a future literary advisor to the IWGC, wrote of a battlefield that
had obliterated not just the individuality of the fighting man but
his very physical integrity,

> on the map a trench called St Martin's led forward; unhappy
> he who got into it! It was blasted out by intense bombardment

5   'It was all Australia to me,' Kipling, the poet of Empire, had written of
the homesick scent of wattle (*Acacia*) for an Australian volunteer in the Boer
War. 'All I had found or missed, Every face I was crazy to see, And every
woman I'd kissed: All that I shouldn't ha' done, God knows! (As he knows I'll
do it again) The smell of the wattle round Lichtenberg, Riding in, in the rain!'

into a broad shapeless gorge, and pools of mortar-like mud filled most of it. A few duckboards lay half submerged along the parapet, and these were perforce used by our companies, and calculatingly and fiercely shelled at moments by the enemy. The wooden track ended, and then the men fought their way on through the gluey morass, until not one nor two were reduced to tears and impotent wild cries to God. They were not yet at the worst of their duty, for the Schwaben Redoubt ahead was an almost obliterated cocoon of trenches in which mud, and death, and life were much the same thing – and there, the deep dugouts, which faced the German guns, were cancerous with torn bodies, and to pass an entrance was to gulp poison; in one place a corpse had apparently been thrust in to stop up a doorway's dangerous displacement, and an arm swung stupidly. Men of the next battalion were found in mud up to the armpits, and their fate was not spoken of; those who found them could not get them out. The whole zone was a corpse, and the mud itself mortified.

It was a world where the dead had precious little claim on the living. 'Crossing the Ancre again . . .,' recalled Blunden,

and climbing the dirty little road over the steep bank, one immediately entered the land of despair. Bodies, bodies and their useless gear heaped the gross waste ground. The shell-holes were mostly small lakes of what was no doubt merely rusty water, but had a red and foul semblance of blood . . . Of the dead, one was conspicuous. He was a Scottish soldier, and was kneeling, facing east, so that one could scarcely credit death in him; he was at some little distance from the usual tracks, and no one had much time in Thiepval just then for sight-seeing, or burying. Death could not kneel so, I thought, and approaching I ascertained with a sudden shrivelling of spirit that Death could and did.

The sustained sacrifice of the offensive over more than four months, the range and destructiveness of the artillery, the capture and recapture of enemy positions, all made it often impossible to observe prescribed burial regulations. In the middle of the battle, an Army Order introduced, on Ware's initiative, a new double identity disc made of pressed fibre. But when a shell could obliterate all trace of a man's existence even the most scrupulous search for regimental badges, tabs, discs, chaplain's and unit returns or – most fantastic of all – 'the measurements and description of the body', was impotent to scratch even the surface of the problem.[6]

In the face of this destructive power – and it was not just bodies and graves that were obliterated, but the landscape itself, with all those defining features, natural and man-made, that Ware's men relied on in their searches – there seems something simultaneously heroic and impossible in the dogged labours of the DGR&E. Over the nine months that followed the first day of the Somme, the Directorate added another 100,000 graves to its register, but one look at the great Thiepval Memorial to the Missing of the Somme with its 72,000 names is reminder enough

6   The horrors had been, if anything, worse at Gallipoli, where in the fierce summer heat the state of a bloated and blackened corpse often meant that a burial party simply could not bear to rescue identity discs.

that Ware's work would, in the future, be as much with those who could not be identified as those who could.

Third Ypres in 1917 and the German Spring Offensive of 1918 would make things only worse, but with corpses still littering the Somme battlefield almost a year after the offensive had begun, Ware's resources were already stretched to the limit. The responsibility for burial lay with the Army and not the Graves Directorate, but as the conduit between relatives and the Army and the official 'face' of death – 'Lord Wargraves' as Ware was irreverently nicknamed – he increasingly took the full brunt of a growing public resentment. 'We are on the verge over here of serious trouble about the number of bodies lying out still unburied on the Somme battlefields,' he wrote almost a year to the day after the start of the battle.

The soldiers returning wounded or on leave to England are complaining bitterly about it and the War Office has already received letters on the subject. There is every reason to expect that the question may be raised in Parliament any day and I do not see what defence the Government could offer for the neglect of the Army in the Field in this connection. We of course have no responsibility in the matter but I feel a lot of the good impression our work has created will be undone if a public scandal should arise in regard to this and Colonel Whitehead will be the first to appreciate that this kind of scandal will be used immediately and with great effect by the pacifists, and by others who are endeavouring to assist the enemy by obstructing the proper prosecution of the war.

The use of 'over here' to mean Britain and not France shows a shift in Ware's perspective since the early months of the war. While he had been based with the Army in the field he could preserve some kind of distance from domestic opinion but ensconced in Winchester House, St James's Square, and inundated with queries and demands from distraught relatives, there was no escaping. 'I am held up on my work,' an overstretched and understaffed Ware complained to Macready, also now back in London as Adjutant General to the Forces,

> My staff is unable to deal with [letters] and cannot offer relatives the true explanation of my inability to answer many of their enquiries. It is small satisfaction in connection with work of this kind to think that this most regrettable state of affairs is not due to any lack of foresight on my part but is entirely due to the action of the Treasury.[7]

7   The Office of Works had not forgotten old enmities either. 'My Dear Ware,' Lionel Earle wrote on 13 December 1916, an average enough sort of day on the Western Front: 'It has been brought to my notice that Colonel Stobart of your department, whose staff occupy Room 21 on the ground floor of Winchester House, insists on open fireplaces being used as well as radiators. As this is absolutely contrary to the instructions issued by order of the First Commissioner, I feel bound to call your attention unofficially in the first place, to the deviation from the rule, and shall have to do so officially unless I am absolutely convinced that it is necessary to disregard the rule in this instance. I have various reports before me as to the temperatures of the room at various times, and I find that, even at 8.10 a.m., the radiators were hot and the temperature stood at 60 [degrees].' Earle, himself, was the hardy soul who had had to flee the bathroom in his French inn when he found a cockroach in it.

It was little use, either, expounding the virtues of 'attrition' to this Britain or telling it that the Somme had relieved pressure on their French allies or on the Eastern Front; the loss was too stark and immediate for that. 'The field of Gommecourt is heaped with the bodies of Londoners,' the future Poet Laureate John Masefield wrote, evoking the Britain of cities, towns, villages and farms that had to face up to this loss,

> The London Scottish lie at the Sixteen Poplars; the Yorkshires are outside Serre; the Warwickshires lie in Serre itself; all the great hill of the Hawthorn Ridge is littered with Middlesex; the Irish are at Hamel, the Kents on the Schwaben, and the Wilts and Dorset on the Leipzig. Men of all the towns and counties of England, Wales and Scotland lie scattered among the slopes from Ovillers to Maricourt. English dead pave the road to La Boiselle, the Welsh and Scotch are in Mametz. In gullies and sheltered places, where wounded could be brought during the fighting, there are little towns of dead in all these places.

It is worth remembering this perspective, because here was the Britain – not forgetting the Newfoundland that left its dead at Beaumont-Hamel, the South Africa at Delville Wood or Australia at Pozières – to which Ware would have to answer for the rest of his working life. Over the last two years of the war the workload of the Graves Directorate would increase massively, but Ware's real battles from now on were to be on the home front. He had won over the Army; the harder task, now, was to win over the public.

95

FIVE

The Imperial War Graves Commission

In the spring of 1917, the old Mobile Ambulance Unit that had gone to France in the September of 1914 began the penultimate and decisive step in its metamorphosis into the modern Commonwealth War Graves Commission. The National Committee for the Care of Soldiers' Graves had served its purpose well enough, but with 'the great expansion and development of the work of the Directorate', Ware recalled in his first General Report on the origins of the new organisation, 'it was felt that . . . the organisation of the National Committee needed to be brought into line with [its] greatly extended scope . . . and to be placed on a permanent basis'.

The initiative for the new body had formally come from the Prince of Wales, as president of the National Committee, Ware explained, and in March 1917 the Prince had submitted a memorandum to the Prime Minister requesting that the question should be raised at the forthcoming Imperial War Conference. At the conference in April the 'matter accordingly formed one of the chief subjects of the deliberations', and on 13 April a resolution was passed 'praying His Majesty to grant a Royal Charter for the constitution of an Imperial War Graves Commission', with the power to maintain the graves of those fallen in the war, to acquire land for new burial places, 'and to erect permanent memorials in the cemeteries and elsewhere. The Royal Charter was granted on the 21st May, 1917, and the Imperial War Graves Commission was duly constituted thereunder.'

Not for the first time in this story, there is something deceptively anodyne about the official version that disguises not just Ware's role in the whole process, but also how much blood was left on the carpet. It is a nice question whether it was character or policy that dictated his show of modesty, but behind the graceful fiction of the Prince of Wales's initiative and the easy, consensual move to an imperial solution lay a familiar, dogged campaign of lobbying and departmental manoeuvring.

The issue was in part simply one of power and control – a battle between Ware and his alter ego, the bruising and immensely able, German-Jewish empire-building Alfred Mond – but beneath it lay Ware's determination that the care of the Empire's dead would be the Empire's responsibility. It was vital to get this right. Ware had briefed the Prince, so that,

the Empire will be spared the reflection that weighed on the conscience of the British nation when, nearly twenty years after the conclusion of the Crimean War, it became known that the last resting place of those who had fallen in that war had, except in individual instances, remained uncared for and neglected.

When Ware talked about the Empire he was invariably talking about himself of course, but in this case the moral argument and the mood of the country were both on his side. The Office of Works was prepared to offer India and the Dominions an 'advisory or consultative' role, but after Gallipoli and Delville Wood and Beaumont-Hamel and Neuve-Chapelle it was hard to see why the Empire should fall for the 'old bait' – as Ware called it – that Mond dangled in front of them. 'In looking forward to the time when peace may be restored,' a well-drilled Prince wrote to Lloyd George,

> the thoughts of all turn instinctively to the honoured dead who rest in many lands across the seas and to whose memory the Empire owes a duty which must never be forgotten. Future generations will judge us by the effort we made to fulfil that duty, and I hope that in undertaking it it will be possible to enlist the representatives of all those who came forward to help the Empire in the hour of need.

The creation of the IWGC was, as the Commission's official historian Philip Longworth claimed, an historic moment: 'the first organisation charged with the care of the dead in any war . . . the only permanent institutional reflection [pre-1965] of a common spirit in the Empire, of an equal partnership of nations', and it would be churlish to see it in the first place as anything other than Ware's triumph. It is possible that Mond and his Office of Works possessed the physical resources to carry out the job, but it is hard to see how any government department, committed to its own architects, hierarchies, internal ideologies and 'baggage' – not to mention monitoring room temperatures in Winchester House – could ever have risen to the challenge in the way that a new and more widely based body could do.

The Commission inevitably included the usual suspects – and, predictably, no woman (what an addition Gertrude Bell might have made!) – but one look at the first list of ex-officio and non-official members appointed by Royal Warrant in October 1917 shows a maverick breadth of representation that reflects Ware's influence. The Prince of Wales remained president with the Secretary of State for War as its ex-officio chairman, but then alongside the First Commissioner of Works and the Secretaries of State for the Colonies and for India are names that one would never have seen if Mond had had his way: the representative for Newfoundland and the High Commissioners for Canada, Australia, New Zealand and South Africa; the architect of Egypt's irrigation system and stalwart of the Red Cross, Sir William Garstin; the former Thames waterman and trade union leader, Harry Gosling; the great weaver of imperial dreams (and future arbiter of all Commission inscriptions) Rudyard Kipling; and there, finally, nestling humbly at the foot of the list, below his old ally Macready and an ageing relic of pre-Fisher naval days, Admiral Sir Edmund Poe – 'Major-General Fabian Ware, CB, CMG (Vice-Chairman)'.

The War Graves Commission was fortunate that in these first, crucial years it could call on men of such varying abilities and influence. In the propaganda battles ahead the industrial muscle of Harry Gosling and the pen of Kipling would be equally needed, and in such early chairmen as Churchill and Milner, and Empire representatives of the calibre of

William Schreiner – the brother of the novelist and campaigner, Olive Schreiner, and a former Cape Colony Prime Minister of great intellect and probity – it had men with the experience, authority and vision to make sure that government and Dominions shared the same agenda.

There would be internal strains and disagreements – Sir James Allen, the dourly formidable New Zealand High Commissioner after the war, could never be bullied into anything – but both the personnel and the powers invested in them perfectly reflected Ware's ambitions for the Commission. As the heir to the defunct Prince of Wales's Committee, it inherited all the legal authority defined by the French law of 29 December 1915. In addition, Ware had sought and got a remit that extended beyond France and Belgium to the care and maintenance of every imperial grave on land or sea of those who had died on active service,

> to keep alive the ideals for the maintenance and defence of which they have laid down their lives, to strengthen the bonds of union between all classes and races in Our Dominions, and to promote a feeling of common citizenship and of loyalty and devotion to Us and to the Empire of which they are subjects.

The Commission had been invested with all the powers that went with these duties – the acquisition and care of land for cemeteries and memorials, the keeping of records and registers, the maintenance of isolated graves, the limited purchase of land in Britain, the administration of funds voted it by the Empire's legislatures – but it was its 'policing' role that crucially defined its future. In the long negotiations of 1915, Ware had been as determined as his French colleagues to prevent a commemorative free-for-all, and enshrined in the Charter was a clause empowering the new authority to prohibit or permit 'the erection by any person other than the Commission of permanent memorials' in any cemetery under its control.

Ware was lucky in his timing in so much as the creation of this powerfully authoritarian and centralised body coincided with the growing interference of the state in the private lives of the individual. The average law-abiding citizen in 1914, as A. J. P. Taylor once memorably pointed out, could have lived out his life more or less ignorant of the state's existence, but three years of war, the Defence of the Realm Act, economic intervention and – from 1916, conscription – had intruded the state into every aspect of public and private life from the bedroom to the grave.

In the growing industrial and party political turmoil of the pre-war period, Ware had privately toyed with the notion of a Cromwellian dictatorship under Milner to put the country to rights, and war had come very close to delivering him his wish. The formation of a coalition government in 1915 had effectively emasculated a Parliament that had already outlived its elected term, and the replacement of the consensual Asquith by Lloyd George further accelerated the trend towards autocracy, concentrating effective power in a small War Cabinet and reinforcing the doctrine that, as one economist in early 1917 insisted, 'the freedom of the individual must be absorbed in the national effort' if Britain was to survive.

It is one of the ironies of the war, in fact, that the liberal democracies were prepared to watch the erosion of their civil liberties in search of victory. In the years after the war, Ware would face a backlash against the Commission's authoritarianism, but in 1917, when only the brilliant Canadian action at Vimy Ridge and the Battle of Messines offered fleeting hopes that the lessons of 1916 had been learned, the country was, as one future War Graves Commissioner put it, prepared to out-Prussian the Prussians if that was what it would take to beat them.

It was perhaps not surprising in such a climate that the Hesse-born Milner – the 'Prussian', as the American President Woodrow Wilson dubbed him – should again find himself at the centre of political life as one of the five-strong War Cabinet. The British public would never really forgive Milner his German grand-mother, but his administrative abilities were not in question, and with the Kindergarten's Philip Kerr as Lloyd George's Private Secretary, John Buchan his Director of Information, Leo Amery Assistant Secretary to the War Cabinet, and Robert Brand an influential figure in Washington, Ware's old South African friends had never been closer to real power or – momentarily it seemed – the fulfilment of their imperial dreams.

'Democracy is not going to win this war or any other,' F. S. Oliver, another imperialist intimately associated with Milner and the fall of Asquith, had insisted, and in a year of unrestricted U-boat activity and massive shipping losses, of continued military stalemate and failed peace feelers, of growing disillusionment and exhaustion, of Caporetto and Passchendaele, Ware for one needed no convincing. There were moments in the summer of 1917 when even he would succumb to the general exhaustion, and yet there are few things more remarkable about the Imperial War Graves

Commission than its dedication to the future at a time when any future favourable to the Allies seemed a remote possibility.

Against the backdrop of an ever-swelling graves register – a quarter of a million casualties and another 70,000 dead by the time Haig called off Third Ypres in November 1917 – Ware and the Commission began to plan for their post-war task. The Charter that brought it into existence had only been signed by the King towards the end of May, but within less than a month Ware had taken soundings among London's art establishment and in the July of 1917 a small advisory committee, consisting of the director of the Tate Gallery, Charles Aitken, and two of the Empire's leading architects, Edwin Lutyens and Herbert Baker, was on its way out to France to report back on the future treatment of the war graves.

There was a case that nothing, or at least as near to nothing as was compatible with the decencies, should be done to them and, oddly, that case was never so superficially compelling as it was in that summer of 1917. 'When I visited the region [the Somme] in July 1917,' Arthur Hill, Kew's advisor to the Commission, recalled in a lecture to the Royal Horticultural Society after the war,

the whole of that desolate shell-hole region was transfigured and glorified by the common scarlet poppy, and the sight was more beautiful than any words of mine can express.

Picture to yourselves a vast undulating landscape, a blaze of scarlet unbroken by tree or hedgerow, with here and there long stretches of white Camomile and patches of yellow Charlock, dotted over with the half-hidden white crosses of the dead.

Smaller patches of Charlock were often conspicuous, and these usually marked the more recently dug graves where seeds, doubtless long buried, had been brought to the surface.

In no cemetery, large or small, however beautiful or impressive it may be, can the same sentiment be evoked or feelings be so deeply stirred. Nowhere, I imagine, could the magnitude of the struggle be better appreciated than in that peaceful, poppy-covered battlefield, hallowed by its many scattered crosses.

There was something profoundly seductive in Hill's pantheism – the same vague paganism would predictably attract Lutyens – but neither national sentiment nor political realities were going to leave the Empire's dead to nature. The French authorities had been immensely generous with their gifts of burial land to Britain; this, however, was not the vast solitude of the South African veldt, where Thomas Hardy's Drummer Hodge could safely be left to lie beneath the strange constellations of the southern skies, but a continuous line of cemeteries, burial grounds and individual graves that stretched from the Ypres Salient and the coalfields of northern France to the rolling arable lands of the Somme and beyond to the Marne. 'The Commission recognised the existence of a sentiment in favour of leaving the bodies of the dead where they fell,' Ware would later explain,

but in view of the critical conditions regarded it as impracticable. Over 150,000 scattered graves are known in France and Belgium . . . Either they must be removed to cemeteries where they can be reverently cared for, or they must be ploughed up with the soil. The Commission felt that the latter course would be excessively painful to relatives and discreditable to the country, besides being unspeakably revolting to the cultivators of the land.

There might not have been anything that could compete with the poppies and the camomile, but if Ware had set out to make life difficult for himself when he chose Baker and Lutyens he could hardly have done better than send out the two men who had just fallen out so bitterly over their work on New Delhi. As young apprentices in London, Herbert Baker and Edwin Lutyens had shared the same architectural ideals, but in their early twenties they had gone their separate ways, Baker to South Africa where his magpie eclecticism – Cape Dutch, Roman, Greek, Mogul – combined with sound Empire opinions to make him Rhodes's and Milner's Imperial Architect of Choice, while Lutyens remained at home to create a series of English country houses that would inextricably link his name with a doomed world and the dying culture of Edwardian England.

From his earliest days there had been an intellectual quality beneath the charm of his houses, but even when he moved towards the more disciplined language of the Italian Renaissance, he remained so ineluctably English in his feel for material and place and the organic quality of country architecture, that it was easy to be blinded to the rigour and deep seriousness of what he was doing. 'There is in art that which transcends all rules,' he wrote to his Theosophist wife in 1907,

It is the divine . . . To short sight it is a miracle, to those a little longer sighted it is Godhead, if we could see yet better, these facts may be revealed before which the [V]ery Godhead as we conceive him will fade dim. It is the point of view that ought to ring all arts, Architecture, Sculpture, Painting, Literature and Music etc. into sympathy and there is no ploy that cannot be lifted to the divine level by its creation as an art.

Lutyens has eclipsed Baker's reputation so completely that it is hard now to remember that Baker was the man with the track record, and Lutyens the imperial novice, when the decision in 1911 to move India's capital from Calcutta to New Delhi at last gave Lutyens his chance to build on the grand scale. In later years Baker would claim that he had been brought out to India to keep Lutyens in check, but if that was the plan it gloriously failed to prevent his rival producing, in Viceroy's House, a fusion of East and West that in its originality and boldness seemed a dazzling reproach to everything that the British Raj, institutional mediocrity or poor Herbert Baker had ever dreamed of. 'For its character,' Robert Byron wrote of the great dome that crowned Lutyens's masterpiece when he first saw it in 1931,

> is so arresting, so unprecedented, so uninviting of comparison with known architecture, that like a sovereign crowned and throned, it subordinates everything within view to increase its own state, and stands not to be judged by, but to judge, its attendants.

The Secretariats, remarkable buildings in themselves, exist

only in relation to it, and in as much as they administer to its success.

It cannot have been an easy thing for Baker – the architect of Groote Schuure, the Rhodes Memorial (the finest thing done since the Greeks, Lord Curzon reckoned) and the Union Building in Pretoria – to take, and Lutyens was not the man to play down the distinction. Baker had always been generous and clear-eyed enough to recognise Lutyens's greatness, and yet it must still have been galling to have to play the Salieri to his buffooning Mozart and watch a man who hated the Oriental's 'slimy mind' produce an intuitive but classically disciplined response to the East that made a mockery of his own earnest and deeply researched symbolism.

Vanities and jealousies played a part in the subsequent drama, but if there had been friction between the two men before they reached India it was New Delhi that brought them to a head. In his original plans, Lutyens had seen his domed central palace rising high above Baker's flanking Secretariats, but when in some baffling moment of inattention he agreed to a levelling of the hill that effectively obscured the view of his own portico from the ceremonial approach route, it sparked off a feud that would rumble on for years.

There were good practical reasons for the change to Lutyens's plan – and political and ideological ones for the symbolically minded Baker – but it was a battle between aesthetic absolutism and government tampering, between the inviolable demands of art and expediency, between an incontinently punning, joking, irreverent artist paradoxically dedicated to the high seriousness of his art, and an earnest, scholarly, high-principled 'trimmer'.

'Schooled under Rhodes and Milner rather than Wren and Newton,' Lutyens's biographer and champion, Christopher Hussey wrote, Baker's 'ultimate allegiance was to statesmanship and he recognised all too clearly its paramountcy over art'. For Lutyens, 'the purpose of life was the embodiment of divine order in finite form, and when a man fell short in this endeavour he fell from grace, became a bad man'.

The two men had infinitely more in common, in fact, than either of them would have cared to admit – their shared roots in the Arts and Crafts Movement, a facility with classical forms, a deep-felt 'Englishness', an ability to give physical expression to abstract ideas – but they had brought India to France with them and the War Graves Commission would pay the price. 'I realised from experience at Delhi that there would be a conflict inherent in our different natures and outlook,' Baker later wrote of their journey to inspect the cemeteries,

that he would be propelled towards abstract monumental design, and I would place more importance on sentiment; and sentiment, the association with English traditional burial places, I felt, should be a prevailing factor in the design of the Shrines of the Dead . . . An English churchyard was always the idea in my thoughts – from a humble 'Stoke Poges' to a Cathedral precinct like Canterbury or Winchester, its trees and gardens surrounded by stone walls with an arched gateway and chapel, perhaps, and covered cloister walks. This sentiment seemed better to express the British feeling for their honoured Dead than the intellectual Grand Manner, or its converse, an unordered towering mass of

masonry ill-set with sculpture and undisciplined by the
Mistress Art . . . My answer to Ware's invitation was that,
while it would not be wise to attempt any close collaboration
in design, I would willingly serve as an independent architect
with Lutyens on the Commission.

It might have made some difference if Charles Aitken had
been anything more than a cipher – 'a namby-pamby ass' as
Lutyens dismissed him – but with his preference for some utilitarian or educational commemoration dead in the water before
they had even left for France, the ring was left to the old sparring
partners. 'The cemeteries, the dotted graves, are the most pathetic
thing,' Lutyens wrote back to his wife, Emily, his egotistical
detachment from the war gone in one comprehensive act of
surrender to the scale of the sacrifice,

What humanity can endure and suffer is beyond belief. The
battlefields – the obliteration of all human endeavour and
achievement and the human achievement of destruction is
bettered by the poppies and wild flowers that are as friendly
to an unexploded shell as they are to the leg of a garden
seat in Surrey . . . The graveyards, haphazard from the needs
of much to do and little time for thought. And then a
ribbon of isolated graves like a milky way across miles of
country where men were tucked in where they fell. Ribbons
of little crosses each touching each other across a cemetery,
set in wilderness of annuals and where one sort of flower
is grown the effect is charming, easy and oh so pathetic.
One thinks for a moment that no other monument is

needed. Evanescent but for the moment is almost perfect and how misleading to sermonise in this emotion and how some love to sermonise. But the only monument can be one where the endeavour is sincere to make such monument permanent – a solid ball of Bronze.

Between Lutyens's solid bronze – a great, Marvellian 'wrecking ball' swinging through his quiet and cloistered retreats, it must have seemed to Baker – and a prettified Bourton-sur-Somme, there was little room for accommodation, and what there was had soon disappeared. By the time they left France, Lutyens had given up on his bronze, but the solution for the permanent memorial he was suggesting in its place only advertised just how far apart they were. 'I most earnestly advise that there shall be one kind of monument throughout, whether in Europe, Asia or Africa,' he wrote at the end of August in a memorandum for the Commission, the architectural purist and the pantheist in him in perfect harmony,

and that it shall take the form of one great fair stone of fine proportions, twelve feet in length, lying raised upon three steps, of which the first and third shall be twice the width of the second; and each stone shall bear in indelible lettering, some fine thought or words of sacred dedication. They should be known in all places and for all time, as the Great War Stones, and should stand, though in three Continents, as equal monuments of devotion, suggesting the thought of memorial Chapels in one vast Cathedral.

Lutyens's great monolith – the 'Stone of Remembrance' as it came, feebly, to be known – might now have the inevitability about it of an accomplished fact, but between Anglican demands for a cross and Presbyterian objections to anything suggesting an altar, it had a tricky birth. Labour MPs, Jews, Roman Catholics (oddly), Nonconformists and 'ladies of fashion' had all come on board, Lutyens cheerfully told Ware – '*Mon General*' as he addressed him – but,

> I have not had the courage to tackle a bishop, but do you think it wise if I asked Cantuar [Randall Davidson, Archbishop of Canterbury] to see me, he would I think, but if I catch sight of the apron it is apt at a critical moment, to give me the giggles, especially when they get pompous and hold their hands over their knees – Why?

The Scots could be bought off with a change of name – 'stone' for 'altar' – the playwright James Barrie had reassured him, but the Anglican establishment was another matter. 'The first person I saw [at the Athenaeum] was Bernard Mallet,' Lutyens wrote to his wife four days later,

> I told him of France – he said Cantuar is upstairs why don't you tell him. So I went upstairs and there was Cantuar and some fellow bishop. I said I want to speak to you, Sir. He said All right, wait a mo'. So I waited a mo and he came up and I told him of my big stone idea as against the cross – the permanency, the non-denominationalism etc. He was

very kind and said he was greatly and favourably impressed but would think it over.

'I bearded the Archbishop of C., in this the above Pot House,' he scrawled a jubilant note to Ware that same night, anxious to share the news of his most important convert,

> and laid with all due humility the Big Stone idea in his apron – and made him a little *croquis* (French!) thereof . . . He said he could certainly (my word perform) the sacrament on such a stone, and he should think his R.C. brother of Westminster – as well as our Brer Hindu. Etc. Etc.
>
> Montagu was pleased too. The Jew.
>
> Am I behaving properly,
>
> *Votre Toujours* Subaltern.

Lutyens could not have stopped the jokes if he tried – they were a compulsion with him, a kind of comic Tourette's – but behind them lay a deepening commitment to his ideas for commemorating the dead. He had never bought in to the ludicrous trappings of his wife's Theosophy, but he had always felt a yearning for some universal truth that transcended the boundaries of creeds and denominations, some substitute, like Ware himself needed, for the faith of his own childhood and his mother's evangelical fire. 'There must be nothing trivial or petty where our valiant dead lie in oneness of sacrifice and in glorious community of Brotherhood in Arms,' he insisted in his memorandum to the Commission,

All that is done of structure should be for endurance for all time and for equality of honour, for besides Christians of all denominations, there will be Jews, Mussulmens, Hindus and men of other creeds, their glorious names and their mortal bodies all equally deserving enduring record and seemly sepulture.

There could be no discrimination, he insisted, no exceptions to this equality, no judgments made, no 'worldly value' put on the dead. 'The most beautiful sites should be selected [for Monuments],' he told Emily the same day, echoing Lionel Earle's disquiet,

not where the victories were and all that snobbery, for I hold that there is equality in sacrifice and the men who fell at Quatre Bras are just as worthy of honour as those who fell at Waterloo . . . They put 'killed in action' or 'died from wounds', 'died'. Died alone means some defalcation and shot for it. I don't like it. The mother lost her boy and it was in the interests of the country and she had to suffer – her boy. Do you see what I mean? But then I don't fight nor do I fight yet for the seemly sepulture of the Germans when they lie along with our men.

If he thought, however, that he had 'Cantuar' in the bag, his optimism was premature – the more the Archbishop thought about it the more hostile he became – and in Baker, the 'Cross Party' had found a dogged champion. 'Such a rush,' Lutyens reported again to Emily on 23 August,

At 12 to General Ware who kept me more than an hour, full of sympathy and fight for the big stone, furious with Baker and almost at breaking point with him and Aitken. Baker's last idea is a five pointed cross, one point for each colony. India, Ware pointed out, was forgotten, but what does a five pointed cross mean? Ware bids me courage.

Baker's slavishly literal use of symbolism would always make him vulnerable to ridicule – 'Baker must be dotty! . . . Too silly', was Emily's reply – but there would seem nothing 'dotty' about the Cross of Lorraine when it became the symbol of the Free French in the Second World War. Baker had, in fact, found his inspiration among the ruins of Ypres, where the sight of such a cross standing unscathed in the cathedral precinct – a symbol of Christian redemption in a city that had itself become the symbol of British resistance to German militarism – crystallised all those 'sentiments' and values and associations of place that he wanted to bring to the design of the war cemeteries.

The future would show that Baker was not just speaking for himself either – Ware, Lutyens and the anti-cross brigade were making a bad mistake if they imagined they were dealing with a bigoted High Church rump – but the argument had become too entwined with personalities to be sensibly resolved. 'Afterwards went and saw Fabian Ware,' Lutyens wrote after another six weeks had brought the two sides no nearer and Ware, himself, to the point of throwing in the towel,

He was 'shocked, grieved' at the Archbishop's letter – expected a neutral attitude not a narrow antagonistic view.

He says the clergy in France are most tiresome – always trying to upset the applecart. But he thinks the 'stone' will win yet, and he may chuck the whole thing and let the Office of Works do it all with lych-gates complete. He liked my grave head-stones and did not like Baker's and was cross at his being so difficult and petty. He said he would consult General Macready and if he agreed would announce that I was appointed Hon. architect to the whole caboodle. He wanted to know if I could afford it.

It was probably just as well that the answer to that was 'no' – Ware knew that he had to take the whole country with him and not just the dissenters, Jews and ladies of fashion – but consensus and committees had never been either man's preferred route. 'Lytton said that if a man – like L[ord] Salisbury – who he knows very well,' Lutyens complained, 'gets into the chair – with 2 opinions before him – he is bound to compromise and then we should get a stone which is not a cross and a cross which is not a stone – or some such absurd finding.'

The more opinions were canvassed too, the less consensus they found. Balfour and Buchan were all for the stone, Poynter favoured Victorian sentiment; Reginald Blomfield wanted the Royal Academy more involved, Earle lych-gates and rose gardens and Worrall wrought iron. 'I see a bell-fry,' Barrie wrote to Ware with a characteristic mix of imagination and whimsy,

and I see the bells ringing at some particular moment of the evening. This should go on thro' the centuries. My idea is not that they should ring quite simultaneously but that one should wake up another (working, say, from north–south). The message each bell is sending to the next is 'All's Well'. Almost more impressive than bells would be bugles but when peace time comes they might seem too military.

The Commission did not make life any easier for itself by bringing in a third architect and former President of the RIBA, Reginald Blomfield. The son of a clergyman and grandson of one of Victorian England's great bully-bishops, Blomfield was about as unlike Baker and Lutyens as they were each other, a hard-fighting, hard-swearing bull of a man, as proud of his cricket or his fast, sliced underhand tennis serve as he was of anything he built, and prouder still of once nearly killing Henry James when he took a wall on his hunter only to find the alarmed old ninny sitting on the other side.

The triple entente was not helped by the fact that Blomfield thought he should have had New Delhi – Lutyens had asked and then dropped him, he claimed – but architects have never needed much of a reason to hate each other. During their time together on the Royal Fine Arts Commission, the only thing Lutyens and Blomfield ever agreed on was the 'ghastliness' of Baker's South Africa House in Trafalgar Square, but then Lutyens was probably prepared to agree with anyone on anything if it meant doing his old friend and walking companion down: 'Professional jealousy I have encountered,' Lord Crawford, the chairman of the Commission recalled, deeply shocked by the violence of Lutyens's hostility to Baker, 'but never anything quite so cynical or uncompromising.'

There was a comic element to it all – 'you are a werry nice man, but a werry, werry bad architect', Lutyens told 'Bloomy' before

ve: Etaples. A view back to the cemetery entrance, showing one of the two arched pylons, with the perpetually onless stone flags that Lutyens had wanted to employ on his Whitehall Cenotaph.

Above: *Etaples, 1919: Life and death.* Sir John Lavery's beautiful painting of the great base-camp cemetery, and i distance a passing train. Fabian Ware had been determined that trains should be able to pause here for passenger pay their moment's respect to the cemetery's 11,000 dead.

ve: A stonemason works on the headstone of a Canadian soldier buried in France. Simplicity, equality and uniformity the guiding principles of its design but nothing in the Commission's history would cause such bitter debate.

: Lutyens's Memorial to the Missing of the Somme, the greatest and most challenging of all the Commission's **s.** On it are inscribed the names of 72,085 soldiers who were killed on the Somme and Ancre and have no known **.** On the slope below are the graves of 300 British dead and alongside them and visible here, of 300 French.

Above: The devastated town of Ypres, as the architect Reginald Blomfield **(left)** first saw it in 1919, when he began preparations for his great Memorial to the missing of the Ypres Salient. The war-artist Will Longstaff attended the unveiling ceremony in 1927, and the result was his visionary 'Menin Gate at Midnight' **(far left)**, with its ghost army marching out over the same moonlit landscape across which almost every British and Empire army unit had once gone into battle.

Above: *'These intolerably nameless names.'* The central arch of Blomfield's Menin Gate, where the names of almost 55,000 'officers and men who fell in the Ypres Salient but to whom the fortunes of war denied the known and honoured burial given to their comrades in death' are recorded.

deciding that he was not even a nice man – but the comedy was lost on Ware, and with the first meeting of the Imperial War Graves Commission scheduled for 20 November, the only solution seemed to be to bring in an outside referee. 'The Commission recognised that there would inevitably be considerable difference of opinion on how the cemeteries abroad should be laid out, and what form of permanent memorial should be erected in them,' Ware later wrote with rather more charity than he had felt at the time,

They felt, moreover, that a matter of this kind should not become the subject of controversy, if it could be avoided. The appointment of Sir Frederic Kenyon therefore was made with a view to focussing, and, if possible, reconciling the various opinions on the subject that had found expression among the Armies at the front and the general public at home, and particularly in artistic circles. His terms of reference were as follows:–

Sir Frederic Kenyon's duties will be to decide between the various proposals submitted to him as to the architectural treatment and laying out of cemeteries, and to report his recommendations to the Commission at the earliest possible date

1) He will consult the representatives of the various churches and religious bodies on any religious questions involved.

2) He will report as to the desirability of forming

an advisory Committee from among those who
have been consulted, for the purpose of carrying
out the proposals agreed on.

There was only one restriction that the Commission placed
on Kenyon's freedom: there was to be no 'distinction . . . made
between officers and men lying in the same cemeteries in the
form or nature of the memorials'. With that proviso, the world
was Kenyon's oyster: and some very large and irritating bits of
grit he was to get with it.

SIX

Kenyon

With the sole exception of Fabian Ware, Sir Frederic Kenyon's was arguably the most important appointment that the Commission made. Kenyon was director of the British Museum when he accepted the job in 1917, a fifty-four-year-old biblical, classical and Browning scholar of great distinction, with 'the clipped moustache and upright carriage' of an army officer, the trained and analytical mind of the caricature Wykehamist, and a string of public achievements behind and in front of him that ranged from the funding for T. E. Lawrence's Carchemish dig, to the purchase of the *Codex Sinaiticus*. 'He is an interesting combination, this pleasant, erect Englishman,' the *Chicago Tribune* wrote of him,

> the jovial, gentlemanly type of Englishman that is so well liked wherever one finds it, who left his desk of director of the British Museum to come over to France in 1914, with, as he put it, the first army that left Southampton for Le Havre since the expedition of Henry V in 1415 before the battle of Agincourt.

Kenyon had been brought back from France at the behest of the British Museum's trustees, but it was as much that military experience as his academic distinction that equipped him for his new task. In the decades ahead, two world wars would make the scholar-soldier a more familiar type, but in 1917 there were few who combined the intellectual and cultural standing demanded of the job – the young Kenneth Clarke, for instance, would eventually be Kenyon's suggestion for his replacement – with the sympathies and experience that enabled him to mediate between the Army and a tricky artistic community. 'The first official meeting of the Commission was held in November 1917,' recalled Reginald Blomfield – who had come to sneer and stayed to admire,

> when Sir Frederic Kenyon . . . was appointed 'adviser' to the Commission, 'in regard to the architectural treatment and lay-out of cemeteries'. The Commission had the usual English distrust of experts, for Kenyon, though a fine scholar and a very distinguished man, was not an architect, or familiar with that art, and of course we did not fail to shoot our cheerful jibes at 'the art adviser'. But Kenyon did invaluable work. He at once visited some cemeteries in France, and in January 1918 made a very able report to the Commission, in which he laid down the broad lines of treatment for the cemeteries, and made suggestions as to organization.

The danger of bringing in a 'referee', of course, was that all you would get is 'building by committee' – the pursuit of the

second class and the attainment of the third, as Lutyens put it
– but Kenyon had at least one important factor going for him
in the work ahead. The antagonism between the three chief
architects was certainly genuine enough, but beneath the endless
frictions and jealousies that had brought Ware to the point of
quitting, lay a common allegiance to the standards and principles
of the Arts and Crafts Movement under which they had all been
brought up that would give the cemeteries their unmistakable
identity.

In the end it was this adherence to quality as much as the
dominant classicism of the day that would be the hallmark of
the Commission's work in France and elsewhere. In the years
after the First World War, Lutyens, Blomfield and Baker would
all build memorials for the Commission in the grand manner,
but if one wanted to identify what it is that gives the cemeteries
their distinct feel, what it is that saves them from the bombast
and the rhetoric of so much commemorative art or prevents the
Commission's hundreds of cemeteries descending into a repetitive
and mechanical uniformity, the answer lies in those traditions of
honesty, simplicity and good design that, from planting to the
use of materials and sense of place, would inform everything that
they built. 'The cemeteries, carefully tended, will rely for their
effect on the dignity of their layout and the beauty of the trees,
the grass and the flowers,' Blomfield would tell an audience in
1920. 'You may recollect those lines of Andrew Marvell, "He
nothing common did or mean/ Upon that memorable scene."
This might, I think, be the spirit inspiring and directing all that
is done to commemorate the war and those who have died
in it.'

This spirit, though, needed to be harnessed, and the directives and framework within which the architects and gardeners would work was the task that had been given to Kenyon. He had been appointed to the job just five days after Haig finally called off the nightmare of Third Ypres, and in the lull between Passchendaele and the German Spring Offensive of March 1918 he visited France twice, inspecting every kind of burial ground from the large base cemeteries of Boulogne and Etaples to the little clusters of graves 'in the squalid surrounding of the mud of Ploegsteert' and the 'immense number of single burials' that lay 'on either side of the road from Albert to Bapaume. I was able to visit cemeteries along all parts of the front,' he reported back to the Commission. 'In the areas of Ypres . . . Festubert . . . Arras . . . the Somme, and also those which fringe the coast . . . and thereby was able to form an idea of the variety of problems in connection with their arrangement, decoration and upkeep.'

There were the most basic questions to be answered. Would every grave be separately identified? Would each have its own headstone? Would that headstone be in the form of plain stone or cross? What kind of permanent memorials should there be in the cemeteries? What kind of character should those cemeteries aim at? Kenyon cast his net wide for answers. 'I have also had opportunities, both abroad and at home, of consulting representatives of the principal interests involved,' he continued,

> the Army, the relatives of the fallen, the religious denominations, and the artists and others whose judgment may be of value in a work demanding imagination and taste and good feeling . . . Among others, I have made a point of

obtaining opinions from those who are qualified to speak for India and the Dominions which have sent so many of their sons to lie in the graves which for generations to come will mark the line of our front in France and Flanders.

Kenyon and the Commission would be absolutely punctilious in their respect for Hindu or Muslim practices, but his first readers cannot have got far into his report before feeling that the public at home might get a rather more cavalier treatment. There is no reason to think that he was anything other than sincere in these consultations, but implicit in that telling category – 'those whose judgment may be of value' – is a very Ware-like assumption that when it came to matters of taste and feeling, the public were better off being told what to do by their betters than left to their own unlettered devices.

Kenyon was justly insistent in his report that all must be treated the same – as he and Ware would point out repeatedly, only the rich would be able to erect their monuments if they were allowed – but inside the great wooden horse called 'Equality' a very different standard was being smuggled. On the matter of individual graves, he continued his urbane exposition of the Commission's thinking:

It was felt that the provision of monuments could not be left to individual initiative. In a few cases, where money and good taste were not wanting, a satisfactory result would be obtained, in the sense that a fine individual monument would be erected. In the large majority of cases either no monument would be erected, or it would be poor in quality;

and the total result would be one of inequality, haphazard and disorder. The cemetery would become a collection of individual memorials, a few good, but many bad, and with a total want of congruity and uniformity.

The argument has drifted a long way from mere 'equality' – this was now about *quality*, taste and artistic judgment – but there would be no going back and no softening of the Commission's stance. 'It is necessary to face the fact that this decision has given pain in some quarters,' Kenyon admitted, 'yet it is hoped' that relatives who had planned to erect their own memorials,

> will realize that they are asked to join in an action of even higher significance. The sacrifice of the individual is a great idea and worthy of commemoration; but the community of sacrifice, the service of a common cause, the comradeship of arms which has brought together men of all ranks and grades – these are greater ideas, which should be commemorated in those cemeteries where they lie together, the representatives of their country in the lands in which they served. The place for the individual memorial is at home.

It was a moot point even then whether the mindless slaughter of more than a million men was a 'great idea worthy of commemoration', however the Commission was designed as an agent of imperial will and not a critic of it. In the years after the Armistice it would stumble upon the idea that there could be no more eloquent argument against war than its cemeteries, but this was an afterthought that had no place in Kenyon's original report. 'My endeavour,' he proudly wrote – determined to maintain the high moral ground at a moment when the chivalrous idealism of 1914 had come to seem a very tarnished thing,

has been to arrive at a result which will, so far as may be, satisfy the feelings of relatives and comrades of those who lie in these cemeteries; which will represent the soldierly spirit and discipline in which they fought and fell: which will typify the Army to which they belonged; which will give expression to those deeper emotions, of regimental comradeship, of service to their Army, their King, their country and their God, which underlay (perhaps often unconsciously) their sacrifice of themselves for the cause in which they fought, and which in ages to come will be a dignified memorial, worthy of the nation and the men who gave their lives for it, in the lands of the Allies with whom and for whom they fought.

It would be hard to guess from this that Kenyon's 'cause' and Siegfried Sassoon's 'crime against humanity' were one and the same thing, but these were military cemeteries and if they were never intended to be triumphalist they were never going to be apologetic. One of the possibilities he examined would have given relatives something closer to a memorial park than a cemetery, but for Kenyon anything that obscured or 'fudged' their military identity was a betrayal of the men who lay there. The cemeteries, he recommended, should have a central monument or monuments and, be marked by rows of headstones of uniform height and width . . . Although it is not desired that our war cemeteries should be gloomy places, it is right that the fact that they are cemeteries, containing the bodies of hundreds and thousands of men who have given their lives for their country, should be evident at first sight, and should be constantly present to the minds of those who pass by or who visit them.

Here essentially was Lutyens's vision: identical headstones 2 feet 6 inches by 1 foot 3 in size, arranged in the 'ordered ranks . . . of a battalion on parade', facing east towards the enemy (ready to spring up and face him again at the Last Trump in the less forgiving interpretations), complete with name, rank, date of death and regimental insignia, and all that was required was the refinement of detail. 'There is some difference of opinion as to whether leave should be given to relatives to add anything further,' he added with the *de haut en bas* air of a man more used to dealing with Greek papyri than with the Kensal Green Cemetery School of Poetry,

It is clearly undesirable to allow free scope for the effusions of the mortuary mason, the sentimental versifier, or the crank; nor can space be given for a lengthy epitaph. On the other hand it would give satisfaction in many individual instances to be allowed to add an appropriate text or prayer or words of dedication; and notably it is certain that in the case of members of the Roman Catholic communion there would be a strong desire to place a customary formula beneath the name. I am inclined, therefore, to recommend that leave should be given for a short inscription of not more than three lines, to be added on the application of the next-of-kin, or other person or organisation . . . and at the cost of the applicant [a cost never levied]; but that the inscription must be of the nature of a text or prayer, and that the Commission shall have absolute power of rejection or acceptance.

With the question of the graves settled, Kenyon turned to the question of 'the central monument' for the cemeteries and here there had to be compromise. In his heart he probably agreed with Ware that Lutyens's 'Great Stone' was the answer, but whatever else it might symbolise (and the comic 'Stoneology' that Lutyens scrawled down for Barrie – 'War Stone', 'Stone of Peace', 'Stone of Watching', 'Stone of Sleep' . . . forty-odd names in all shows just how flexible a concept it was) the one thing his great, uncompromising monolith did not embody was Christian love. 'It would meet many forms of religious feeling,' Kenyon wrote,

To some it would merely be a memorial stone, such as those of which we read in the Old Testament. To others it would be an altar, one of the most ancient and general of symbols, and would serve as the centre of religious services. As an altar, it would represent one side of the idea of sacrifice, the sacrifice which the Empire had made of its youth, in the great cause for which it sent them forth . . . [But] it lacks what many (probably a large majority) would desire, the definitely Christian character; and it does not represent the idea of self-sacrifice. For this the one essential symbol is the cross; and I have no doubt that great distress would be felt if our cemeteries lacked the recognition of the fact that we are a Christian Empire, and this symbol of self-sacrifice made by those who lie in them.

There was a certain amount of agonising over what this cross should look like, and a very English and Protestant dread that it should in any way resemble the kind of 'horrors' that filled French and Belgian cemeteries, but a report that had taken Kenyon no more than two months had effectively created a blueprint for the Commission's future. There were a number of modifications and refinements that time and experience would suggest, but in essence the cemetery Kenyon describes, with its Lutyens stone and great cross and regimented headstones and shelter and plantings and low boundary walls, was the cemetery that can be found in its hundreds up and down the old Western Front.

Kenyon's 'recommendations', Ware recorded in his first General Report, 'were adopted by the Commission at their meeting of the 18th February, 1918, in the following form':

(1) That the principle of equality of treatment laid down by the Commission should be carried out by the erection over the graves of all officers and men in the war cemeteries abroad of headstones of uniform dimensions, though with some variety of pattern.

(2) That each regiment should have its own pattern of headstone . . . and that regimental feeling should be consulted.

(3)   That there should be carved on the headstone the rank, name, regiment and date of death of the man buried beneath it, and that relatives should be allowed at their own cost to add a short inscription of the nature of a text or prayer, subject to the approval of the Commission.

(4)   That in every cemetery there should be two central monuments; (a) at the eastern end, a great memorial stone upon broad steps and bearing some appropriate phrase or text; and (b) elsewhere in the cemetery, a cross.

(5)   That in every cemetery there should be some form of building, either covering the memorial stone or separate from it, as a shelter for visitors . . . and as a place where religious services might be held.

(6)   That the cemeteries should be laid out and planted with flowers and shrubs . . . The surfaces of the graves should be levelled, for reasons of convenience and economy.

(7)   That each cemetery should be fenced in by some durable boundary.

(8)   That each cemetery should have a printed register of the burials in it, which should be easily accessible to visitors.

(9)   That, in consultation with the French authorities, the principle of concentrating in selected cemeteries the bodies at present buried in isolated graves or in small groups should be settled in advance . . .

It was an impressive and disciplined piece of thinking and more surprisingly perhaps, an extraordinary act of imagination from a not particularly imaginative man. Lutyens and Hill had seen the Western Front when the poppies and larks were out in force, but Kenyon had toured it in all its winter ugliness and out of the chaos and horror of Ypres he had somehow managed to extrapolate a vision of order and peace – out of an exhausted and embittered Britain, torn by strikes and doubts and disillusionment, he had created a metaphor for national and imperial unity; out of the sustained and complicit failure of the Churches, a perfect 'type' of Christian sacrifice; out of the psychic and physical mangling of a whole generation, a picture of ordered sanity – out of a troglodytic war of shell-holes and bunkers and mud and filth and corpses, rats and lice, and trench fever and disappointment, a vision of an army that, in its smart and disciplined ranks and parade ground order, had not existed since 1914 and First Ypres.

The Imperial War Graves Commission did not invent these myths about the war and the Army, but what Kenyon had effectively mapped out here were the cemeteries that would become the cultural spaces in which they took on their most persuasive physical and permanent expression. It is important to remember that he was writing his report while the war was still going on, and if it was not propaganda in any overt sense, it was a blueprint for an idealised Britain and Army that had no place in it for doubt, disunity or self-questioning.

There was no room in his vision for the 'crokers' Ware had complained of, no recognition that Sassoon's conscripted 'droves of victims' would fill his cemeteries, no admission of the divisions, inequalities and brutalities that were as much a part of the Army's experience as courage, comradeship and endurance, and above all no confronting that great taboo of the war, Death. From the day that Ware was appointed to head the Graves Registration Commission, death was the reason for everything he did, but perhaps nothing is more extraordinary about the cemeteries he and Kenyon were creating than the discreet cult of Omertà that surrounds them or their strange sense of disconnection with the realities that lay beneath Blunden's 'green coverlets' of lawn.

'The beauty, the serenity', Blunden would later write of them – an old and astonished Silas Marner in reverse, revisiting the dystopic landscape of his youth to find in its place a world of 'lovely, elegiac closes' which 'almost cause me to deny my own experience in the acres they now grace' – but that was precisely what Kenyon had intended. It is no coincidence that it took more than a decade for Remarque's great novel of death, *All Quiet on the Western Front*, to emerge, because nobody before that – and certainly nobody in the early months of 1918 – could have borne the truth that behind all the euphemisms of the 'Fallen' and the 'Glorious Dead' and 'Sacred Places' was nothing but the grim, annihilating fact of death.

Even the possible texts for Lutyens's Great Stone – some variant on 'Rest in Peace' or 'They Lie in Peace' – had to be quietly shelved in case some disgruntled veteran changed the 'peace' to 'pieces'; between the man at the front and his wife or parent or child at home was a gulf that neither side wished to bridge. The ignorance and jingoism of the home front might provoke fantasies of hatred and revenge in a soldier-poet like Sassoon, but for the vast, decent majority of men in the trenches and their families the only salvation or sanity lay in silence. 'You biddie people at home have no idea what sort of hell this is,' the sculptor Charles Jagger wrote from Gallipoli, but the reception of his Hyde Park Memorial after the war shows how little they wanted or could have borne to know. 'Those gruesome rags,' Vera Brittain recalled, the physical horror of returning to find a parcel with her dead fiancé's uniform lying on the floor still vivid after nearly twenty years: they 'made me realise as I had never realised before, all that France really meant'.

'Everything was damp and worn and simply caked with mud,' she had written at the time to her brother Edward, another of the headmaster of Uppingham's boys about to die,

> The smell of those clothes was the smell of graveyards and the Dead. The mud of France that covered them was not ordinary mud; it had not the usual clean pure smell of earth, but it was as though it was saturated with dead bodies – dead that had been dead a long, long time.

There is no need here to rehearse the gothic horrors of the trenches – the skeletal hands and feet jutting out of the Flanders mud, the fly-blown corpses of Gallipoli, the grave-robbing of Mesopotamia – these are among the abiding visual clichés of the war, but it needs remembering that death was not the quiet sleep of Kenyon's sleight of hand. 'We see men go on living with the top of their skulls missing. We see soldiers go on running when both their feet have been shot away . . . we find someone who has gripped the main artery in his arm between his teeth for two hours so that he doesn't bleed to death,' wrote Remarque of the visceral fear, the soldier's primal urge to cling on to life in a world where every instinct was 'on guard against death'.

A hole has been blown in the ground right in front of me. I can just about make it out . . . and I want to get into that hole. Without stopping, I wriggle across the earth as fast as I can, flat as an eel on the ground – there is a whistling noise again, I curl up quickly and grab for some cover, feel something to my left and press against it, it gives, I groan . . . I crawl under whatever it was that gave away when I touched it, pull it over me – it is wood, cloth, cover, cover . . . then I remember we've taken cover in a cemetery.

But the shelling is stronger than anything else. It wipes out all other considerations and I just crawl deeper and deeper beneath the coffin so that it will protect me, even if Death himself is already in it.

'Good God, did we really send men to fight in that?' one general is supposed to have wept when he saw for the first time for himself the swampland of the Ypres Salient, and the cemeteries seemed to offer the reassuring answer of 'no'. It was one thing to nurse memories of a 'Happy Warrior' like Julian Grenfell, but the alien world of terror, pity, horror, curiosity, forensic interest and brute indifference that soldiers inhabited needed to be kept at bay. Death for one Highland officer had been 'three rather gamy Germans . . . but one gets used to that sort of thing'. At Festubert, in May 1915, it was 'an enormous Hun' dressed in spite of the heat in 'two pairs of trousers and thick pants below them'. For Remarque there was the eternal, accusing stare of a French soldier slowly slipping away in the same dug-out; for Francis Law, a callow subaltern in the Irish Guards, the face of a young Irish lad, lying alone on a stretcher at the end of a support trench, waiting to be taken away. For the Australian volunteer, Albert Facey, it was reassembling his brother's arm with the other fragments of his body in a mass grave at Gallipoli; for the Reverend Julian Bickersteth, a boy who had volunteered under age in 1914, 'turning his blind-fold face to me and [saying] in a voice which wrung my heart, "Kiss me, Sir, kiss me", before a firing-party sent him into the Great Unseen'.

'Covered with snow, as with a sheet, lay the body of a Boche,' recalled Edwin Vaughan,

> looking calm and, I somehow felt, happy. Yet the sight of him made me feel icily alone. It seemed such a terrible thing to be alone, covered with snow throughout the night, with never a sound until we came along . . . never spoke, and then went away for ever. It seemed so unfriendly, and for a long time I sat wishing we could do something for him.

This was a world that nobody wanted to know of during the war – the world that divided the man at the front from the civilian at home – and the surprise would have been if Kenyon's blueprint had been any different. From the earliest days of the Mobile Unit, grave work had been marked by an instinct of patriotic faith, and if there was ever a time to hold on to the certainties and beliefs that had driven Ware from the beginning, it was the early months of 1918.

At the end of 1917, the Bolsheviks had effectively brought an end to the fighting in the East, and on 21 March 1918, free at last to concentrate on one front, Ludendorff launched astride the Somme the first of five massive offensives that brought the Allies as close to losing the war as at any time since the Marne in 1914. On that first day alone the British sustained casualties of over 38,000, with 21,000 surrendering. By the twenty-third the Germans had advanced twenty-five miles in a return to the open warfare of 1914 that made all the derisory gains of the intervening years seem more pointless than ever. On 9 April a second offensive was launched along the River Lys, and by the end of the month – almost before the ink on Kenyon's report was dry – the old battlefields of the Somme and the Ypres Salient, and something like half those cemeteries that Kenyon had visited over the winter, were in enemy hands.

A third hammer blow in late May along the Chemin des Dames brought Paris within range of German shells, but with that checked the worst was past and Ludendorff's gamble all but lost. Over the next weeks the offensive continued in the Champagne region until by the middle of July the German army had shot its bolt, a victim of its own territorial gains and over-extension, of inadequate logistical support and falling manpower, of stiffening Allied resolve, influenza, incoherent strategy, wavering morale, economic blockade, dwindling production, Allied air superiority and the mounting influence of American troops.

For Ware and the Commission, however, the offensives had left a grim double legacy, because in addition to another 350,000

Allied killed and wounded from the first two attacks alone, there was the inevitable ravage done to existing graves. In 1916 the German withdrawal to the Hindenburg Line had been marked by a barbaric programme of destruction, and while Ware found no single case of deliberate desecration of British cemeteries, the subsequent battles and bombardments had more than done Alberich's work. On that morning of 21 March, in a space of just five hours, the Germans fired 1.16 million shells – over two-thirds of the number fired in the entire seven-day Allied bombardment that preceded the Somme – promiscuously mingling the living, the dead, and the long dead of both armies in one giant charnel house. And with each battle fought, the geological layering of the war grew ever more chaotic. In his report to the Commission, Ware remained confident that their records were detailed enough to reconstruct any cemetery, but as defence turned to attack and the Allied armies advanced again over the same devastated battlefields, the sheer numbers of missing and unidentified that they had left behind on the Somme alone – 73,000 of them – was already pointing to the greatest challenge that the post-war Commission would face.

It was a challenge, too, that they would be facing sooner than anyone could have expected. Even after 8 August, 'the black day in the history of the German army', the Allies' commanders were still thinking in terms of limited offensives and a 1919 campaign. One hundred days later a war that had seemed interminable was over: the 'long war' illusion of 1917 had proved no more accurate than the 'short war' illusion of 1914. A summer that had opened with Britain's armies standing with their 'backs to the wall' on the outskirts of Amiens had turned into an autumn campaign that swept them eastward to where it had all started for the BEF in 1914. It was an extraordinary turnaround. Few people reading in January 1918 Sir Frederic Kenyon's scholarly musings on where and how Britain's victories should be commemorated, could have thought it the most pressing of the War Graves Commission's concerns; fewer still, who buried the first British casualties in St Symphorien near Mons in August 1914, can have ever dreamed that four years later the same cemetery would take almost the last of the million dead that the war had cost the British Empire.

SEVEN

Opposition

The real work of the Commission in France and Belgium would only properly begin when the war was over, but it was against this shifting background of retreat and advance that the first tentative steps were taken. There was little to be done on the ground in areas where the fighting continued, but that was possibly just as well because there was still one key issue that Kenyon's report had left unresolved. 'I have not considered that question of finance came within my terms of reference,' he had concluded, before highlighting the awkward balance between economy and quality that the Commission would have to maintain,

but it is obvious that it has an important bearing on the subject of this report. However carefully the cost of each cemetery is limited, the number of these cemeteries is so large that the total expenditure must be very great. On this ground alone, if on no other, it is essential that the general principles of cemetery design should be determined without delay . . . It is also essential that the architects employed should make their designs as simple and inexpensive as possible, since extravagant cost must inevitably lead to the rejection of the design. The country needs dignity and refined taste, not ostentation, and then it will not grudge the cost. It surely will not refuse the cost of one day of war in order to honour for centuries the memory of those who fell.

There was, unusually, no difficulty from the Treasury and none from the Empire – in June 1917 the representatives at the Imperial War Conference agreed to share the costs in proportion to the numbers of their dead – but the problem was that the Commission had no real idea at all as to what those costs might be. At that June conference Ware had produced a figure of £10 per grave; although this was adopted and became the measure of subsequent budgeting, it was no more than guesswork, an arbitrary figure pulled out of a hat by a Commission so ignorant of their business, according to Blomfield, that they needed the meaning 'of specifications and quantities, and the ordinary methods of obtaining tenders and ordering of building contracts' explained to them.

Blomfield was never one to underplay his own role in things, and the Commission had the Office of Works' experience to call on, but he was only exaggerating an essential truth. The Commission's remit stretched to every theatre of the war, and in June 1918 they could have had no more idea of what challenges Gallipoli had in store than they had of the costs there might be in East Africa or Mesopotamia. 'The resting places are in every conceivable site,' Kipling, the Commission's literary arbiter and public spokesman, would have to remind an impatient public, 'on bare hills flayed by years of battle, in orchards and meadows, besides populous towns or little villages, in jungle-glades and coast ports, in far-away islands, among desert sands, and desolate ravines.'

The graves on the Gallipoli peninsula, in particular, would present the Commission with a problem that could not even be addressed until after the war. For the greater part of the conflict, Britain's cemeteries along the Western Front had been in or behind the lines, but from the night in early January 1916, when the last Allied soldier slipped away under the cover of darkness from Gallipoli, the makeshift graves and snow-covered corpses of a nine-month-long campaign had been left to the mercy of an Ottoman foe and hostile climate.

This was distressing enough for relatives who had been forced to live in almost total ignorance for three years, who often did not even know whether or not their son or husband had a grave, and it was exacerbated by the peculiar associations that had wrapped themselves around the name of Gallipoli. The campaign had been fought by a combined force of French, British and Empire units, but for the ANZAC troops and their governments and populations who had sent them to war in 1914 the peninsula and its landmarks – Anzac Cove, Lone Pine, Chunuk Bair, the Nek – had assumed a significance that transcended the military or strategic to become a proving ground of courage and a mythic part of national identity.

The 8,709 Australian dead were just the beginning of the challenge awaiting the War Graves Commission – the British had lost 20,000 during the campaign, the New Zealanders 2,721 or almost a third of their troops, the Indian units more than fifteen hundred, even the tiny Newfoundland contingent, bound for annihilation on the Somme, forty-nine – but Ware had no answers to give relatives. In the last days of the campaign, an Australian padre had scattered wattle seeds among the Australian graves and made a rough map of the cemeteries, but when the burials had almost all been at night in shallow, hastily dug holes the chances of identifications were slipping away with every year.

There was nothing either that Ware could do – approaches through American and papal channels had produced little – and even in France and Belgium the ebb and flow of battle in 1918 had made the most basic reconnaissance a challenge. 'The cemeteries were often very difficult to find,' recalled Reginald Blomfield, whose own prior experience of the front had been limited to digging trenches around London with the Inns of Court, 'as in many cases the roads shown on our maps had been obliterated by shell fire, and we had to leave our cars and wander over what had been battle-fields in search of graves hastily made and planted anywhere.'

The end of hostilities on 11 November showed too the numbing scale of exhumations and reburials that the concentration of graves into selected cemeteries would entail. For obvious reasons the Commission wished to disturb as few graves as possible, but the figures involved were still staggering: 128,577 re-interments in the first fifteen months of peace, a further 76,073 over the next eighteen months and 38,000 more over the following three years, disinterred by chance and the plough after the official search programme was closed at the end of 1921. 'The total number of graves in France and Belgium when this work has been completed will probably be over 500,000,' Ware predicted in March 1920, writing with his Graves Directorate hat on, and the number of cemeteries requiring architectural treatment . . . will exceed 1,200 . . .

When the Directorate has completed the marking and registration of the graves in a cemetery, and the cemetery is tidy and in good order, the complete records, after being checked and verified, are handed over to the Commission who then take charge of the cemetery. A survey is then made in order to furnish the French or Belgian authorities with the information requisite for the acquisition of the land.

Only photographs now – wooden crosses lurching drunkenly on the edge of flooded craters, the pathetic scraps of a body lying beneath a blanket, a fleshless arm jutting out of a buried dug-out, long lines of searchers steadily moving across a morass of mud with that intent air of a police cordon searching for a missing child – can give any faint sense of the reality that lay behind these figures, but after four years of war there seemed nothing that people could not endure. 'Exhumation was a routine job despite its grimness,' one Australian officer remembered. 'The grave would be opened and the body uncovered. The body was checked for identity discs, paybooks, papers or anything else that could be used in identification. Then the body was wrapped in a blanket, sewn up and marked with an identifying tag for future occasions.'

The work was carried out by soldiers awaiting demob, divided into Grave Concentration Units of twelve men each under a senior NCO, but it was still the forensic skills honed by the successors to the old Mobile Ambulance Unit and Ware's double identity discs that offered relatives the best hope of reclaiming their dead. For each soldier whom they managed to identify there would be ten who remained unknown, and yet every badge, wedding ring, tattoo or distinguishing shade of khaki that yielded a positive identification saved another family from that 'dreadful uncertainty' and unresolved grief that so many, including Kipling, had known since 1914.

It would be another two decades before the task of commemorating the missing would end with Villers-Bretonneux, but for the Commission's own credibility and for public morale it was vital that a start was made on the cemeteries as soon as possible. In February 1918, the Treasury had made an initial grant of £15,000 for the construction of three 'experimental' cemeteries situated safely behind the lines, and in November 1918 a contract was placed for the first of these at Le Treport, a medium-sized cemetery situated on the French coast.

Le Treport offered the chance of gaining a more accurate estimate of costs and the physical and logistical realities of the task ahead and it also provided a first test for the whole design system on which the Commission's work was to be based. Kenyon had learned only too well the difficulties of getting anyone to agree on anything, and in place of a 'committee of architects or art critics' he had proposed a solution that went back to the 'medieval tradition' of 'master' and 'disciple' idealised by the Arts and Crafts Movement, with the cemeteries divided into 'a few large groups' under a 'Principal Architect' and a team of younger architects, ideally recruited from the forces, answerable to him but – within the general principles laid down by the Commission – 'free to work in accordance with the dictates of their genius'.

It might have seemed a quaintly medieval solution to death

on an industrial scale, but Kenyon's report dovetailed with both a wish to employ young architects and draughtsmen who had served with the Army and with the personalities the Commission had landed itself with. 'The Principal Architects had areas assigned to them,' Blomfield recalled with a degree of smugness that suggests how right Kenyon was to keep the three principals apart,

> The three cemeteries at Ypres, for example . . . the great cemetery of Lystenhoek near Poperinghe, and several of the more important cemeteries in the Ypres area and the Somme district, and the large and important cemetery of St Sever at Rouen, were designed by me in this way . . . As far as I can recollect, the cemetery of Le Treport on the coast, which was designed by me, was actually the first cemetery that was completed. It was regarded by the Commission as in the nature of an experiment both as to cost and effect, and Kipling having said some nice things as to its beauty, this cemetery became more or less a prototype for subsequent designs.

There were difficulties and delays on the ground that are glossed over here, problems with transport and labour and the scale and speed of demobilisation, but these were nothing compared with the troubles the Commission was brewing for itself at home. The Anglican mutterings over Lutyens's Great Stone ought to have warned them, because while Kenyon's compromise of two central monuments – cross and stone – had successfully brought Baker into line, there was an intransigent and vociferous element that was not going to be bought off so easily.

There were other strands of opposition – the people ask for housing and we give them stones, the architect and influential teacher, William Lethaby, complained – but it was the old issues of repatriation, freedom, religious sentiment and the headstone around which the principal opposition rallied. In his original report Kenyon had strongly advocated the plain, simple stone that is now so familiar, but with the end of the war and the public's first chance to see what was being planned for them, a thin trickle of protest letters turned into a vituperative parliamentary and press campaign against the Commission's 'unspeakable tyranny'.

They were 'the most heartless and soulless' of all official bodies . . . 'no government would dare to attempt such an outrage . . . under the eyes of the public' . . . 'desecration' . . . 'monstrous' . . . 'bureaucracy run mad' . . . 'against the custom of all civilised nations' . . . 'Never before in the history of man has a parent or widow been deprived of her right to show their love by a personal memorial' – week in, week out, letters in *The Times* show the depth of anger at the refusal 'to allow bereaved parents, widows, and orphans to have any say in regard to the graves of their loved-ones', and the Commission's problem was that it was only too true. As a former newspaper editor, Ware was acutely aware of public opinion, yet whenever it came to any specific issue, whether it was the latitude allowed to the lettering on a grave-stone, or a request for the Hand of Ulster or the Maltese Cross or school emblem to replace a regimental badge, the 'Old Milner' in him would always out. 'I know how English people dislike (more than ever after these five years of bureaucratic control) any interference with their liberty in any way,' he wrote to one widow who had been palmed off with the usual official high-handedness, but 'they do not understand that such committees as this . . . are really designed to help them'.

The problem rested in that patronising use of 'they' – another relative was breezily dismissed as one of those people 'who prefer modern translations of the Old and New Testament to the Authorised Version' – and Lord Wolmer was not lying in *The Times* when he promised the War Graves Commission a fight. 'Nothing could put a harsher touch upon the underlying sorrow with which innumerable hearts are now stricken,' a *Spectator* editorial lamented, putting its finger unerringly on the weaknesses and subterfuges in the Kenyon Report,

than that there should be a bitter public dispute over the war graves. That would be a humiliation when everything should be done in the spirit that makes sorrow and sacrifice ennobling . . . For our part we have read the Report by Sir Frederic Kenyon, whose recommendations have been accepted by the Commission, with a full appreciation of the anxious care which he brought to his task, of his evident sense of responsibility and of his recognition of the dignity and significance which should properly belong to the war cemeteries. But when all has been said, we fear that the recommendations lack just that touch of sympathetic understanding and indulgence which would have made allowance for the almost uncontrollable individual cravings that have expressed themselves and are rapidly growing. On the artistic side we admit there is everything to be said for uniformity and for strict regulations, but this leaves out the question of what is more important than grandeur or austerity of design, and that is the passionate and incalculable longing of the individual – of the wife, the mother, the brother or sister – to express devotion to the dead in his or her own way.

It was a difficult case to answer, and all the more so for the unusual moderation with which it was expressed. 'The last thing we want to do is to be unjust,' the editorial went on in its measured *ex cathedra* tones,

but we cannot help thinking that, whether unconsciously or not, the idea of 'equality of treatment' – the idea that the officers and men must be treated alike is made unduly to come to the rescue of the desiderated artistic principles . . . Correctness of taste is good, but the sincere outpouring of a wife's or mother's love, may be even better than good taste. We do not know how far women were consulted in this matter, if they were consulted at all; but if a single mother had helped to draw up the Report we feel pretty sure that it would have caused less pain.

Who would have thought, one embittered mother wrote, 'when they left us in 1914 in their boyish vigour that not even in death should we be allowed to choose for them', and it was a cry from a pre-war world to which Ware was determined there would be no return. In the early days of the fighting he had glimpsed the democratic possibilities latent in his work, and he had no intention of seeing the vision of national and imperial unity enshrined in his cemeteries high-jacked now by what he saw as a narrowly self-interested, patrician clique, dominated by the extended Cecil clan for whom his old colleague from the early days in France, Lord Robert Cecil, was the chief spokesman.

It is important to realise too that this was as passionately a matter of 'religion' to Ware, who had been brought up in the evangelical dissenting tradition of Victorian England, as it was for the Anglican opposition to their plans. By the last quarter of the nineteenth century, evangelicalism had lost much of the high ground in national affairs it once owned, and yet the cemeteries that he and the Commission were planning were as much an expression of that deflected Victorian evangelical energy and high earnestness as was the Empire they were built to honour.

The cemeteries seem in so many ways now the product of a new century of democracy, equality and agnosticism that it is easy to forget that they were in a very real sense the last great achievement of the Victorian Age of Faith. By the time that they were realised, the missionary zeal and dreams that had inspired that Age belonged to a fading past, but it is no coincidence that the men who shared Ware's vision at the Commission were the same men who had given India New Delhi, South Africa its parliament building, Egypt the Aswan Dam and the Mother Country her last monumental proofs of her special place in God's dispensation.

The opposition was not, of course, the privileged Anglican clique Ware liked to pretend it was – it was something that transcended wealth, party, denomination – but it suited him to pull out the 'class card' now as it had when William Gladstone's body was repatriated to England in 1915. In the spring of 1920, a petition with more than eight thousand signatures was presented to the Prince of Wales, and yet all Ware could see, or was prepared to see, were the same old Cecil names that figured in every protest from the letter pages of *The Times* to the Canterbury House of Laymen. 'Your Royal Highness,' began Lady Florence Cecil's petition, a gold-embossed and vellum-bound volume, ivory in colour, 10½ x 8½ inches x 3½ deep, crammed with line after line of signatures and pasted-in slips of paper,

In the name of thousands of heartbroken parents, wives, brothers and sisters of those who have fallen in the war, we, the undersigned, appeal most earnestly to Your Royal Highness as President of the Imperial War Graves Commission to help us.

We have been deeply wounded by the decision of the Commission that no crosses (other than those engraved on the headstone, which time and the weather will soon deface) are to be allowed over the individual graves of those who gave their lives to preserve the lives and liberty of others.

It was through the strength of the Cross that many of them were enabled to do so. It is through the hope of the Cross that most of us are able to carry on the life from which all the sunshine seems to have gone, and to deny us the emblem of that strength and hope adds heavily to the burden of our sorrow.

We do not ask that all should have crosses. Some may prefer headstones, but for those of us who so deeply desire it – is it too much to ask that the present wooden cross may be replaced at our expense, by more durable ones of stone . . .

> We pray Your Royal Highness most fervently to grant
> that right which has been from all time the privilege of the
> bereaved may not be denied us.

It was a powerful and moving document – 'Lost three sons . . .
Three brothers . . . Three brothers . . . 3 sons killed in action
. . . Four dear sons out of five having given their lives for King
and Country . . . Mother of only son . . . Mother of two sons
. . . Five nephews . . . My only child . . . Son aged 18 years . . .
Bereaved of Chums . . . Bereaved of Pals . . . Fiancé . . .' – but
the 'Cecil clan' were not the only ones ready to mobilise their
support.[8]

'When the widows and mothers of our dead go out to France

---

8   There was one abortive attempt at compromise when at a private
meeting with Balfour (another of the Cecil clan) it was agreed that he
should present designs to their artistic advisors for an alternative cruciform
gravestone. There was a very strong instinct within the Commission to rest
its argument on principles, but nothing could have made the aesthetic case
for their own simple headstone better than the squat and bulbous confection that looked as if it might have been the product of a game of
'Consequences' among Balfour's 'Souls'. 'I should much regret its adoption,
both on artistic grounds and as a matter of principle,' Kenyon responded
to his design. 'Artistically it seems to me thoroughly ugly.' It was open
house at the IWGC, with Commissioners, artistic advisors and Principal
Architects competing in their abuse. MacDonald Gill did at least made an
effort to find 'a good word for it' before giving up the attempt as impossible, but from Lutyens to Baker, from General Cox of the India office to
South Africa's Reginald Blankenberg and Sir Alfred Mond, there was no
such charity: 'extraordinarily ugly' . . . 'ugly and ungainly' . . . 'appalling'
. . . 'disastrous' . . . 'a humpty-dumpty design' . . . 'a bottle' . . . 'a sort of
thing you shoot at' – just the sort of thing, in fact, that you could expect,
as Blomfield predictably reminded the Commission, the moment that you
didn't leave everything to your Principal Architects.

to visit the graves,' a counter-memorandum from the Trades Union Congress Parliamentary Committee, representing four and a half million working men, declared,

> they will expect to find that equal honour has been paid to all who have made the same sacrifice, and this result cannot be attained if differences, however restricted, are allowed in the character and design of the memorials erected.

The Imperial War Graves Commission was showing the benefit of having Harry Gosling, an old and experienced trade union activist, as one of its Commissioners, and with 'The Comrades of the Great War' and 'The National Federation of Discharged Sailors and Soldiers' weighing in with their own resolutions in favour of equality, the battle-lines were drawn. 'As I see the position now,' one sympathetic MP, the Unionist Member for Westminster, William Burdett-Coutts wrote in April 1920, after Lord Robert Cecil had demanded a division of the House over the war graves question,

> the Commission has been roundly attacked by private influence, by a particular set of people whose names give a superficial weight to their views, and by methods of persistent personal persuasion, including not a little misrepresentation.
>
> The House of Commons is apt to be led by sentiment, and has not a very long memory. The sentiment in this case has been confined to sympathise with the harrowing appeal on behalf of a comparative few individuals.

In all the history of the Commission there is perhaps nothing odder than the intervention of a man who in thirty-five years as an MP had scarcely so much as troubled the House. With a name like 'Burdett' and the constituency of Westminster, he might have seemed born to take such a stand, but this particular Burdett was not all he seemed, having only adopted the name by Royal Licence in 1881, when, to a good deal of ribald gossip, he had married the great Victorian philanthropist and heiress to the Burdett political inheritance and Coutts banking fortune, Angela Burdett-Coutts.

William Ashmead-Bartlett, as he then was, was thirty at the time of his marriage, Angela Burdett-Coutts sixty-seven and, unfairly or not, a faint air of improbability seems to have surrounded him ever after. Her closest friends always insisted on the contribution he made to her work and happiness, but even if that were true it is not just imagination that detects a note of mild surprise in Commission circles that their democratic champion in Parliament should turn out to be the sixty-nine-year-old widower of the Victorian age's richest heiress.

Until this moment, in fact, William Burdett-Coutts had spent his whole life in the shadow of either wife or brother or, when they were both safely dead, of a war-correspondent nephew who had made his name with his Gallipoli despatches. His widowed mother had brought him and his four siblings from America to England while they were all still young, but while the older and flashier Ellis was progressing from a double First at Christ Church – where he routed Asquith for the presidency of the Oxford Union – to full-blown Disraelian imperialism and an unchallenged position as the rabble-rousing Michael Heseltine of the late nineteenth-century Conservative faithful, William was making his plodding way through Keble into the Burdett-Coutts philanthropic empire.

If Burdett-Coutts had spent thirty-five years in Parliament in virtual silence, however, he was ready when his chance came. He had first publicised his sympathy with the Commission in a letter to *The Times* in February, and when the following month Cecil tabled a question in the House demanding his debate, Burdett-Coutts rose 'as one who is strongly and conscientiously opposed to the policy of the Noble Lord', to echo the demand as the clearest way of endorsing Commission policies.

Ware had probably been hoping that someone more prominent would take up their cause, but after three weeks had produced no one else, he made his first overtures. 'An attack on the general policy of the Commission will shortly be made in the House of Commons,' Ware wrote to Burdett-Coutts in mid-April, thanking him for his earlier contribution in *The Times*,

> and I understand that you intend to speak on the occasion. I should be glad to give you any information you may desire on the subject . . . I would be much obliged if you could give me the names of any members likely to be interested in the matter . . . and would care to be supplied with the facts.

Ware needed to maintain a delicate balance here, because while he was keen to maintain at least the appearance of Burdett-Coutts's independence, he was determined that he was going to be well coached. 'I understand that you are going to draw up a statement and send it over here,' he wrote again on 19 April, forwarding on with his offer of help the trade union statement of support that Harry Gosling had orchestrated: 'If you wish me to draw up a skeleton statement of headings I shall be happy to do so.'

The statement when it came at the end of the month, printed at Burdett-Coutts's expense and over his name and circulated to MPs, had, like so many apparently independent documents, Ware's signature all over it. 'The Imperial War Graves Commission was constituted by Royal Charter in 1917,' the statement began, reminding Members that the money involved was 'imperial' money and not simply 'national' money, and the principles on which it had been pledged imperial principles that the House had no business interfering with. 'It is of the utmost importance that the House should realise the position in which the Imperial War Graves Commission is now placed by the Motions [demanding a change of policy],' Burdett-Coutts concluded, his final paragraphs set in a bold type for emphasis,

It is not too much to say that the whole work of this great Imperial and National Memorial is now paralysed by this fatal atmosphere of doubt. The way of the Commission must be cleared once for all, so that they can be free to get on.

Under these circumstances it will not be sufficient to defeat the motion under notice, if the House should so decide, when it is brought forward. A negative decision would still leave the matter open and the commission liable to some new attack . . . Therefore, if the motion is made, an Amendment will be moved which will enable the House, if it so wills, to directly confirm the principle of equality of treatment . . . and the entire policy connected therewith.

There was the flimsiest of olive branches from Churchill in the form of a letter to the Archbishop of Canterbury inviting a text for the great Cross of Sacrifice, but any last-minute nerves disappeared the moment in the late afternoon of 4 May 1920 that the Member for Westminster rose to a packed House to reply to the motion. 'No one could be more reluctant than I am to deprive relatives of anything that can in any way assuage the irreparable loss that they will carry to the end of their days,' Burdett-Coutts began, an elderly and childless widower transparently, almost humbly, conscious of the grief that separated him from so many of those to whom he was speaking,

They have had to meet awful trials in this War and they have borne themselves in their darkest hour with a heroism that seems to reflect and form a very part of that shown by those whom they mourn. The women: the mothers, the wives, the daughters and sisters of England and Great Britain! We used to read of the Roman women in this connection. But classic story contains no examples of mingled resignation and pride comparable to that shown by British women in the 20th century of the Christian era. Can I say less of the men – the fathers who lost their sons, often an only son. I can only say, and I think many hon. Members have felt the same thing, that when one met them for the first time after the blow had fallen, something came into your throat that almost prevented your speaking. And there they have stood, speechless too perhaps, but brave, proud, calm and uncomplaining. It has been wonderful throughout the War, but what is clear is that it is they themselves whose light has gone out who seemed to have died the death for their country. No, it is not want of sympathy that will lead a single member of the Commission to go into the Lobby, as I hope a large majority will do, to confirm once for all the policy of the Commission . . . It is rather the natural movement of sympathy into the largest channel, and one where it is most needed, that will do it.

It might not have been the kind of language that Kenyon or Macready would have used, perhaps, but age demands and gets a different sort of licence, and it was an astute opening from a man defending a Commission that stood accused of bureaucratic heartlessness. 'I approached this subject with an absolutely fresh mind,' Burdett-Coutts went on, keen to erase any impression that he was the Commission's poodle; he 'was only the man in the street' . . . 'knew nothing of the discussions that had taken place' in the House over the last year and knew nobody on the Commission 'except one man, the great poet of Empire' who 'kindly came down to this House the other day and made a most convincing speech to a meeting of hon Members'.

It would be intriguing to know how much of this was coaching and how much spontaneous. Whichever way it was, it is impossible to believe that Ware did not know what was coming next. 'At the time I speak of, [Kipling] was away, and I could not get at him,' Burdett-Coutts continued – and across the century one can see the House in the subfusc shades of mourning, many of them men who had fought in the trenches, men who had lost their own sons; men whose decisions had sent a million troops to their deaths, Asquith, Churchill, Lloyd George . . . and on his feet the sixty-nine-year-old Member for Westminster, only a year from his own death, the seeming incarnation of disinterested and diffident simplicity, carefully unfolding a letter as he softened up his audience for a *coup de théâtre* that his brother in his Gladstone-baiting heyday would have been proud of.

> I cannot help, however, reading one sentence from a letter I received from him a day or two ago. The letter is marked 'private', but I do not think he will object to my quoting this sentence . . . The words are these: 'You see we shall never have any grave to go to. Our boy was missing at Loos. The ground is of course battered and mined past all hope of any trace being recovered. I wish some of the people who are making this trouble realise how more than fortunate they are to have a name on a headstone in a known place.'

It was a crucial moment in the debate and with Kipling's letter, Burdett-Coutts had given the Commission the human face it needed. 'In my communications with the Commission,' he went on, clawing back yard by yard the emotional high ground that the opposition had held unchallenged over the past year, two things had struck him: the 'infinite consideration' of the Commission to 'all classes of relatives' and,

> what I call the genius of this War . . . which has never in history had an opportunity of expressing itself before. That is the solid and united effort, embodying its unity in forces drawn from every island and continent under the British Flag, fused and welded into one, without distinction of

race, colour or creed, fighting, ready to die, and dying for one common cause that they all understood. It is that great union, both in action and in death, that the Commission seeks nobly to commemorate and make perpetual by its policy and design.

The debate had just begun, though, and if some of the rancour had momentarily gone out of it, the truce was only temporary. In his opening speech Sir James Remnant had paid a warm tribute to his 'old personal friend' Ware, but when Viscount Wolmer – a Cecil grandson – rose in his turn, a cursory nod in the direction of the Commission's 'fine' motives was the most they were going to get. 'I listened to my hon. Friend very carefully,' Wolmer went on, successfully turning the whole argument of equality and compulsory uniformity on its head before going straight for the heart of Ware's imperial dream. So long as there were clear guidelines as to size and cost there could be no conceivable objection to variety, he argued,

> But there is a further point . . . the conception that you have in the graveyards designed by the War Graves Commission is of a great national Imperial memorial, a great war memorial, a great memorial to the British Army . . . By all means have memorials. Make them out of Government stone if you like. Make them uniform. But you have no right to employ, in making these memorials, the bodies of other people's relatives. It is not decent, it is not reasonable, it is not right. A memorial is something to be seen. There will be two classes of people who will visit these

graveyards: there will be the idle tourists in the first place, and secondly there will be the bereaved relatives. Are you going to consider the feelings of the bereaved relatives or the artistic susceptibilities of the casual tourist? These graveyards are not and cannot be war memorials. Have your war memorials in England or in France or wherever you like . . . but you have no right to take the precious remains of bereaved widows, parents and orphans and build them into a monument which is distasteful and hateful to those relatives, as in many cases it is.

It must have made uncomfortable listening for the Commissioners because Wolmer was largely right – uniformity *was* a matter of aesthetics and not principles; nine people of ten *would* choose their own stone if allowed, the English did *not* like conformity – and the old alliance of patrician and people was in full cry. 'I must ask the House to bear with me while I read some of the hundreds of letters I have received from bereaved relatives . . . who feel most terribly and acutely on this subject,' he continued – Hansard captures the exchange:

The hon. Member for Westminster spoke about the voice of the dead. No doubt it may be the case that some of the men who have died would have liked to be buried in the way that the War Graves Commission has decided.
Captain BROWN All of them!
Viscount WOLMER . . . How does the hon. Member know? What right has he to say that? I know of the case of a boy who told his mother that he would 'hate to be buried

like a dog'. Those were the words he used. The boy is
dead, and that is how he is going to be treated.

'How does the hon. Member know? What right has he to say
that?' – these were questions to which the Commission had no
real answers. There was nobody on Wolmer's side who would
have denied an equal freedom to those who chose a 'Commission
stone', and all they wanted to know was by what conceivable
right – even if the Imperial War Graves Commission party were
in a clear majority, even if there was only one mother, one son,
one husband who did not want the stone – did a country that
had publicly gone to war to defend Little Belgium against the
militarist might of Germany now trample over the wishes of its
bereaved relatives?

'My hon. Friend in his most interesting memorandum calls it
an Imperial memorial for the freedom of men,' Wolmer continued.
'What freedom is it if you will not even allow the dead bodies of
the people's relatives to be cared for and looked after in the way
they like? It is a memorial, not to freedom, but to rigid militarism,
not in intention, but in effect.' It was not as though it was the
'country' speaking, either, Wolmer reminded the House, or as if
Parliament had been given a say in the matter, only an unrepre-
sentative and dictatorial coterie of like-minded men without a
single representative of any religion on it. 'I think it extremely
unfortunate that the whole scope of the Commission's activities
was not discussed in Parliament,' he concluded, and while the case
against the narrow elitism of the Commission might have carried
more weight if it had not come from a member of the extended
Cecil clan, Wolmer was on solid ground on at least one point:

and it is extremely unfortunate that there is not a single woman upon that Commission. I listened with admiration to the Hon member for Westminster when he spoke about the women of England. Why are they not represented upon the Commission? Of the hundreds of letters that I have received the greater part of them come from women. Women feel more acutely upon this question than men. That is only natural. Why are women not represented on the War Graves Commission? We come here, not to ask that relatives should be allowed to display wealth or privilege upon the graves, but only that they may show their love, the love which itself is stronger than death, the only thing that is, that love which makes the churchyards of our countryside beautiful in spite of the uncouthness of many of the tombstones or the lack of taste in particular ornaments . . . It is that love which will carry mourners to these grave yards in France, and it is to that love to which we as a nation owe a debt which we never can repay and which we ought in a matter of this sort primarily to consider.

Wolmer's had been an impressive performance, but for every letter produced against the Commission another could be produced for it, for every report of the Commission's 'intolerance and high-handed insolence' the gratitude of a grateful widow or mother. As Wolmer sat down Asquith rose to declare his support in the shortest and simplest of terms, and one by one Members followed him with their stories and praise for the work already completed in France. 'I have suffered in this war like my right hon. Friend,' Colonel Burn, just back from seeing the first completed cemeteries, told the House,

> I know not where my boy's body is. His grave is not known, and whether he is buried or not is more than I can say, because the Germans came into the trenches where he was killed, and when I looked and saw the grave of a General and on either side that of an unknown British soldier, I felt proud to think that my boy may have been one of these unknown British soldiers.

'Long before there was controversy on this question,' Mr Thomas, the Member for Derby, took up the theme, he had received a letter 'which reflected the opinion of humble people'. He had been visiting France shortly after the death of 'that brilliant young man, Mr Raymond Asquith' and had seen his grave and near it that of his cousin, 'young Tennant'. 'Between them were the graves of humble British soldiers,' Thomas went on,

> and as I stood there I thought of the . . . events that had brought the statesman's son, the peer's son, and the humble British soldier together, all with the same kind of tombstone, each burial place indicated in the same way . . . At Derby, later, I was speaking at a meeting of my constituents, and I told them of the incident . . . [and] a few days later I received a letter from Leicester, and it was something like this effect. 'I see in the press that you have been near the grave of Raymond Asquith. I lost my only boy in the War. I am blind and his mother is deaf. I was told by some friends

that he was buried near the grave of Raymond Asquith, and I wonder whether you could tell me that the grave is well kept.' The name was Simon. I looked into my book and I found that was the lad whose name I had put down merely by chance. I replied . . . that not only could I say the grave was well kept, but that I had picked up a leaf from the grave and that perhaps he would like to have it. I leave Members of this House to imagine the reply I got.[9]

There seemed no reason why the debate should ever stop and no reason why it should go on. Few on either side had wanted to air their bitter divide in the first place but no one now was going to change sides. Something good, though, had come out of it: not an emotional exhaustion, exactly, but a sad-eyed recognition of a universal grief that made rancour and division – emotional or parliamentary – seem somehow indecent. There was more to unite than separate them. Mr Turton would have given all that he had to have brought his only son home from Poperinghe to lie in their own churchyard 'where Sunday after Sunday we could see the grave'. Colonel Burn found solace in the thought that one of those unknown graves in France was his son's, but in their common loss was a common call to consideration, decency and humanity. It would, Burn told the House, be an ingratitude and insult to the dead to 'come to a division'. 'I appeal to my

9   It does not change the argument but it is, sadly, no longer true. Raymond Asquith, the Prime Minister's son, is buried between two fellow officers in Guillemont Cemetery, which was constructed after the war. Lieutenant the Honourable Edward Tennant is buried in the same row, but there is no Simon.

hon. Friend (Sir James Remnant) with whom I completely sympathise,' responded Mr Thorne for the opposition, 'not to force this
to a Division. A Division on such a subject would harass every
one of us. Our men, officers and men alike, on every stricken
field have fallen together. In their death they were not divided.
Let us, their fathers, not be divided here.'

The House agreed. To the bitter end, Lord Robert Cecil
promised to fight on but there would be no division.[10] The War
Graves Commission could now go ahead and Churchill, their
new chairman, summing up the debate, painted for them the future.
'The cemeteries which are going to be erected to the British dead
on all the battlefields in all the theatres of war, will be entirely
different from the ordinary cemeteries which mark the resting
place of those who pass out in the common flow of human fate
from year to year,' he declared with his own inimitable and
overweening sense of history,

10   It is ironic that a rare beneficiary of Commission flexibility on burial
should in fact be a Cecil. Lady Violet Cecil – a Cecil by marriage, and a
reluctant one at that – had lost her son at Villers-Cotterêts in the early
fighting of September 1914. On the death of her husband she had married
Lord Milner, with whom, it seems, she had been in love for twenty years.
In 1922 a distressed Ware wrote to Milner to say that he had received a
request from the families of the three officers buried with George Cecil in
a single grave known as the 'Guards' Grave'. They wanted the bodies
exhumed and reburied with their comrades. This could not be done without
moving all four. What, Ware wanted to know, would Lady Milner wish?
It is hard to imagine that anyone but Milner's wife would have got this
letter, but on 11 April 1922 the four bodies were 'carried under a Union
Jack to the Guards' Cemetery where a service was held by the Chaplain'.
Lady Milner visited her son's grave every year until the Second World War
made it impossible.

They will be supported and sustained by the wealth of this great nation and Empire, as long as we remain a nation and an Empire, and there is no reason at all why, in periods as remote from our own as we ourselves are from the Tudors, the graveyards in France of this Great War, shall not remain an abiding and supreme memorial to the efforts and glory of the British Army, and the sacrifices made in that great cause.

Some decried Lutyens's Great Stones as meaningless, he went on, but they too were part of this great feat of commemoration. 'I have been speaking of periods of 200 or 300 years,' he concluded,

but these great stones of which I speak are of Portland stone, weighing about 10 tons . . . and there will be 1,500 or 2,000 of them on the plains of France alone, and these stones will certainly be in existence 2,000 or 3,000 years hence . . . [and] even if our language, our institutions, and our Empire all have faded from the memory of man, these great stones will still preserve the memory of a common purpose pursued by a great nation in the remote past, and will undoubtedly excite the wonder and reverence of a future age.

Now all the Commission had to do was build the cemeteries.

EIGHT

The Task

In all the arguments over principles it is easy to lose sight of the sheer scale of the physical task that the Imperial War Graves Commission had set itself. In the months immediately after the war it was naturally impossible to put a precise figure on the Empire's dead, but as prisoners returned and the exhumations and discoveries continued and the Gallipoli peninsula was opened, the numbers of dead and missing began to assume something like their familiar, neatly rounded totals.

There may possibly never be a final figure – bodies are still found, identifications made, the missing given a name and grave, a whole new cemetery constructed – but there would be over 580,000 separate burials before the Commission had completed its immediate task. By the time that another war had added its own grim toll, the Commission had more than 23,000 burial sites under its control, but for all the global scale of its later work nothing in its history can begin to compare with the physical, logistical and administrative feat of burying or commemorating those half a million and more dead of the First World War who have their individual Commission graves.

These figures need to be put in their wider context of course – France had lost 1,398,000 men, Russia 1,811,000, Germany 2,037,000, Austria-Hungary 1,100,000, Italy 578,000, the USA 114,000, Turkey and Bulgaria 892,000, a grand total of 9,450,000 even before civilian deaths are taken into account – but no country was planning to do quite what Britain was. It should be remembered too that France and Belgium had a devastated country to reconstruct but that also made the Commission's task harder. They were starting from scratch in a shattered land; they were struggling against a chronic shortage of labour, gardening and clerical staff; they were working in the aftermath of the greatest cataclysm in Europe's history; they were competing with the rival claims of agriculture and demobilisation, and while numbers conjure up something of the challenge – 580,000 gravestones to be quarried, shaped, incised and lettered, to take just the most obvious example – they cannot remotely suggest the difficulties against which it was met. 'The Commission itself started its work on the Continent with a staff of only eight operating from headquarters buried in the forests near Hesdin,' the Commission's official historian wrote,

hard put to it to find even basic necessities. Enterprising officers went out on the scrounge returning with quantities of supplies that had been begged or borrowed from the withdrawing army units . . . Gradually they built up stores, commandeered camps, and built others, and soon they acquired a miscellaneous collection of vehicles.

It was much the same story in London, where temporary huts had to be erected on the bed of the drained lake in St James's

Park to accommodate a growing Commission staff. But it was the itinerant labour force levelling and preparing the hundreds of cemeteries that stretched like a chain down the line of the Western Front who had it hardest. 'Life in that wilderness was dismal,' Longworth wrote of the Commission's migrant bands of ex-soldier-gardeners, cut off from all outside contact except for the occasional messenger bringing up mail.

> In some ways their existence bore similarities to that of the cattle drovers of the pioneering West. Many went out armed, to shoot rabbits, or any other game that lingered on the battlefields, and towards the end of the week their return to camp would be punctuated by often riotous visits to every cafe or estaminet along the way. But these 'travelling circuses', as they were called, did their job, putting as many as 1,375 cemeteries in order in one year.

The hard physical labour was only part of the task, because for every cemetery that the Commission took over, there was the legal and surveying work to be done, photographs to be taken, preliminary sketches to be made, the Principal Architect to be consulted, designs to be finalised, a horticultural programme to be agreed, Kenyon to be placated and the chastening lessons of the first three 'experimental cemeteries' implemented.

These three cemeteries were all, in the end, designed under Blomfield's aegis and had inevitably thrown up the need for future modifications. Their enthusiastic reception in the press was all that Ware and Kenyon could possibly have hoped for, but with fluctuating exchange rates and tenders exceeding estimates by anything up to two and three hundred per cent – prices had gone up by two and a half times from their pre-war levels – the costs had come in far above the £10 a grave to which the Commission had tied itself.

Ware knew the picture was not as disheartening as these first experiments suggested – with the great cemeteries like Etaples or Tyne Cot, economies of scale would automatically kick in – and yet even the imposition of a 'Unit Cost Schedule' to keep their architects 'honest' was not enough to bring ambition and expenditure into line. The Principal Architects were naturally reluctant to see any of their designs compromised by 'niggardly' economies, but with Lutyens's great monoliths alone costing £500 each it was soon clear that in the smallest cemeteries both the War Stone and the shelters on which Baker had placed such stress would have to be sacrificed.

It is characteristic that of the three Principal Architects for the Western Front (a fourth, Charles Holden was added in 1920), it was the disarming, incorrigibly joking and punning Lutyens who was least biddable when it came to changes. For all his bluster, Blomfield had been prepared to see his Cross of Sacrifice scaled down where it was suitable, but for Lutyens the integrity and permanence of his Great Stone, with its complex geometry and subtle use of entasis – the corrective use of curved surfaces learned from the Greeks – lay as much in its mathematical and quasi-mystical perfection as it did in the sheer mass of stone that loomed so large in Churchill's historic imagination.

The issue for the Commission was fundamentally one of costs, but if anyone had dared raise it there was also an aesthetic case to be made against the ubiquitous use of Lutyens's stone. In the great formal cemeteries like Etaples, his altar – inscribed with the words 'Their Name Liveth For Evermore' – creates a powerful focus, but in even the medium-size cemeteries it can sometimes feel an intrusion, the intellectual plaything of a stubborn egotist, the overbearing extravagance of an Edwardian Timon, or, more charitably, the calculated concession of a secular age to a vaguely religious sentiment.

Lutyens eventually, and only very reluctantly, agreed to it being assembled in pieces where nothing else was possible, and Baker submitted designs for standardised shelters. The one element that no one was prepared to budge on was the bitterly won gravestone. In an attempt to hold down costs the Commission had been tempted to make the headstone smaller, but with the savings from mass production and the development of a pantograph engraving machine coming to their rescue, they were able to hold to the original proportions and standards that Kenyon's report had demanded and still keep well within their budget. There was the occasional problem in the mid-1920s, with substandard seams in the quarries and the Middle Eastern and Gallipoli cemeteries bringing their own serious complications, but the astonishing thing is how smoothly the operation went. In the last year of the war, the Commission had taken some early soundings around the building trade, and after an initial 850 stones for the 'experimental' cemeteries had been contracted out, headstones were soon being shipped over to the continent at a rate of more than four thousand a week.

After consultations with the Curator of the Geological Survey Museum, Portland and Hopton Wood stone were chosen for their durability and cheapness; again aesthetics and economy marched hand in hand. In the different climatic and soil conditions across the world, other stones would eventually have to be used, but the quintessential War Graves Commission headstone is made of English limestone and stands in one of the Western Front cemeteries, 2 feet 6 tall, by 1 foot 3 inches, by 3 inches deep, the head slightly rounded to carry off the rain, its crisp Roman lettering equally legible from above or the sides, the regimental badge unfussy, the incised cross everything, as Kenyon had always insisted it would be, that Christian sentiment could ask: a piece of design that in its perfect marriage of utility, simplicity and dignity has an air of inevitability about it that makes the bitter heartache that preceded it all the more baffling. 'It is the simplest, it is the grandest place I ever saw,' a *Times* correspondent wrote in 1920 when he first visited Blomfield's 'experimental' cemetery at Forceville on the Somme,

The most perfect, the noblest, the most classically beautiful memorial that any loving heart or any proud nation could desire for their heroes fallen in a foreign land. Picture this strangely stirring place. A lawn enclosed of close clipped turf, banded across with line on line of flowers, and linked by these bands of flowers; uncrowded, at stately intervals stand in soldierly ranks the white headstones. And while they form as perfect, as orderly a whole as any regiment on parade, yet they do not shoulder each other. Every one is set apart in flowers, every one casts its shadow upon a gracious space of green. Each one, so stern in outline, is most rich in surface, for the crest of each regiment stands out with a bold and arresting distinction above the strongly incised names.

There was the odd niggle from the Commission – too much ornament, the walls at Le Treport far too high to please the Canadian High Commissioner – but Blomfield's 'experimental' cemeteries marked the beginning of an immense programme of building that would redefine the landscape over which Britain's armies had once fought. For practical reasons the first cemeteries tackled were those situated behind the old front line, but by the spring of 1920, Ware was able to announce the construction of some fifty cemeteries in two waves, an initial group of thirty-one, which made up what he called 'The First Priority Programme' and included the 11,000 dead of Lutyens's great cemetery at Etaples, followed by a 'Second Priority Programme' that ranged in scale from the forty-four graves of the Gouy-en-Artois Communal Cemetery Extension to Ecoivres and its 1,725 dead.

Calais Southern Cemetery, 720 graves; Les Baraques British Cemetery, Sangatte, 919; Wimereux Communal Cemetery, 2,847; Lijssenthoek Military Cemetery, Poperinghe, 9,887; Poperinghe New Military Cemetery, 677, Villers-Bocage Communal Cemetery Extension, 59; Doullens No 1, Doullens No 2 . . . Fifteen miles of hedges by the spring of 1921, seventy-five miles of flower borders, 200 acres of sown grass. 'In France and Belgium alone there are 970 cemeteries,' Ware would eventually be able to write of an achievement that Kipling called the greatest work attempted since the Pyramids, 'surrounded by 50 miles of walling in brick or stone, with nearly one thousand Crosses of Sacrifice and 560 Stones of Remembrance, and many chapels, record buildings and shelters; there are some 600,000 headstones resting on nearly 250 miles of concrete beam foundations.'

For all the building and planting and sowing of these post-war years – 'The Strenuous Years' as the Commission's historian proudly dubbed them – and for all the establishment of nurseries, the compilation and printing of cemetery registers, the daunting task of verification and the garnering of personal inscriptions, there remained one issue that sheer slog could not resolve. In the grim process of exhumation, every conceivable effort had been made to identify remains, but what was to be done about all those who could not be identified? What of the hundreds of thousands who had graves but no names or had been obliterated or lost without trace? 'I, for one, would not have risen but for the fact that I desire, if I may be permitted to do so, to impress one aspect of this matter which has been very little dwelt on,' one MP had begun his reluctant contribution to the war graves debate in Parliament,

Like my hon. Friend opposite, I am one of those who will never have even the melancholy consolation of mourning at the grave of my son. The appeal I desire to make is on behalf of those, of whom I think there are some in this Commission, and many thousand outside, that in these cemeteries which will be scattered over the world even we may have some share in the memorial which will be erected to our honoured dead. May I convey what is in my mind by an illustration?

The illustration was a familiar one: a young officer leads his 'gallant men' into an enemy trench, the Germans evacuate and shell it, the officer and his men are shelled, the trench becomes their tomb, it is retaken by the Germans, and their bodies are lost forever. 'It is impossible thus to secure individual graves for our boys,' he went on,

> but those boys are as much loved by us as any of those who have individual graves, and we would, therefore, without any controversy whatever, appeal to the Commission to see whether it is not possible that in the cemetery nearest where many came to their death there cannot be some memorial where their names are recorded, so that all dying in that locality may have the honour of being recognised by this country? If under the conditions we cannot go and kneel by the side of the individual grave, we can at least go to the memorial where our boys' names will remind us of what they suffered and sacrificed for us. I do not know whether it is possible . . . I hope it is possible, because it will bring satisfaction to tens of thousands of hearts in this country.

'It will certainly be possible to meet the wish my hon. Friend has just expressed,' Churchill had assured him, but the problem was more complex than his confidence suggested and if the Commission had not yet come up with an answer it was not for any want of trying. In December 1918, Kenyon had proposed inscribing the names of the missing on panels in the cemetery closest to their deaths, but whichever way the Commission turned – geographical, regimental, monumental, individual graves or tablets – all the old passions and divisions stirred by the headstone and cross controversies only resurfaced in aggravated form.

It had seemed relatively simple to deal with the graves of the unidentified dead – in his role as literary advisor, responsible for all the Commission's texts, Kipling came up with the haunting formula that in its variations can be found on 180,000 headstones, 'A Soldier of the Great War Known unto God' – but that still left relatives of the missing exactly where they were. 'My own feeling,' one bereaved mother, Mary Elwood, who had lost her son on 14 July 1916, two weeks into the Battle of the Somme, wrote to Ware,

is that I should much prefer his name being recorded on a headstone exactly the same as all those whose graves *are* known . . . this would make all the memorials the same, which is to my mind such a *very* nice idea. I like the feeling of all the headstones being the same, for officers and men, & personally I feel I should like a headstone to my son in the cemetery amongst his men, who fell with him, and who all loved him.

'Sir, my son is one of the missing,' another parent, N. Smith of 180 Canterbury Rd., Croydon wrote,

Could I have a stone instead of a tablet if I paid for it? ['No' was Ware's answer.] I should like a stone the same as the soldiers have if it is possible. My son's address is Pte. S. Smith 10999 1st Queen RWSB Company, BEF France. I could send the money if it could be done if you would please let me know what it would be,

Yours respectfully,
N. Smith

There was another 'No' to a Mrs Christie who wanted her two sons' memorials near each other, and it was not only individuals who felt that every missing soldier was 'entitled to his six feet of ground'. 'In my recollection,' Ware was reminded in the spring of 1919 by a representative of Hughes's Australian government, especially sensitive to the issue on account of the heavy toll of unidentified bodies that still had to be dealt with from the Gallipoli campaign,

> the idea of the Commission was to avoid dogmatising as to any particular treatment and to invite some suggestion from parties who were interested.
>
> So far as Australia is concerned, the Prime Minister after giving the matter due consideration on the spot, has decided that Australia deserves that each man should have his place in a cemetery whether his burial has been ascertained or not, together with a temporary cross, at once, and a permanent headstone at a later date. The cross and the headstone would, of course, not bear any statement as to the fact that the body had not been discovered.

The South Africa government wanted the same for the dead of Delville Wood – their own Gallipoli – but if there was one thing the Commission was adamant on it was that there should be no 'fake' or 'dud' graves. They were prepared to allow the erection of temporary wooden crosses so long as it was clear that they did not mark actual burials. But with more than half a million men missing, how on earth, as Macready wanted to know, could they ask a French government struggling with reconstruction and the problems of commemorating its own dead to double the gift of land that they had ceded in 1915?

There were strong practical reasons against it from the Commission's point of view as well – changes of design, delays in construction, uncertainties over numbers, that would all mean extra costs and time – but in the end it was a matter of gut instinct rather than economics. 'I may tell you confidentially,' Ware wrote to a Mrs Anstruther, leaking the Australian proposal that a headstone and 'grave space' should be allowed to every missing soldier, 'this met with bitter opposition, with which I am bound to say I sympathise, from those on the Commission who have lost their own sons. Mr Kipling very strongly rejected the idea of what he called a "dud grave".'

It is one of the more curious ironies of an organisation devoted to equality, unity and, ultimately, reconciliation, that its chosen spokesman was one of the most brilliant and talented 'haters' of the age. It was perhaps understandable that Kipling hated the Hun, but he hated politicians and priests as well, he hated liberal anti-imperialists and organised labour and the miners and the strikers and the Chinese and the 'Yids' and the Vatican and democracy and parliaments and, possibly above all – an oddity from the author of the history of the Irish Guards with whom his son served – he hated the Irish and their 'pernicious little bitch of a country' with a violent and dangerous passion.

In many respects Kipling's prejudices were those of the age – it simply seems to matter more with a man of his extraordinary gifts – but in his hands prejudice took on a savage and vindictive harshness. 'Allah, for his own purposes, has created a pig called Mond, Head of the Public Works,' he wrote of his fellow

Commissioner, the future Lord Melchett, 'an 'Ebrew whose mere voice and presence is enough to put up the back of any and every committee that he presides over' – and the tone was not untypical. 'He was a man of the strongest political prejudice,' even Ware, a staunch friend and ally on the Commission, was forced to confess,

> and would never meet my more radical friends such as Shaw, who always wanted to meet Kipling. His only excuse was that he was always preoccupied with foreign dangers, loathed those who ignored them, and happened to be right. He loved people who shared his opinions absolutely, such as Gwynne and Lady Bathurst. Everything was either black or white. There were no other colours.

It took a lot to make Ware seem a political moderate, however, and any political differences between the two men were swallowed up in their shared belief in Empire. In the years before the war, Kipling's stock as a writer and public Jeremiah had taken a steep fall, but for men of the generation that made up the Commission, for old South Africa hands and imperialists like Ware who shared Kipling's sense of national election, the idea of an Imperial War Graves Commission without the great poet and mythologiser of Empire would have been unthinkable.

When it came to the question of 'the missing', though, it was not the name but the authority of a father to whom the war had dealt a numbing personal tragedy that gave Kipling the decisive voice within the Commission. His son, John, had been just sixteen when war broke out. On his seventeenth birthday, less than two weeks later, he had tried to volunteer. When he was rejected on account of poor eyesight, Kipling used his influence with Lord Roberts to get John a nomination into Roberts's old regiment. His influence worked its grim magic. By 14 September, John was on his way to Warley Barracks and on 15 August 1915 to France with the Irish Guards. 'One mustn't let one's friends and neighbours sons be killed in order to save us and our son,' his mother Carrie – one of the mothers of ancient Rome, Burdett-Coutts spoke of – had written,

> There is no chance John will survive unless he is so maimed from a wound as to be unfit to fight. We know it and he does. We all know it, but we all must give and do what we can and live on the shadow of a hope that our boy will be the one to escape.

He was not. 'He looks very straight and smart and young,' she noted in her diary the day he left, 'as he turned at the top of the stairs to say: "Send my love to Dad-o".' Six weeks later – that familiar timescale in the short lives of Great War subalterns – the news they dreaded and expected arrived. 'Two of my men say they saw your son limping,' John's company commander wrote to tell the Kiplings,

> just by the Red House, and one said he saw him fall, and somebody ran to his assistance, probably his orderly who is also missing. The Platoon Sergeant of No.5, however, tells me your son did not go to the Red House, but remained with the rest of the 2nd Btn. digging themselves in just

outside the wood, but I think the former story the more correct.

The body was not found.[11] 'Have you news of my boy Jack?' Kipling wrote in 1916, putting into the mouth of the bereaved mother of a lost sailor all the hard, implacable grief and stoic pride he felt in the loss of his own short-sighted, eighteen-year-old boy,

> 'Have you news of my boy Jack?'
> *Not this tide.*
> 'When do you think that he'll come back?'
> *Not with this wind blowing . . .*
>
> 'Oh, dear, what comfort can I find?'
> *None this tide,*
> *Nor any tide,*
> *Except he did not shame his kind –*
> *Not even with that wind blowing, and that tide,*
>
> *Then hold your head up all the more,*
> *This tide,*
> *And every tide;*
> *Because he was the son you bore,*
> *And gave to the wind blowing and that tide.*

11   The Kiplings did not live to know it, but their son's body was eventually identified by a process of detection and elimination some seventy years later. Another 'Unknown' was given a name.

It was a poem and a yearning to which tens and hundreds of thousands of parents across the Empire could relate. In 1931, an Australian mother was found sobbing with relief at the grave on Gallipoli of a son who she had thought among the missing. 'If only I could see your grave, I would die happy,' another Australian, the mother of Jack Fothergill, killed on the first day of the Gallipoli landings in 1915, wrote in the memorial column of the *Melbourne Argus* eight years later. 'After nearly two years' private enquiry,' a London father, whose son had been 'reported missing presumed killed' in the summer of 1917, wrote to Burdett-Coutts in 1920,

> I got into touch with a man serving in the same company who saw my son fall, in the morning of August 17th, in the advance on Passchendaele; the spot immediately above the 'pill boxes' known as Tower Hamlets. He was carrying a watch, automatic pistol etc., and it appears probable that his identity disc was destroyed by the RAMC bearers who removed his body. I traced the automatic to an officer who purchased it from one of the orderlies, but by the time the information reached me, both orderly and officer had been killed in Italy and it was useless pressing the matter further.

Was there to be no memorial to his son? he wanted to know. Could at least his name be inscribed somewhere? On a stone? 'By taking up this matter and securing the adoption of some such suggestion,' he finished, 'you would earn the gratitude of many parents to whose sons no visible memorial has been erected.'

There was, inevitably, no shortage of suggestions from families as to what form that memorial should take. One wanted to commemorate the missing with a 'Grand Statue of our Saviour as the Light of the World', in place of the Blomfield stone cross. Another suggested a sundial carved from the rock of the Giants' Causeway and inscribed beneath the head of the King with the gladiators' *Morituri te Salutant*. 'There should be a granite or marble soldier lying dead,' Lena Hunter wrote to Ware, 'with a half circle of Angels standing around him with bent heads & the text beneath "He shall give his angels charge over thee" – Ps XCI. II. I might tell you,' she went on to explain,

> that I had a vision of my son, the late Captain N. D. D. Hunter, climbing a hill with determined face, with a half circle of five angels behind him; and he met his death, when climbing an embankment to locate the enemy's machine gun, which was enfilading his men, and was killed while pointing at the position of the gun to his men, & his body could not be recovered, as the enemy were pressing forward in overwhelming numbers.

It was the Commission's nightmare made marble, and the letters and proposals – 'Via Sacra', 'Campo Santo', 'Iona' Cross – kept coming. The mother of one Australian lieutenant proposed a giant stone of the kind Lutyens had designed, but with the face decorated with relief carving running from the top left to bottom right and showing,

> fragments of destroyed wire entanglements. In bottom left corner foreground a large shell hole containing one or more

deceased soldiers partly buried by fallen debris, shells bursting overhead and on ground. A township under bombardment and on fire or similar battle scene on top left hand corner. The stone should be surmounted by the figure of an Angel bearing a large open scroll or book which is inscribed: 'The Book of Life'. Rev XX 12.

The Commission knew that they did not want angels at any price, but what they did want remained as elusive as ever. In the early stages of the process Lieutenant Colonel Durham, Ware's Director of Works, had put forward a scheme for commemorating the missing in 'regimental chapels', but to the men of Kitchener's New Army – and still more their relatives – the old loyalties and pride that had made the 'regiment' Captain Oates's last thought as he stumbled out into the Antarctic blizzard meant little or 'practically nothing'.

There were sound economic and practical arguments for Durham's scheme but the Commission could not afford to allow 'economy' to be their only watchword. The single thing that was important to relatives, Kipling warned them, was 'that little piece of France' where their son or husband had fallen and anything that divorced remembrance from 'place' could only seem 'heartless and official'. What consolation to a mother was a 'regimental' memorial on the Somme to a son whose body lay in the Ypres mud? 'The policy of the Commission in dealing with a matter which affects almost every home in England has, up to the present been entirely & may I say – cruelly practical,' one widow, Mrs Una Langton, eloquently put it, all these poor souls [the relatives of the missing] know is the 'place' where their dear one was last seen, & naturally that 'place' holds a peculiar sacredness in their eyes.

Why therefore cannot the Commission give a *sympathetic* consideration to these cases, & overlook the fact that to commemorate the missing in the nearest Cemetery to the place of death 'will mean so much extra work'; 'take so much longer'; 'present such great difficulty' & similar unsatisfactory reasons which I have heard expressed . . .

The War Office has recognised with sympathy the sorrow of the next of kin in these sad cases by the erection of memorial crosses, an action which has given intense satisfaction to many, & I cannot conceive the Commission can ruthlessly take these down & substitute a name on a memorial in some cases miles away. This is what would happen in my own husband's case.

It was an unanswerable argument, and the Commission felt it, but the problems of verification were not to be shrugged off as easily as Mrs Langton suggested. 'During the past week I received 78 queries from you,' an irascible Brigadier Edmonds, of the Historical Section, Military Branch, Committee of Imperial Defence, complained to Ware in January 1921, finally snapping under the immense burden that the Commission's demands were putting on his hopelessly overstretched staff,

they took two experts in classification of the records three complete working days to investigate and answer.

This section exists for the purpose of writing a history

of the war . . . I must therefore finally decline to deal with further queries, unless you can give me clerical assistance in compensation for the time spent on your work by my trained staff . . .

'Where [for example] was 10th Battalion, Argyll & Sutherland Highlanders operating on 10th October 1915?' the Brigadier went on, warming to the task of demonstrating just what each verification request from Ware entailed,

The War Diary for that date reads:
10/10/15 (no place stated) The battalion took over Trench 29 in addition to trenches 27 and 28.
    For description of Trench 29 see Appendix 2 attached (Appendix 2 NOT ATTACHED)
    The Infantry Brigade Diary was then consulted and the only clue was 'Nr Ypres'. In this case also the Divisional Diary was then consulted. (Approximate time, half-an-hour.)

Other problems existed, too, in an area like the Ypres Salient where there had been more or less continuous fighting for four years. There were, of course, still graves and burial grounds surviving from 1914, but when even in 1921 so few true battlefield cemeteries in the Salient remained how was that 'sacred' connection between death and commemoration to be preserved? What was to stop memorial tablets, split up between the post-war cemeteries, as Kipling put it, looking more like notice boards than anything else? And what of the time factor? Were relatives prepared to wait the five years that the Director of Records reckoned it would take to establish the place of death of each missing man? And would the country wait when the United States and the Dominions were pressing ahead with their own plans for commemoration?

'Clearly,' as the Commission's official historian wrote, 'some compromise was necessary', and for a while it looked as if that compromise had been found. If it was not possible to honour Kenyon's original 'geographical' commitment to the missing, then a commemoration based around the eighty-five major battlefields into which the wonderfully named 'Battles Nomenclature Committee' had divided the Western Front might offer a practical way forward. More land would have to be purchased and that would take six months, but by February 1921, Ware was reporting better progress than they could have hoped. And to the country at large, as Kipling pointed out, it was the generic names – Ypres, Somme, Marne, Loos – that exercised the strongest imaginative and emotional pull.

The idea of dedicating eighty-five cemeteries to the memory of the missing was a compromise, but then compromise was in the air. An organisation that had been founded on absolutes and fixed principles was learning to bend with the wind. At home, where there was no land law of the kind Ware had negotiated abroad, and no means of compulsion, Kenyon's insistence that Britain was the proper place for private memorials was coming home to roost. The Commission could acquire plots by private purchase, they could negotiate with churches and local authorities, but they could not insist on their headstone or prevent a wife from being buried in the same grave as her husband. Across the globe, too, politics, religion and climatic conditions meant that anomalies and exceptions were unavoidable. On Gallipoli, the standing headstone would have to be abandoned for a sloping 'headstone block' set on the ground. In Macedonia religious hatreds and violence saw the substitution of Blomfield's Cross of Sacrifice by a great stone cairn. In Iraq, the Army, just as in the Crimea fifty years before, had been forced to obliterate graves rather than see them desecrated.[12]

Even on the Western Front – still, as ever, the focus of the Commission's energies – experience was throwing up challenges that demanded a softening of bureaucratic rigour. The old embargo on 'fake graves' was as strict as ever, but the 'Kipling memorial' – an additional, larger stone, carrying an explanatory inscription – would eventually allow individual headstones to men whose bodies had been lost as the war swept over the cemeteries in which they originally lay. In a similar way, common humanity demanded and won a more flexible application of the burden of proof when it came to identification. Many families needed their 'place', needed that six feet of France they could call their own, needed to believe that the body in a grave was theirs; and who, as their Director of Records asked, were the Commission to insist on rigour and the ugly, bureaucratic formulation of 'Believed to Be' in the face of that?

---

12   During the fighting in Mesopotamia, at least one unit found its own macabre solution to the problem. The Methodist chaplain with the Leicestershires (the father of 'E.P.' and of Frank Thompson, executed by Bulgarian fascists and buried in a ditch after a botched SOE operation in 1944) remembered how his battalion would dig a 'dud grave' alongside a new burial, remove the pin from a Mills bomb, place the bomb carefully in the 'grave', weight it with earth, and retire to the nearest cover to await the grave-robbers and the explosion.

Compromises then, but compromises of detail that if anything strengthened the Commission without threatening its essential values. Whether, though, that can be said of another shift in policy that the Commission made in the summer of 1921 is a matter of opinion. It represented either a great opportunity seized or the loosening of their most fundamental principles. Either way, it was to nullify the whole previous debate on the missing and define, as nothing else but the individual gravestones do, the work of the Commission and the way that we now remember the war.

NINE

Completion

One of the great tenets on which Commission policy had always rested was a strict demarcation between commemoration and military celebration. As the 'sole authority' involved in the control of monuments, some kind of 'brokering' role was unavoidable, but from the very first Kenyon had been clear that this was and should be the limit of their involvement. 'The design of such memorials does not appear to come within the scope of the Commission,' he wrote of the 'battle memorials' that the Army and Dominions would undoubtedly want to mark their 'most notable triumphs':

> The site of these monuments will not usually compete with those required for cemeteries . . . ordinarily the battle memorials will be on high and conspicuous spots, while cemeteries will be in villages and folds of the ground which have the air of shelter and of rest appropriate to a place of burial. It will confuse and obliterate the ground idea our cemeteries are intended to embody, if it is attempted to make them serve the turn of battle memorials also.

Kenyon had been right about both the popular demand for public memorials and the proactive role of the Dominions, and in the November of 1919, Winston Churchill, the Secretary of State for War, circulated a memorandum to the Cabinet on the need for government action. In the months since the war, Churchill explained, individual Army units had taken steps to commemorate their own exploits, and if memorials were not simply to be limited to units who could afford them and 'the dignity of the Imperial Government' compromised by the Dominions and India it 'should erect at the public expense general memorials to the Army' on certain symbolic sites.

Things were seldom quite as easy as Churchill could make them sound, however, and beyond the creation of a National Battlefield Memorial Committee (NBMC) under the Earl of Midleton, six months of departmental rivalries, personal animosities and institutional jealousies had left everything more or less where it was. In the November of 1920, a small subcommittee of Midleton's NBMC went out to inspect the battlefields, but it would no sooner decide on a suitable site for a memorial – Villers-Bretonneux, where the great German spring advance of 1918 was finally halted or Vimy Ridge – than it would discover that the Australians or Canadians had got in first or that some division had already built its own private memorial.

There was not just a problem with sites, but also potentially with a resurgence of the 'Little Englander' attitudes that had dogged Ware in his early days with the Mobile Ambulance Unit. During the negotiations in Paris in 1915 he had done all in his power to prevent Britain turning France into a monumental theme park, but any thought now that their old allies might not want 'perpetual reminders' of their indebtedness looming over them from every ridge on the Western Front seemed utterly lost in a surge of competitive national dignity he was helpless to stop.

The generals wanted their own 'victories' marked of course, newspaper magnates lobbied for 'great upstanding monuments that will strike the popular imagination'; Churchill wanted the whole of Ypres kept as a ruin, others, more modestly, merely its great Cloth Hall – the only feelings, in fact, not consulted were French or Belgian but then, as the Midleton committee put it, what was the point of a monument on the Hindenburg Line that 'only a very few French peasants' would see? There was a rare cautionary voice from Lord Crawford, the new First Commissioner of Works – a hint to tread carefully in French cathedrals with plans for commemorative plaques, a suggestion that Parisians might not take kindly to a major British monument in the centre of their city – but it was again Ware who came to France and Belgium's rescue.

The issue at stake was, as ever in these negotiations, one of jurisdiction and from a position of impotence Ware found himself on strong ground. Under the terms of an Anglo-Belgian agreement of 1919, the Commission had sole responsibility for licensing memorials in Belgium as well as France, and when in April 1921 the Office of Works made the mistake of directly notifying Brussels of their plans to rebuild the Menin Gate, Ware stepped in to warn them off his patch.

In the ensuing argument the Foreign Office came down on the Commission's side, and subsequent discussions made it clear to both sides that the Midleton committee's plans for battle memorials and the Commission's scheme to commemorate the missing must either lead to duplication or convergence. On 8 July, the Secretary of State for War circulated a Cabinet memorandum suggesting a fusion of the two schemes, and just under a month later the Cabinet, as Lieutenant Colonel Chettle, the Commission's Director of Records, ingenuously put it, 'agreed to abandon all general memorials other then the Commission's; to regard the National Battlefield Committee as "having completed its functions" . . . Thus, by general consent, a new and independent duty was laid on the Commission.'

'Thou hast it now – King, Cawdor, Glamis', and if there is no suggestion that he 'play'd most foully for it' – it is worth remembering that what Chettle is talking about here is not so much 'convergence' as 'takeover'. In the official history of the Imperial War Graves Commission, Philip Longworth conjured up a picture of a passive and almost reluctant Commission, but everything we know about Ware and his methods makes a nonsense of the notion that the whole thing simply fell into his lap.

Given the previous bad blood between the Commission and the Office of Works, it had been as Colonel Lord Arthur Browne smoothly explained, 'rather necessary to scotch this later serpent', but it was more than simply another of Ware's turf wars. Throughout the summer and autumn of 1915 he had spent his time negotiating for this very moment, and he had not successfully fought off opposition in England to see his vision of imperial unity fragment on the continent into 135 private divisional memorials and a plethora of separate Dominion monuments.

The Canadians had voted a million dollars for monuments, the Australians already had two under construction with another £100,000 budgeted for a general memorial at Villers-Bretonneux;

South Africa had purchased Delville Wood on the Somme; the Indian government had allocated £10,000 for a memorial at Neuve-Chapelle; the Newfoundlanders were buying at Beaumont-Hamel; the Anzac forces were going their own way on the Gallipoli peninsula – the mounting list of monuments must have made strange reading for Ware, because in one sense this was the future he had seen and preached in his last book before the war. In *The Worker and His Country* he had pictured a day when the leadership of the Empire would pass from the 'weary Titan' to the younger nations of the Empire, but it had clearly never occurred to him that an Imperial Victory would have the centrifugal influence that it had, or that Third Ypres or Gallipoli might add a different note to the Dominions' burgeoning sense of national pride and self-reliance.

If the idea of Empire was Ware's motivation for moving in on Midleton's territory, the clinching argument for a government anxious to placate public opinion and still save money was a financial one. The Commission had already budgeted £5 for every name to be commemorated on their own proposed memorials to the missing, and with 'at least 200,000 missing in France and Belgium alone', and a further £100,000 of Empire money earmarked for an Ypres memorial, the saving to the government, as the Secretary for War reminded the Cabinet in a memorandum drafted by Ware, was 'considerable'.

In a serendipitous sort of way, too, the 'merger' fitted in conveniently with the Imperial War Graves Commission's more limited plans for their memorials to the missing. In Kenyon's original scheme the geographical link between the place of death and commemoration had been as close as humanly possible, but once the topographical link was snapped there was no argument for eighty-five memorial cemeteries that would not equally apply to the four great monuments that Midleton's committee had finally proposed for the Western Front.

One of these – the memorial in Paris – died its predictable silent death, but the Midleton plans for monuments at Ypres and on the Marne and Somme offered the Commission not just a way forward but possibly a way *out*. There had been absolutely no thought in its early days of building on a monumental scale, but as the business of squaring war diaries and casualty lists proved not just difficult but insuperable, the attractions of a chain of a dozen great memorials to the missing stretching down the length of the Western Front from Nieuport in Belgium to Soissons near the Chemin des Dames were increasingly obvious.

Few who have stood beneath the great arch of the Menin Gate at eight on a winter's night when the Last Post is sounded, or seen Lutyens's astonishing Thiepval Memorial towering above the Ancre, could wish it different, but it still needs remembering what a volte face this was. For many families it had been hard enough to see their dead commandeered by the state, but this merger of the War Graves Commission and Battlefield Memorial Committee represented an abrogation of the fundamental principle on which the whole work of the Commission had been based.

'It will confuse and obliterate the ground idea which our cemeteries are intended to embody' – it is worth repeating Kenyon's words – 'if it is attempted to make them serve the turn of battle memorials also', and that was precisely what the Commission was now planning to do. It could be fairly argued that the temper of the memorials they produced is hardly

194

triumphalist, and yet if nothing else or worse they are a reminder that while the Commission served two masters, its first allegiance, as it had already demonstrated, was always to the Empire and not to the bereaved relative.

The Commission faced a formidable new task, with monuments to build across the globe, and if they wanted a preview of the challenges ahead then their first involvement on British soil, with the Royal Navy, was probably the perfect introduction. Under its original Charter, the Commission had a duty to commemorate all the missing of the war, but it was a particularly tough irony that an organisation that had grown organically out of the peculiar culture and circumstances of the Western Front and the Army, should have to cut its new teeth on a service that proudly stood as one of the last great bastions between Victorian Britain and the kind of democratic sentiment that the Commission stood for.

When it came to the subject of memorials, or most other subjects for that matter, there seemed no middle ground for the Admiralty between lordly indifference and a confident assumption that they could do what and where they wanted. In the immediate aftermath of war there had been only the vaguest idea of any commemorative monument at the Admiralty, and yet within the year they had swung from one extreme to another, coolly proposing to an un-amused King that the Army's Duke of York should be replaced on his London column by Britannia, before making moves to appropriate the whole north side of Trafalgar Square. 'The [Naval Memorials] Committee . . . visited Trafalgar Square' – Admiralty minutes beautifully capture the tone of their deliberations,

The general opinion was that the ideal site in the Square for a Naval Memorial would be that occupied by General Gordon's statue, but that site against the North parapet of the Square . . . was practicable and had much to recommend it. The First Lord repeated to the Committee his view that they were inclined to under-estimate the indignation which was invariably aroused by any proposal to move an existing statue from a desirable site, adding that the partisans of General Gordon might be expected to prove formidable.

With their tradition of burial at sea, and a resolutely unsentimental world vision, the Admiralty were no more sensitive to the claims of the missing than they were to General Gordon's, and they had moved as slowly as possible to meet their obligations. The War Graves Commission had first tried to prod them into action as early as June 1919, but it was another eighteen months of internal dithering and external prompting before they were ready to come back to the Commission with their own inimitably unimaginative solution to the problem.

It was not possible to commemorate the dead of Jutland, say, on the site of the battle – the North Sea was hardly Navarino harbour – and as it made no sense to site a memorial on the nearest landfall on the Danish coast, the Naval Memorials Committee had finally decided on three identical monuments at the three principal manning ports. There were still other plans in the air for a general naval memorial in London, but with Trafalgar Square blocked by the wretched Gordon et al., and an alternative site on the Thames Embankment filched from under their noses by the submariners, it would in the end be these three

e: *Sacred Places*. Lone Pine Cemetery, Turkey. Nowhere have the Imperial War Graves Commission Cemeteries and attles they commemorate played so important a part in the creation of national identities as here in Gallipoli. The Pine Memorial records the names of almost 5,000 Australian and New Zealand soldiers who have no known grave.

Above: *Etaples.* The funeral of a St John's Ambulance Brigade nursing siste[r] Annie Bain, killed in an air raid on 1 June 1918, and (**inset**) the Commissio[n] headstone over her grave. She lies among the 10,816 who are buried here.

Top left: *Cultural differences*. Käthe Kollwitz's deeply moving 'Mourning Parents', a portrait of grief and a monum to her son, Peter, killed in the early, heady days of war and buried here in the Vladslo German war cemetery.

Top right: The graves of French dead from Verdun, and in the background the monstrous Douaumont ossuary.

*ve: **Tyne Cot Cemetery, near Ypres.** The work of Sir Herbert Baker, and the largest of the Commission ...teries in Belgium. In the foreground can be seen Lutyens's Stone of Remembrance, and beyond it and the ...al scattering of graves, covered in stone and surmounted by Blomfield's Cross of Sacrifice, the German ...house that gave the cemetery its name.

Above: *11 November 1920.* The funeral procession of the Unknown Warrior, an outpouring of national grief and one of the great cathartic moments in the post-War history of a Britain coming to terms with its immense losses.

Right: *'Done at dinner.'* Lutyens's rapid sketch of a monument for the Peace Day Celebrations of July 1919. Originally made of wood and plaster, it immediately became such a popular focus of national mourning that the Government decided to replicate it in stone on the same site in Whitehall.

Far right: *Armistice Day 1920, the unveiling of Lutyens's cenotaph, or 'empty tomb'.* 'The majestic unveiling ceremony by the king … is part of our national history,' wrote Lutyens. 'My hope is that, as the years pass into centuries, the cenotaph will endure as a sacred symbol of remembrance.'

Overleaf: *Sandham Memorial Chapel, Burghclere.* The great centrepiece of Stanley Spencer's extraordinary commemoration of the War, painted for the Oratory commissioned by the Behrends in memory of Henry Sandham who died in 1919 from an illness contracted during the Macedonian Campaign.

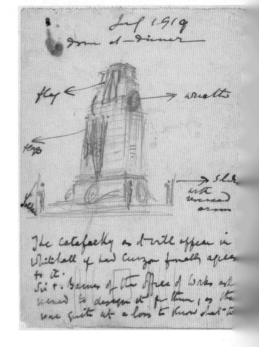

monuments of Sir Robert Lorimer's at Chatham, Portsmouth and Plymouth – giant obelisks, with lions couchant at each corner and surmounted by an allegorical confection of globe and winds – that became the chief memorials to the Royal Navy's contribution to victory.

They are odd monuments, impressive enough from a distance, but ugly in detail and cold and predictably unlovable. The Admiralty had never wholly embraced a commemoration that was alien to all their traditions, and this was reflected in Lorimer's obelisks – naval monuments of a resolutely old-fashioned kind, designed as leading marks for ships at sea, official and establishment monuments to a service that had always, historically, been a world within a world and, quite rightly, harboured a suspicion that the rest of the nation did not quite see what it had done to win the war.

Ware hated working with the Admiralty – the idea of them being involved in anything 'fills me with dismay' he complained – and it was not as if the Navy was the only problem when it came to putting up memorials on home soil. It can sometimes seem, in fact, as if post-war Britain was determined to get its own back for the Commission's autocratic high-handedness, determined to avenge its impotence overseas in a domestic campaign of obstruction, snobbery, entrenched interests and petty jealousies that has effectively robbed England of a single First World War Commission memorial (the Cenotaph would not be the Commission's work) of any real distinction.

There were again the usual suspects – the Treasury, the Office of Works, the RIBA – but there were also the Royal Parks, the London County Council, the rivalries between local and national government, and the Royal Fine Arts Commission, to remind

Ware what an extraordinarily free hand the Commission actually enjoyed in its work abroad. There could be practical and political difficulties of a different sort of course, but if they wanted to commandeer the high ground over the Ancre, or erect a Gallipoli memorial that would dominate the sea lanes of the Eastern Mediterranean, there was no Fine Arts Commission to tell them – as they told Lutyens when they thwarted his plans for a mercantile marine memorial on the river side of Temple Gardens – that it would interfere with Sir Joseph Bazalgette's 'great scheme of decoration' along the Embankment.[13]

For all the political and religious challenges of building in Iraq or Jerusalem in fact, or the desire of the Ypres citizens to reclaim their city, the real cultural battle-line was between the new, democratic Britain enshrined in the Commission's principles and those thousands of families who had spoken so movingly in Lady Cecil's petition to the Prince of Wales. In the great debate in the House of Commons, the Commission

13 The redevelopment of London's Docklands has given Lutyens's Mercantile Memorial a second chance, though it has never really recovered from its miserable start. It offers a classic illustration of the snobberies and class assumptions that the Commission was up against in its work in Britain. Abroad, all could be treated equally: at home, Blomfield advised the Office of Works, men should be 'classed according to their occupations' and commemorated accordingly in some appropriate place. On this basis, the Fine Arts Commission suggested Tower Hill for Lutyens's memorial as the area was 'devoted to sea-going occupations' with the result that it is the least well known of all the great First World War memorials. The decision infuriated Lutyens. The thousand men commemorated on it deserved the same treatment as everyone else, he insisted, not some 'hole in the corner because they happen to have been low in social status'. Let the beggars be commemorated in Parliament, he added, and 'the Earls at Shoreditch or better to the Tower'.

had effectively won its battle over its central policies, but if the country's parish churches and their stained-glass windows, kneeling Galahads and weeping angels are any guide, there remained a great swath of the British public stubbornly resistant to the vision of secularised, democratic uniformity that was unfolding on the other side of the Channel.

There is a danger here, however, of politicising something that had nothing to do with politics, and Ware's old habit of demonising his opponents has seeped into the way the Commission has presented its story. In his official history, Philip Longworth wrote censoriously of a reactionary rump that 'unfortunately did not understand' the new spirit of democracy, and yet a simpler and more profoundly human explanation for their opposition is that a deeply traumatised, grieving society needed far more than the Commission was prepared to give it.

They certainly wanted their own individual memorials, their crosses and their freedom of choice, but more importantly than that they wanted and needed some tangible connection with their dead that the Commission policies on repatriation denied them. They wanted a focus for their mourning. One wanted to see his son's grave beside the pathway into his church and know that one day he would be buried with him. Will Gladstone's mother wanted to have her son in the family plot surrounded by the graves of everyone who had ever cared for him. Australian parents wanted tracings of their sons' names from memorials. Others wanted the 'sacred earth' of Gallipoli brought home. And many wanted, if they could have nothing else, the temporary crosses that had once stood over the graves of their sons and husbands and brothers. 'May I suggest something,' asked one vicar, the

Reverend F. R. Marriot of Woodstock, whose boy had been killed
with the 1st Cameronians and buried at Inverness Copse before
being moved to Hooge Crater Cemetery near Ypres,

> In this village of 500 people, we lost about 30 of our men.
> I feel sure that many of the parents etc. would like to have
> the Crosses.
>
> I wonder if it could be arranged for the representatives
> of the *Missing Men* never traced and never buried to have
> similar crosses if they made application?
>
> They have had a heavier burden even than us who were
> plainly told of the death of our lads.

The growth of spiritualism during and after the war, the
burgeoning belief in paranormal phenomena, the apparitions and
visions, the unearthly photographs of 'armies of the dead' hovering
over the living in Whitehall, the crowds of thousands who queued
across Australia to see the artist Will Longstaff's ghost army in
'Menin Gate at Midnight' all testify to a yearning that the
Commission had done nothing to ease. 'Oh, the road to En-dor
is the oldest road,' Kipling wrote of the parents' and wives' bitter
search for those who had gone,

> *And the craziest road of all!*
> *Straight it runs to the Witch's abode,*
> *As it did in the days of Saul,*
> *And nothing has changed of the sorrow in store*
> *For such as go down on the road to En-dor!*

There were longings here that neither the War Graves Commission nor any other secular body could satisfy, but that is only part of the case. There was plainly little that could be done to ease the appalling ache of families who had no grave, and yet even men like Marriot who had been notified of his lad's death and grave were necessarily excluded from any share or say in the rituals that form an integral, healing part of grieving.

It must have made it all the more bitter, too, that families would only have to look across to the continent or to America to see their own aspirations fulfilled. At the end of the war the French authorities had imposed a total ban on exhumations within the *Zone rouge* where the fighting had taken place, but a nationwide campaign for repatriation and a booming trade in illicit exhumations had made it unworkable and in the end something like 300,000 bodies would be returned to their villages and towns across France.

The contrast between Britain and France was not simply a matter of finance or logistics either – the American government had pledged to honour the wishes of every family and shipped home sixty per cent of its dead – and paradoxically it was precisely that class that the Commission had set out to honour who would suffer most. It was one thing for Lady Violet Cecil to say that the soil of France would be 'dearer' to her 'because my child is buried there' – she was able to visit his grave every year between 1919 and 1940 – but the irony of the Commission's obsession with 'equality' was that a policy designed to prevent the rich from bringing home their dead now made sure that the poor never got to mourn at their graves. During the 1920s and '30s there was no falling off in the number of visitors to Commission cemeteries, but for most relatives – and virtually all from the Empire – a photograph and, perhaps, a wreath laid on Armistice Day by one of the more (or less) honest businesses that sprang up in Belgium and France to cater for the trade, were as close as they were ever going to get to their sons' or husbands' graves.

It was not enough – it was never going to be enough – but to be fair to the Commission, probably no one realised quite how inadequate it was until the extraordinary reaction to the unveiling of the model for Lutyens's Cenotaph a year after the war. The original design for the monument had been made up in wood and plaster for the celebrations to mark the signing of peace in 1919, and then after the official ceremonies were over and the troops of the fourteen Allied nations had silently filed past 'something'– as Gavin Stamp put it – 'unexpected happened':

> the temporary structure became sacred, 'the people's shrine'. Tens of thousands of women, grieving for husbands or boyfriends or sons who were buried abroad or who had simply disappeared, found that Lutyens had created a visible focus for mourning. A mountain of flowers and wreaths piled up around it, and a million people made pilgrimage.

The slender, tapering pylon shows Lutyens at his most chillingly assured – elegant, austere, intellectual, its deceptive simplicity the simplicity of refined mathematics – but if ever a memorial was sanctified by association, it is the Cenotaph. In his brilliant and partisan celebration of Lutyens's war work, Stamp evoked the immense power of architecture to articulate emotion and loss, and yet the inchoate outpouring of feeling that his empty tomb unleashed had less to do with the subtle use of entasis or classical pedigree than with an overwhelming need to find *some* centre in Britain for a communal act of remembrance and mourning.

This should not be surprising because the 'stiff upper lip' is one of the great fictions of British history – like *rigor mortis* a passing phase in the death of Empire – and the women and children who left their wreaths at the Cenotaph were in some respects truer to the national character than the Edwardian products of a setting Empire who made up the Commission. In his speech in Parliament, Burdett-Coutts had spoken movingly of the 'Roman' dignity and fortitude of Britain's mothers during the war, but in villages, towns, schools, factories, railway stations, clubs, colleges and charitable organisations across Britain, men and women were coming together in acts of communal mourning, remembrance, commemoration and support that had little to do with the stonier virtues of ancient Rome.

It was 'the human sentiment of millions', as Lutyens put it, that forced the government to turn his temporary structure in Whitehall into a permanent national memorial and it was that same sentiment that found its myriad expression in the 54,000 war memorials that would be built across the country. Many of these were erected by families to individuals or by regiments to their dead comrades, but the overwhelming majority were civic or communal in character and raised by precisely the kind of committees of local dignitaries, councillors and clergymen who never had a voice when Kenyon and the Commission were canvassing opinion.

They erected cairns, columns, crenellated towers, crosses, memorial gates and pergolas, they built cottage hospitals, pavilions, village halls, gardens and fountains, they commissioned statues and dedicated plaques – everything, in short, that Kenyon had excluded – but the keynote is always, in the most local sense of the word, community. If Ware had been asked what the men in the Commission's cemeteries had died for, he would unhesitatingly have said 'the British Empire'. If the same question had been put to villagers across Britain the conventional answer of 'King and Country' that is inscribed on a thousand local memorials would have masked a deeper and more intimate sense of debt and belonging.

The villagers of Lydford on Dartmoor were no more thinking of Empire when they commemorated the eighteen-years-old Wilfie Fry, dead from pneumonia before he could even leave the country, than were those of Fulstow, Lincolnshire, who preferred to have no memorial to one that excluded the executed deserter, Charles Kirman. In many final letters from the front, young subalterns would express their hopes that their school or college would be proud, and the village memorial is the other side of the same coin, a mutual recognition of obligation and relationships that is of a different kind from the institutional commemoration of the war cemeteries or the official language of imperial mourning.

There is no engine of social change to match war, however, and while Britain was commemorating a disappearing world of tight-knit communities, it was utterly appropriate that the first monuments to the new spirit should rise above the battlefields where it was forged.[14] 'In the autumn of 1919 I was sent out to Ypres by the War Office,' Blomfield wrote, recalling the origins and long gestation of the most famous of these,

> to report on sites for the great memorial to be built at Ypres to commemorate all those who had died in the war on the Ypres salient and had no known graves . . . After a careful examination . . . I recommended the site of the Menin Gate on the east side of Ypres . . . because it was the way by which most of our men had gone out to fight, and also because I saw a great opportunity here in the reflection of a building in the moat which is here about 100 feet wide.

The site was nothing but 'a great ragged gap' in the ramparts when Blomfield first saw it in 1919 and for 'some little time' nothing more was done. Blomfield later learned that there had been talk behind his back of an open competition for the design, but the problem could only be dealt with by someone 'who had studied on the spot . . . and was familiar with all the problems'. And 'I', he continued with inimitable pomposity,

> was in fact the only person who fulfilled these conditions . . . I should have taken it hardly had the design been taken out of my hands and . . . such a course would not have

14   It is interesting that the village memorial of Lydford, examined in great detail by Clive Aslet in *War Memorial*, reflects the economic realities of rural life that lay behind Ware's sense of Empire. Two of the names on it, Mancel Clark and Samuel Voyzey, were Lydford boys who had emigrated to Canada and fought and died with Canadian battalions on the Somme.

been in the public interest. Fortunately, Ware and his colleagues on the Commission were men of sagacity and abundant common sense, who did not allow themselves to be paralysed by red tape, and, finding that they had the power to undertake the memorial themselves, they took the matter into their own hands and in 1922 instructed me to proceed with my designs.

The challenge presented by the site was, as Blomfield was at great pains to point out, 'a very difficult one', and made more so by the irritating determination of the citizens of Ypres to behave as if they owned their city. 'I tried hard to get the building line on the north side of the road leading from the Cloth Hall to the Menin Gate set back a few feet, in order to get a vista through from the Cloth Hall,' Blomfield later grumbled,

but plans had already been got out for the building, and the citizens of Ypres were as tenacious of their sites as the citizens of London had been when Wren made his splendid plans for rebuilding London after the Great Fire. I had also hoped to be able to form a spacious 'Place' on the east side . . . but here also I was beaten by the indomitable proprietary instincts of the Belgians.

If it wasn't the Belgians, it was the Belgian subsoil: he had been promised a solid bed of clay running from Ypres to Tournai and found running sand instead, but with the aid of a two-feet-thick concrete raft sunk on to massive concrete piles 36 feet long and 16 feet square he was ready to build. The challenge for Blomfield was to produce a design that would simultaneously celebrate Britain's victory and commemorate its missing, and for inspiration he turned to a long and vaulted tunnel-like gateway he had once seen in the seventeenth-century fortifications of Nancy. The area covered by his monument was a massive 104 feet wide, 133 feet deep, and, somehow, on its 69-feet-high walls, he

had to find space for a vast number of names, estimated at first at some 40,000, but increased as we went on to about 58,600 . . .

Between the inner and outer arches I designed a Hall of Memory, 115ft. long by 66ft. wide, covered in by a half-elliptical coffered concrete vault, with a span of 66ft. A suggestion was made to me by Webb that I should deal with the archway by means of columns along the curb of the footpaths on either side of the road in the manner of the Mall Archway, but this would have ruined the design. The columns would have upset the scale; they would have been in the way, and it would have been impossible to light the inscription panels, an absolutely vital condition of the design.

It would probably have been enough for Blomfield that the proposal had come from Aston Webb to reject it, but he also had a deeply English suspicion of what foreigners would get up to if you did not watch them like a hawk. The Commission had already warned Lorimer against using any metals on his Salonika memorial that the 'inhabitants' could steal, and behind Blomfield's insistence on an uninterrupted single span lay a similar fear that the Belgians would turn the whole thing into a giant *pissoir* if he gave them half a chance. 'Having regard to the peculiar habits of the Belgian populace,' he replied to Webb and the Commission's Menin Gate subcommittee's proposed alterations, 'it is desirable that there should be as few points as possible behind which, or against which, people can take cover.'

There were, though, good architectural reasons for Blomfield's preference and there is nowhere that can stop the heart quite like the Menin Gate. In his original plans he had envisaged a long brick vault above the road out of Ypres, but in the end engineering triumphed over prettiness and concrete over brick to produce the great, coffered vault we now have, with its three circular 'eyes' let into the crown to shed a calm, even light over the endless columns of the missing dead inscribed on the walls below. 'It is a memorial . . . offered not to victory but to the dead – the victims,' Stefan Zweig, the Austrian novelist, wrote of the result,

Here there is no image of the King, no mention of victories, no genuflection to generals of genius, no prattle about Archdukes and princes: only a laconic, noble inscription – *Pro Rege Pro Patria.* In its really Roman simplicity this monument to the six and fifty thousand is more impressive than any triumphal arch or monument to victory that I have ever seen.

The response might have been scripted by Blomfield and was gratefully quoted by him – it was his one building in which he would have changed nothing, he later said – and to his great credit there is nothing in that 'Hall of Memory' to distract attention from the impact of those names. Above the eastern arch a recumbent lion offers a reminder that this is also a battle memorial, but beneath the vault and along the flanking loggias on each side of the gate there are only the names – 54,986 of them in all, engraved by unit, rank and alphabet into panels of Portland stone – to bring home the sheer scale of slaughter recorded in Kipling's measured inscription: 'HERE ARE RECORDED NAMES OF OFFICERS AND MEN WHO FELL IN THE YPRES SALIENT BUT TO WHOM THE FORTUNE OF WAR DENIED THE KNOWN AND HONOURED BURIAL GIVEN TO THEIR COMRADES IN DEATH.'

The memorial was not to everyone's taste – 'Was ever an Immolation so belied/ As these intolerably nameless names?' Sassoon famously demanded – but in his understandable bitterness he had missed the way in which Blomfield's 'sepulchre of crime' works on the imagination. The slight air of imperial afflatus might offer its hostages, but is there anywhere that exposes the conventional piety of the text inscribed on Lutyens's Stone of Remembrance – 'Their Name Liveth for Evermore' – quite so vividly as the Menin Gate? Anything that so numbingly emphasises the anonymity of an army its politicians and generals sacrificed with such an utter indifference to human values or scale as those neatly lettered and carefully costed columns of 'intolerably nameless names'?

Craig, Crawford, Cresswell, Cripps, Cross – try as you will, concentrate as hard as you like, it is impossible to scan those columns of the missing without losing all meaning or individuality in a hypnotic repetition of names that, when rank, initials and regiment have rendered their all, have only their numbers to differentiate them. 'For instance,' a harassed Chettle wrote in a minute that might stand as a kind of clerical metaphor for the industrialisation of death on the Western Front,

the name of 192 Pte H. Robertson, 6/ Royal West Kents, would appear on the 'Missing' memorial at Bethune, and exactly the same particulars (in respect of 1576 Pte H. Robertson, 7/ Royal West Kents) would appear on a grave at Chauny on the Aisne. Pts 14193 H. Robertson, of the 12/East Yorks, might read his own name, initials, rank and regiment on the grave of 733 Pte H. Robertson, 5/East Yorks . . . Pte. H. Robertson, 21st Northumberland Fusiliers, who survived the war, would be equally [surprised to find himself] commemorated on the headstone of Pte. H. Robertson of the same Battalion, at Dozinghem British Cemetery.

'He is not missing, he is here,' Field Marshal Lord Plumer famously told a great crowd and a still vaster radio audience at the unveiling of the gate in July 1927. But for Ware there was one significant omission clouding its success. In the early stages of planning for the memorial, the Dominions had been reluctant to participate in a joint imperial monument, and although Ware had managed to bring round the Australians, New Zealand's High Commissioner, Sir James Allen, had stood firm, refusing to budge on either the original principle of commemoration in the nearest cemetery to the place of death or the strict separation of memorial and battle monument.

If in one sense New Zealand was the only country that could 'afford' to take this approach – its soldiers had fought as a cohesive entity throughout the war and its units knew where their missing were lost – Sir James Allen's austere adherence to principle was a reminder that something had been lost as well as gained when the War Graves Commission and the Midleton committee joined forces. In the end the Menin Gate had only room for the names of those killed in the Salient up until August 1917, but the separate New Zealand memorials at Messines Ridge, Buttes New British Cemetery and – 1,176 names among another 34,887 British and Empire missing – at Baker's Tyne Cot, remain haunting reminders of a road the Commission did not take and of early cracks in Ware's imperial edifice.[15]

For all the dilution of the original ambitions, however, not to mention other important Commission memorials on the Western Front, like Soissons, La Ferté, Truelove's curiously academic cloisters at Le Touret, there is only one monument that can rival and outdo Blomfield's Menin Gate in its impact, and that is the great masterpiece that Lutyens raised to the Missing of the Somme above the River Ancre at Thiepval. In one sense, of course, the difference between the two is simply the difference between competence and genius, and yet it still beggars belief that two memorials, so different in their architectural language, emotional feel, and in what they say about war, could have sprung from the same brief and been conceived at more or less the same time.

If there was not the evidence of Lutyens's first sketch, in fact, drawn in 1923, it would be tempting to think that one memorial

15   The relationship between the Commission and its constituent members was intricate. The Dominions and government of India paid for their separate memorials but the Commission were responsible for the names of the missing inscribed on them.

stands at the end of one phase of remembrance and the other at the beginning of a second. In the years while Blomfield was overseeing his gateway it was still possible to see and think of Haig as the Architect of Victory, but within a year of the dedication of the Menin Gate in 1927, Haig and his reputation were dead and a spate of revisionist texts – *All Quiet on the Western Front*, *Journey's End*, *Memoirs of a Fox-hunting Man*, *Undertones of War* – had created a permanent sea-change in the way the war would be remembered that Lutyens had in some way already anticipated.[16]

In some respects Lutyens was fortunate with his timing, lucky that Thiepval would be almost the last of the great Commission 'Memorials to the Missing', but it was still a long and fraught passage before his first ideas could be realised. The design had originally been intended for a monument straddling a road at St Quentin, but when a growing disquiet about the number and size of foreign monuments on French soil led to a scaling down of Commission plans, St Quentin was scrapped and Lutyens's design transferred to the ridge over the Ancre and dedicated to the Missing of the Somme.

It was an inspired choice of site, as Gavin Stamp has so memorably evoked, because for the army of France, the Somme had the same significance that Ypres had for the army of Belgium,

---

16   A fascinating addition to the standard list is Dorothy L. Sayers's *The Unpleasantness at the Bellona Club* (1928), a murder story set on Armistice Day in a London military club. The plot depends on the fact that the body can be moved at precisely 11 a.m. on 11 November because the whole world will be at the Cenotaph. No civilian in the story can believe anyone could be so callously indifferent to feeling and no ex-officer is in the least surprised; they are broke, unemployed, mentally disturbed and have had enough of all the Commemorative 'gush'.

and Thiepval the same resonance as Passchendaele. The British Army had opened its attack there on the morning of 1 July 1916, and more than three months of heat and rain and blood and mud and shells and untold casualties later it was still in enemy hands, and the long, shattered, corpse-strewn slopes leading up to the heavily fortified German positions had become a landscape that would haunt the imagination of a whole generation.

'One only has to glance at the hill on which they stand,' John Masefield wrote a year after the Schwaben Redoubt had finally fallen into British hands after a last spasm of vicious close fighting,

> to see that it has been more burnt and shell-smitten than most parts of the line. It is as though the fight here had been more than to the death, to beyond death, to the bones and skeleton of the corpse which was as yet unkillable . . . Blasted, dead, pitted stumps of trees, with their bark in rags, grow here and there in a collection of vast holes, ten feet deep and fifteen feet across, with filthy water in them. There is nothing left of the church; a long reddish mound of brick, that seems mainly powder round a core of cement still marks where the chateau stood.

It was here, on a spur of high ground above the Ancre at the northern end of the old British lines, that Lutyens created his masterpiece. He had initially chosen a site on the brow of the hill, but for reasons of economy he was forced to compromise, and his monument rises from a platform near the summit of the hill, a towering 'pyramid' of interrelated arches, with each ascending arch, opening on alternate axes, springing from the keystone height of the arch below to create a structure of massive, lowering solidity and improbable, airy mobility.

In terms of its utilitarian function – a structure that on its outer walls and along its interconnecting catacombs of arched tunnels has to carry the names of 72,085 missing men – it is a brilliant solution, but here, unlike the Menin Gate, it is the monument and not the names that resonate in the imagination. In the development of Lutyens's work, Thiepval clearly stands as a stepping stone towards the designs for Liverpool cathedral, but as an abstract expression of the pity and horror of war, of emptiness and hope, of the triumph of the spirit and the crushing of all humanity – of all the polar opposites of emotion and interpretation that people have brought to it – it is this or any other war's ultimate indictment and commemoration.

For a generation that had gone through the physical and mental degradation of the trenches – for a soldier like the artist and writer Herbert Read – the appeal of abstraction is obvious, but there was nothing escapist about Lutyens's abstract design for Thiepval. In the years after the Boer War he had happily adapted the forms of classicism for his Rand war memorial, but here on the Thiepval ridge, faced by the unimaginable tragedy of the Somme, he stripped them down to their bare bones, paring away all the language and associations of their imperial heritage that Sassoon had so hated on the Menin Gate to leave a structure of pure form, intimidating in its size, admonitory in its grandeur and implacable in its intelligence.

From one aspect it is all air and emptiness, from another solid mass. If no two people see it the same or see it precisely the same way twice that is in part because it is so ambiguous in its message.

As one approaches from the east along the main axis, the immense central arch opens out on to the Picardy sky, and then as one moves around towards the diagonal the whole structure closes in on itself, receding in ascending planes and spiralling upwards with its 70,000 dead, in a kind of architectural 'rapture', before opening out again on to what in 1932, was still the bare, desolate ridge of Blunden's nightmares. 'Its high arch screams . . . [he is] an enormous monster . . . the open mouth of death,' the American historian Vincent Scully wrote of it. 'He is emptiness, meaninglessness, insatiable war and death. There is no victory for the dead. All that courage wasted . . . It is not to be borne.'

This might be no more than anthropomorphising 'histrionics', as Gavin Stamp insisted, but there was something about the memorial that disturbed even Ware. From the earliest days of the Commission he had got on far better with Lutyens than with either Baker or Blomfield, and so it is all the more curious that he should be so reticent about the one monument of genius that the Commission built. 'Many preferred to look forward rather than back,' Stamp wrote of the puzzling conspiracy of silence that met the memorial when it was finally unveiled by the Prince of Wales on 1 August 1932, sixteen years and one month to the day after the greatest single disaster in British military history,

Even so it is hard to understand why even in *The Immortal Heritage,* Fabian Ware's own account of the work and policy of the Imperial War Graves Commission published in 1937, while there are photographs of the Menin Gate, Vimy Ridge, the Ulster tower and many other memorials (including a perspective of Lutyens's as yet unfinished Australian memorial) there is no illustration depicting the sublime grandeur of the Thiepval arch.

With anyone but Ware one might hazard compassion fatigue – the Chatham, Plymouth and Portsmouth dedications in 1924, the Menin Gate, Tyne Cot and Neuve-Chapelle in '27, the Merchant Navy, Nieuport, Soissons and La Ferté-sous-Jouarre all in '28, Le Touret in '30, he had been at them all – but in the simple fact that Thiepval can no more be adequately photographed than described lies perhaps the key to his silence. In the early years of the Commission's history, modesty and restraint had been the ambition and hallmarks of all their work, but whatever else might be said of Lutyens's vast, overpowering memorial to the Missing of the Somme no one could ever call it either restrained or modest or square it with the terms of reference Kenyon had mapped out for the Commission in 1918.

It is not simply a matter of size or position – though at 150 feet high and 185 feet wide by 135 feet deep and visible across the length of the Somme battlefields, that has a lot to do with it – but that it says something about war and commemoration that directly challenges everything that the Commission had done up until this point. There are certainly days in winter, during the brief post-Armistice Day hiatus in the battlefield tourists' year, when the cemeteries of the Ypres Salient or the urban sprawl of northern France can be grim places, but the overwhelming impression of all those Commission cemeteries constructed in the 1920s is one of pride and gratitude without mawkishness that is exactly what Kenyon and Ware had aimed for when they set out their guidelines.

'I wanted a massive lion,' Blomfield wrote of Reid Dick's recumbent creature surmounting the Menin Gate, 'not fierce and truculent, but patient and enduring, looking outward as a symbol of the latent strength and heroism of our race', and the cemeteries insist on the same reading of national character and history. The great fear of the anti-Commission lobby in those early debates was that they would be too 'militarist' in their uniformity, but if this is militarism, the cemeteries proclaim, it is a very British kind of militarism, a militarism of knapped flints and Jekyll-inspired borders and poignant inscriptions and regimental crests and modest neo-classical pavilions that is as far away from 'Prussian-ism' and Prussian aggression as it is from the desperate rows of French crosses or fascist grandiloquence.

There is nothing more British than grass lawns and herbaceous borders, the Commission's horticultural advisor, Arthur Hill, volunteered, and even in the care and beauty of the planting of the war cemeteries Ware saw a moral and cultural significance. 'Let us pass on to the west of the town' – he was speaking of Lorimer's cemetery outside Damascus in an Armistice Day address to the Empire that perfectly encapsulates this sense of 'Britishness',

and there amidst a grove of trees, half concealed, not vaunting itself, we find a British War Cemetery with its six hundred graves – and two smaller Indian cemeteries near it. Rows of simple white headstones bearing the badges of historic British regiments, or the newer heraldry of the Dominions, flowers and shrubs and trees – a peaceful garden, the architectural design purely British . . . solid and foursquare and yet gentle, proclaiming the equality of all

217

beneath the Cross which is graven on the monument facing the gateway. Could the strength and grandeur of the British Commonwealth be displayed to these people of the East in any way more in harmony with the spirit of our heroic dead, and could its character be more nobly expressed than by the constant loving care of those simple graves, thousands of miles from their homes and yet watched over as sacred possessions of the common crown?

The 'typical' Commission cemetery does not exist – on the one hand there are small, hidden 'extension cemeteries' like Oulchy-le-Château, red roses ablaze in mid-June, or pastoral cemeteries like Vendresse set in sloping fields of poppies, and on the other great base cemeteries such as Etaples – but they virtually all share this same unmistakable identity. 'From the great wall or by the cross on the pyramid on a clear day,' wrote John Dove, the editor of the imperialist *The Round Table*, when he visited Baker's Tyne Cot near Passchendaele – in name, power of association, and organic growth, perhaps the most quintessentially *English* of the cemeteries,

> and looking out, as the Germans used to do, westwards, a faint gleam will catch your eye far away to the north. It is the narrow sea, which, thanks to the men who lie there, the Germans never reached; and beyond lies England . . . If there are tears in things, it is here.

Nothing made a 'deeper impression on old soldiers' than Tyne Cot, P. B. Clayton of Toc H told Baker, and that was because

England was not just the other side of that far away gleam to the north, but right *there* beneath the slopes of Passchendaele. 'It was laid out around the graves of those buried on the field of battle, around one of the biggest of the German blockhouses that the Northumberland Regiments had called Tyne Cot,' Baker explained,

I was told that the King, when he was there, said that this blockhouse should remain . . . On the pyramid [built over with stone to hide the concrete] we set up on high the War Cross; thus from the higher ground . . . the cross can be seen against the historic battlefields of the Salient, Ypres, and far and wide beyond . . . Tynecot, when the trees have grown, should have the appearance of a huge, well-ordered English churchyard with its yews and cedars behind the great flint wall, reminiscent of the walls of the precinct at Winchester, and its oak and poplars bordering the cemetery framing the distant view.

Churchyard, yews, oaks, flint walls, cloisters, Winchester – the ancient capital of England – it might be a checklist for a certain, deeply evocative kind of Englishness, but the most telling detail lies in Baker's treatment of the blockhouse. The structure was only left there in the first place because George V had said that it had to stay, but it is characteristic of Baker's whole treatment of the cemeteries that the one relic in the landscape that might bring home the brute ugliness of war – the one thing, too, that because of its ugliness had reminded the North-East troops of home and the ugliness of their lives and *their* England – had to be discreetly disguised. '[The King] expressed a natural sentiment,' Baker explained, architect and devoted imperialist momentarily at odds with each other,

> but in order to avoid the repellent sight of a mass of concrete in the midst of hallowed peace, which we wished to emphasize, a pyramid of stepped stone was built above it, leaving a small square of the concrete exposed in the stonework; and on this we inscribed in large bronze letters these words, suggested by Kipling, 'This was the Tynecot Blockhouse.'

That 'was' says it all, but in spite of the evasions, Tyne Cot is deeply moving in precisely the way Baker wanted and with his memorials to the Indian missing at Neuve-Chapelle and to the South Africans at Delville Wood he works the same magic of dissolving harsh realities in the romance of his architecture. In the hands of anyone else there could feel something saccharine or even fake in these memorials of Baker's, but the quality that invariably keeps them on the right side of pastiche or sentimentality is the utter sincerity and lack of cynicism that he brought to the great imperial project of commemoration.

No one but Baker could have crowned his South African monument with statues of Castor and Pollux to symbolise the peaceful union of the English and Afrikaner races and got away with it, and no one but Baker, in the decade of Amritsar, could have so promiscuously appropriated the symbolism and architecture of India to the cause of Empire. 'It consists of a circular space of green turf,' he wrote of the Neuve-Chapelle memorial, a hallowed space of 'reverence and eternal peace' enclosed at one

end by a solid screen inscribed with the names of the Indian
dead, and at the other by a pierced wall,

> carved with symbols like the railings of Buddha's Shrine at
> Budh Guaya and those surrounding the great Sanchi topes
> – low domes preserving the sacred relics of Buddha. In the
> centre . . . is an Asoka Column raised on high and guarded
> on either side by sculptured tigers. The entrance is through
> a small domed chattri with pierced red-stone grilles or jaalis
> . . . another similar chattri opposite forms a shelter.

In the mean, flat, north French countryside in which it is set,
Neuve-Chapelle is about as congruous as the Prince Regent's
Pavilion at Brighton, but a man who could build Greek and
Romanesque in South Africa and Cape Dutch summer houses
on the Somme was perfectly at ease with that. 'Oaks were planted
in two rows on either side of the avenue,' he wrote of the Delville
Wood memorial, unthinkingly certain of the permanence of what
he was doing and of the Empire he was serving,

> reared from the acorns off the old trees which the early
> Dutch settlers had planted in Capetown, grown from seeds
> brought from Holland. In the centre [of the monument]
> and pathway . . . an archway was built with a flat dome
> on which is set a bronze horse. The idea was suggested to
> me by Macaulay's poem on the Battle of Lake Regullus, telling
> how Great Twin Brethren appeared from the skies to fight
> in the ranks of Rome. Might it not seem miraculous, as
> the coming of the mythical Brethren did to the Romans, that

Dutch and English, such recent enemies should have come overseas to fight for the British Commonwealth against a common foe?

Britain and Rome – Britain the 'New Rome', the old trope reborn in a shattered French wood, and nothing for Baker could be more Roman than the blessings of the gods on the Empire's newest shrine. 'The unveiling ceremony was a dramatic occasion,' Baker recalled, with a blackening sky suddenly 'bursting' into a torrent of rain and hail as the visitors made their way up the long vista from the cemetery to the monument,

> But as they reached the archway the storm disappeared as if by magic, and the sun from a blue sky shone down on General Hertzog, as he spoke, and on Mrs Louis Botha as she unveiled the bronze Twin Brethren above, symbols of the comradeship in arms of the two South African races.

This sense of destiny, the Churchillian perspective on history – and with it the faith and imagination to build for the future – are not just Baker's prerogative, however, but one of the most remarkable aspects of the Commission's work. The South African monument in Delville Wood now sits at the end of a long, beautiful oak avenue against a backcloth of dappled greens, but when Baker began there was nothing there – only one hornbeam survived from the wood in which there were 2,500 South African casualties in July 1916 – and it was the same story wherever along the old front that the Commission built.

Order out of chaos, beauty from ugliness – Kipling's bereaved 'pilgrim' in 'The Gardener' stands in a bewildering forest of black crosses until she sees at the far end of the half-built cemetery the first of the clean, lucid lines of white headstones – it was a compelling vision and one few could resist. In some of his early cemeteries Charles Holden created a raw and desolate response to the carnage of war, but even Holden – 'nine-tenths Quaker' and the most disinterested, the most principled of the Principal Architects – softened in his style, moving from the uncompromising bleakness and horizontal gravestones of Wimereux to the classical refinement of Buttes New British Cemetery and Messines Ridge, mellowed by the passage of time, by the growing distance from the war, or simply converted himself by the note of pathos and proud patriotism that was the hallmark of the Commission's work in the 1920s.

It is revealing to compare the Commission's airy cemeteries with their darkly sylvan German counterparts, because while German sites offer nothing more than a muffled and apologetic echo of the Teutonic spirit, the Britain that went to war to save Plucky Little Belgium and sacrificed a generation in the cause of freedom, could unashamedly bask in its disciplined rows of headstones and crusader swords. 'What I wanted to do in designing this cross was to make it abstract and impersonal,' Blomfield wrote of his ubiquitous Cross of Sacrifice – in its moral smugness perhaps the one genuinely false note that the Commission struck,[17]

---

17   It says a lot about national character and the very different legacies of victory and defeat, that while Britain ended up with Blomfield's cross, German artists like Otto Dix turned for their inspiration to Grünewald's terrifying Isenheim Altarpiece.

to free it from any association with any particular style, and, above all, to keep clear of any of the sentimentalities of Gothic. This was a man's war far too terrible for any fripperies, and I hoped to get within range of the infinite in this symbol of those who had gone out to die. The bronze sword is there to identify it with war – and also there kept ringing in my head that text, 'I came not to bring peace but a sword.'

It would be hard to imagine in a Commission cemetery Käthe Kollwitz's great granite memorial at Vladslo Military Cemetery in Belgium, where her 'Mourning Parents', arms folded across their chests, the mother's head bowed, kneel at their son Peter's grave in a prayer for his forgiveness, because the generation that sent Britain's 'first holocaust of public schoolboys' to their deaths in 1914 were not asking for forgiveness. 'If any question why we died,/ Tell them because our fathers lied,' Kipling wrote, but what he meant by that was something different from what Käthe Kollwitz's kneeling figures mean. There are ambiguities about Kipling's epitaph, but they are ambiguities only on the page. The author, who had done more than anyone to glamorise the brutality of war for the men and boys who filled the cemeteries, was not repenting or recanting. His anger was for the politicians who had not listened and left Britain unprepared, for the unions who had opposed conscription, and for those whose lies, complacency and cowardice had meant – the bitterness is still shocking – that his son John died 'at eighteen instead of between nineteen and twenty, as he ought'.

This is what makes Thiepval so different. 'His loss,' John Kipling's mother wrote of her dead son, 'though so great a thing to us, is a little thing set against this greater.' 'This greater' was the general sacrifice honoured in the Commission's cemeteries but no one could look at the great gaping arch above the Ancre and believe that the mindless waste of the Somme or Passchendaele was a price that anyone should pay. Its impersonal, abstract indifference and intellectual sophistication are in themselves an indictment of the appalling stupidity and destruction of human potential it marks. Could anyone absorb the monstrous size of the thing, with its 70,000 plus names, and still believe his country cared? Could anyone stop to read the names of those under-sized boys of the Pals' battalions – from Accrington, Bradford, Barnsley, Sheffield, Hull, Durham – and not wonder what the England of Gertrude Jekyll had to do with them? Could anyone who had survived, wounded, jobless and houseless, to find every promise of peace disappointed, not see in the beauty and seductive mythology of equality and unity that the Commission offered just one more establishment lie?

'Let us honour if we can,' wrote Auden in 1930, 'The vertical man/ Though we value none/ But the horizontal one' – those were more than just the smart lines of a man too young to have fought in the war to end wars. There was certainly no falling off during the 1930s of visitors to the Western Front cemeteries, but if somehow Thiepval slipped out of the popular consciousness that was because it conjured up a past that no one wanted to recognise and foreshadowed a future no one wanted to see. Memorials, Jay Winter wrote, are as much about forgetting as they are about remembering. But that is not true of Thiepval. It lets you neither forget nor forgive. It is war's answer to Forster's

Marabar Caves, where the last words of Christ on the cross and the striking of a match produce only the same nihilistic echo. 'Honour', 'Glory', 'Valour', 'Love of Country'– the words Roland Leighton grew to hate before a bullet in the stomach finished him – say them at Thiepval and they simply evaporate away through that great arch into the infinite sky, leaving behind only the massive, looming silence and the eternal reprimand of those 70,000 names.

The unveiling of Thiepval marked the end of the heroic period in the Commission's history and if it was an odd irony that the greatest thing that the Commission ever did should be its least loved, it was an irony that Ware could live with. Less than anyone did he wish to hear what the monument said about the past or the future. He had begun his commemorative work to enshrine an idea about nation and Empire, but by the time Thiepval was finished another and even greater vision had grown out of it. Twenty years earlier, writing with his 'filthy French pen' in his Paris room and recalling the sunsets of South Africa, Ware had wondered if the great collective ideal he had learned there at Milner's feet might not ultimately grow beyond the British Empire to embrace all mankind. Now, as the world moved towards another war, it became an old man's dream that the cemeteries that had been born of a deep and inclusive patriotism should and must contribute to a greater unity.

TEN

Keeping the Faith

One of the most engaging things about Fabian Ware was that he never lost the idealism or enthusiasm that had fired his youth. In an interview with him in 1924, Violet Markham wrote that to see him again was to be face to face once more with one's own younger self, and nothing would ever change him in that respect, nothing dim the visionary gleam.

When Kipling wrote his great hymn-like 'Recessional' for Queen Victoria's Diamond Jubilee in 1897, the Reverend F .W. Macdonald, the last of his family to cling to their dissenting origins, wrote to tell him that the Methodist community proudly claimed it and him as its own, and in an odd sort of way the Plymouth Brethren would have said the same of Ware. In the forty years since he had escaped the narrow 'cell' of his parents' faith, he had travelled as far as possible, but the visions that had once filled that cell with glimpses of another and transformed world would burn as bright for him at sixty as they had at six.

Like Lutyens, Ware was something other than he seemed, a religious zealot masquerading as a secularist, a missionary parading as a politician, and his opponents might have made a better fist of opposition if they had only recognised this. It was once said of Baker that he had a 'conviction . . . of the rightness of British Imperialism so strong as to be almost a religion', but there was no 'almost' about Ware, no Anglican fudges or compromises, only that same all-consuming instinct for the 'absolute' and the 'Godhead' that fired Lutyens's art.

Visionaries come in different forms, however, and nothing better illustrates either the fierce power or the limitations of the chiliastic dream that Ware had inherited from his parents than the work of an artist who was to leave Britain with its finest memorial of the First World War: Stanley Spencer. Spencer had served through the conflict as a medical orderly with the RAMC in Bristol and Macedonia, and at the end of the 1920s was asked to paint a series of murals for a memorial chapel that had been commissioned from Charles Holden's architectural partner, Lionel Pearson to commemorate a lieutenant who had died from an illness contracted in Macedonia.

The result was the Sandham Memorial Chapel at Burghclere, near Newbury, a plain brick structure from the outside, and inside as close as one will ever get in England to fourteenth-century Italy. The formal inspiration for Spencer's murals was Giotto and the Arena Chapel in Padua, but it is Giotto mediated through a peculiarly English sensibility that locates the divine and the spiritual in the everyday. Along the flanking walls, the murals record the unheroic world of Spencer's war, of hospital orderlies and delousing, of bathtubs, iodine, stray dogs, idling soldiers, ration tins and angels. And on the end wall, above the altar, Spencer has painted a Resurrection at the last day that is unlike any commemoration of war ever painted. In the foreground, crowding the plane of the painting, tumbling almost into the chapel itself, is a jumble of white crosses and behind it soldiers emerge sleepily from their graves to find themselves in the Macedonian landscape in which they fought and died. Again, though, there is no violence here. They look around them. They carefully unwind their puttees. One, still only half out of his grave, stretches out a hand to stroke a tortoise. Another leans back against a mule, taking silent stock of the situation. At the centre, two white mules, mirror images of each other, stir slowly into life again, and framed between their arched necks, and receding into the background, a long procession of soldiers climbs towards a small and unmemorable seated Christ, carrying their grave crosses with them.

This is the Last Day, but it is the last day in the here and now, and that is where Spencer and Ware's visions are at odds. Spencer dreamed of the resurrected man and painted the ordinary soldier; Ware buried the soldier and dreamed for him a brighter world. It was the future he was concerned with. There was nothing of Spencer's sense of the numinous about him, no sense of the holy in the everyday. He did not see God in the simple act of a soldier unwinding his puttees or treating a wounded man, or cleaning a bath. He did not see God in Spencer's soldier – Ware's double identity discs about his neck – skimming a stone across a shallow stream. He did not see God *in* the world; like his father he wanted a new world, a world that in its promise of human perfectibility offers an oddly secularised version of a re-made world that fuelled the faith of his father's Plymouth Brethren.

'Each stage reproduces the development of that which has

produced it,' he had written before the war, his political vision of the British Empire growing into something still greater, infused with the visionary fervour of his youth,

> and . . . under the influence of some force from the infinite – incomprehensible to the human intelligence because it transcends it, but seized in momentary flashes by the instinct – each succeeding stage . . . passes something of its spirit down . . . And so, in ascending collectivities the human race progresses, the limit – if limit there be – being a united humanity.

It was probably as well that Ware also inherited all the more bruising features of the Brethren tradition because in the years before the struggle with Hitler's Germany came to revalidate his dreams, the street-fighter was as badly needed as the visionary. 'Do you think that they ["the Gallant Dead"] would have wished these Millions to be spent when their Comrades are on the dole?' demanded one furious, six-times wounded veteran, of 'Major-General Sir Fabian Ware, KCVO, KBE, CB, CMG', as he contemptuously addressed him.

> I am unable to ascertain the gallant corps you commanded or is it just an honorary rank you hold like so many more out here in the Commission . . . I wonder what General in the regular army draws your salary? Look at the great Marshall [sic] Foch who could have availed himself of a Field Marshall's [sic] pay of £1,692 a year from our country but patriotically refused although his own pay was far less

a sum – look at the great Marshall [sic] Joffre's salary and realise for one minute what the great French nation must think of this gigantic squandering which is going on . . .

Captain Chanter had only just begun, and in bilious, caricature form, every charge of high-handedness and waste thrown at the Commission in the years between the wars was rolled out. 'Let me invite the public to go to the length and breadth of France and Belgium and see the country plastered with Cemeteries and Monuments and signposts specially designed broadcasting what Britain did in the Great War,' he continued,

– is it dignified? Is it military? Is it British? The French Nation, I would remind you, also fought in the War and . . . they have *not* got their cemeteries all over the country but have concentrated them in certain places . . . Imagine your country plastered from North to South with French Memorials but it is lost on you . . . to see you arrive at an unveiling ceremony puts Napoleon in all his glory in the shade. Those who do not know imagine you to be some Veteran Warrior or 13th Apostle of the Great War.

Ware could cope with a man like Captain Chanter – Chanter was running a business out of La Panne, laying wreaths (or not, as the suggestion was) for relatives too poor to cross the Channel, but his diatribe is just the crank's version of some far wider concerns about the War Graves Commission. From the earliest days there had been a strong feeling in some circles that the Commission's money would be better spent on public projects, and the distressed state of many of the cemeteries by the early 1930s – an inevitable result of the speed and inexperience with which they had been constructed – inevitably added fuel to the sense that this was money that had been misdirected. 'I have just returned lately from placing my wreaths for relatives on the actual graves and what I have seen is simply one gigantic disgrace,' Chanter wrote again – and his letter is dated February 1931, only ten years after the first of Blomfield's 'experimental' cemeteries had been finished,

> there are piles of cheap bricks and stones at nearly every Cemetery where shelters or tool sheds are being built and which look just like Pill Boxes . . . thousands of Headstones are toppling over and you are aware of the numbers that have already cracked in two and which will go on cracking . . . the stones look as if they had been bombarded by shrapnel and in the same Cemetery you see the plain simple White Cross of the French graves which stand out in prominence to the dirty stained Headstones erected by the Commission.

A great deal of this was true, but the real challenge for Ware and the Commission in the inter-war years was not subsidence or crooks or public indifference but the old enemy of the Treasury. As early as 1921 the Treasury had signalled its hope that as interest faded, the cemeteries 'might ultimately be allowed to disappear', and over the next fifteen years a semi-permanent state of war existed, with successive Chancellors determined to control and curb the Commission's expenditure and Ware equally bent on preserving its independence.

As far as the Treasury was concerned, the notion of an independent controlling body was 'inconsistent with the principles of British Government finance' and even when an endowment fund was set up in 1925 they did their best to make life for the Commission as difficult as possible. The other participating governments had all agreed to contribute their shares within six and a half years, but with eighty per cent of the total to find, the Treasury was determined to hold out for longer, insisting that Britain should have fourteen years to pay its instalments – £4,076,000 of the Endowment Fund in mounting increments – and that their contributions to the fund should be confined to investments in UK government securities.

For the Treasury, searching for cuts and economies at a time of depression, the issue at stake was one of money, financial control and the principle of responsibility, but for Ware it was a battle between utilitarian officialdom and the larger imperial dream that had always underpinned his work for the Commission. 'For Ware,' his old friend from South African days, Leo Amery, declared at his memorial service,

> the thought of what the war cemeteries could give in individual consolation was never separated from the thought of what they might mean as a spiritual link between our peoples and an example and model of how a common task might be effectively carried out by a jointly established organisation.

'Think what this organisation of ours means as a model of what Imperial co-operation might do,' he had told Violet

Markham in 1924, and in speeches, memorial services and broadcasts he took every opportunity to make the dream a reality. Who can remember their 200,000 dead 'and falter in his faith in our Empire?' he had asked in a BBC radio address on Armistice Day 1926, calling on a bitterly divided Britain to recall its common heritage of sacrifice,

> Never in the world's history has there been anything like it. And let us here, in this dear land, remember that the imperishable glory and unsurpassed heroism of the greater multitude of dead of the Mother Country, men nurtured in these islands, the home and focus of the freedom . . . gains an added brilliance from the devotion and sacrifice of their fellow-subjects from overseas.

On anniversary after anniversary he would return to the same themes. It was not just a call to unity for a Britain torn apart by the General Strike but for the wider Empire too. 'Can we possibly visualise them to-day, these Anzac graves,' he asked his listeners in an Anzac Day broadcast on 24 April 1933, blissfully unaware, as ever, of the double-edged sword he was unsheathing,[18]

> They are literally scattered over the world . . . they lie in cemeteries whose names are to you household words, names given by these dead themselves and their comrades to nooks and plateaux of that stern promontory lapped by the blue

18   Unfortunate timing too. This Anzac Day came in the wake of the notorious MCC 'Bodyline Tour' of Australia under D. R. Jardine that led to Australian threats to leave the Empire.

234

Aegean Sea, to heights on those arid slopes to which they desperately and heroically clung. Listen to the names of some of them. Just a few: Lone Pine . . . Shrapnel Valley, the Nek . . . Thousands of years hence some of them will still be there to remind [the world] of a British Empire that was one and indivisible when assailed.

To Ware the Empire was not just the political cause that he had espoused in the pages of the *Morning Post* but a religion for which the war and its cemeteries had provided the Holy Places. 'On former Novembers I have given you a general account of the work of the Commission,' he began another of his traditional eve-of-Armistice broadcasts, unashamedly decking out the day's commemorations in the language and rituals of a solemn Holy Day,

But to-night [the 'vigil', as he called it, of 'the greatest human anniversary the world has ever known'] I want you, in preparation for to-morrow, to let your thoughts dwell for a few minutes on some of those who fell so far from these Islands (almost as far away from England as from the overseas Dominions) that their graves can rarely be visited, and then only by a few of those to whom they are dear. I have just returned myself from an inspection of the cemeteries in the Near East and it is about them that I should like to say a few words . . .

Over the last month, he explained in a voice, with its slight lisp, redolent of a pre-war world, he had visited all but one of the thirty-one cemeteries on the Gallipoli peninsula, as well as

Constantinople, Aleppo, Damascus, Beyrouth, Haifa, Jerusalem, Ramleh, Beersheba . . . Cairo, Alexandria. 'I give the individual names to you as some of you who are listening to me may be interested in a particular one,' he went on,

> and I want you to know that in each I found the graves perfectly tended. To get a general idea of the extent of our graves in the Near East, might I suggest that when I have finished you take a map and draw a line *round the Gallipoli Peninsula* passing through *Constantinople to Baghdad,* then on to the *Persian Gulf* and back through the Red Sea across Egypt. Within that curve you will notice almost all the Bible countries, as we called them when I was a boy; within it are 135 of our cemeteries containing 62,727 graves, and in addition twelve monuments commemorating 82,273 men of the British Empire who have no known grave, 33,000 of them Indians. To these lands of ancient holy places the Great War has added our holy places, and believe me, so much they are increasingly regarded by the local inhabitants whatever their race and whatever their creed.

'Enter this zone by the Dardanelles at daybreak as I did,' continued 'the Great Commemorator', deftly drawing in his listeners to share his vision,

> and as you pass the Southern end of the Gallipoli Peninsula, you will see, lit up by the rays of the rising sun, placed on the highest cliff and dominating the blue Aegean Sea, the great British Memorial to 12,000 of the Gallipoli Missing.

They are not forgotten these dead, even by other nations than our own – for some, if not all, of the ships, foreign as well as British, salute the Memorial as they pass, dipping their flag and asking all passengers to observe two minutes silence.

The glamour and physical associations of the classical world had long had a seductive, Byronic pull for Britain's soldiers – many a Philhellene had gone to a miserable end mistaking modern Greece for the Greece of the *Iliad* or Herodotus – but this Armistice it was not Troy but a very un-Homeric ideal of Christian sacrifice Ware wanted to evoke. 'I have only a few minutes with you and cannot describe . . . all the cemeteries in lands within our curve,' he apologised,

> I will therefore select one. At first I was tempted to choose the cemetery in Jerusalem on the Mount of Olives, a very noble monument which we have endeavoured, for reasons which you will appreciate, to make the most beautiful. But I am taking one situated among conditions as foreign as they can possibly be, in a land where the English language is rarely heard and even British visitors are few . . . I have chosen Damascus.

It was not just a single cemetery, however, but a single grave around which he invited his listeners to stand. 'I want to tell you of one selected grave, equal in honour, no more and no less, to all,' he went on, uniting Empire and Motherland, Past and Present in one great continuum spanning the centuries that conjures up the shade of Evelyn Waugh's Guy Crouchback,

In a cemetery in the south of Palestine stands a simple white headstone with its fern badge marking the grave of a trooper of the Dominion cavalry. In the old days of sailing ships, before most of us were born, he left England for New Zealand, the eldest of fifteen children, his father an officer bearing the name of one of the oldest English families; surmounting through years of hardship the obstacles which faced the pioneer in a new colony, he had established himself in that country and founded a branch of his family to carry on its traditions of the New World. The War came; it found him an old man; he enlisted, refusing to accept the rank that was repeatedly offered him, and set out on the homeward journey. He fought gallantly in Palestine – where he fell, in that Holy Land where had fallen before him ancestors who had set out in the ranks of the Crusaders from his own English country . . . In to-morrow's Silence, give a thought to the children of many such men as this; they will not be here in the Motherland by our sides, but their spirits in the great trial were at one with ours and with us to-morrow they will celebrate the eternally binding community of sacrifice.

As Ware got older, his sense of what could and *must* be done through the Commission's work took on an enlarged and increasingly visionary tone. 'In the course of my pilgrimage,' King George V had famously told the crowds at Terlincthun Cemetery at the end of his tour of the Western Front in 1922,

I have many times asked myself whether there can be more potent advocates of peace on earth . . . than this massed multitude of silent witnesses to the desolation of war. And I feel that, so long as we have faith in God's purpose, we cannot but believe that the existence of these visible memorials will, eventually, serve to draw all peoples together in sanity and self-control, even as it has already set the relations between our Empire and our allies on the deep-rooted bases of a common heroism and a common agony.

The speech may have been the King's, the words Kipling's, but the sentiments were Ware's and over the next sixteen years he returned to this vision of the healing power of the dead with ever greater urgency. It is possible that the ideal had been somewhere at the back of his mind from an even earlier date. He would certainly have seen photographs of the ageing Gettysburg veterans, snowy-bearded Unionists and Confederates in their grey and blue, shaking hands over the Stone Wall at the 'Angle' on the fiftieth anniversary of the battle in 1913 in a gesture of reconciliation that provided the romantic theatre for a politically driven belief in the unifying and 'regenerative power of sacrifice'. 'Cold must be the heart of that American,' Champ Clark, the Speaker of the House, had insisted at the ceremonies,

who is not proud to claim as countrymen the flower of the Southern youth who charged up the slippery slopes of Gettysburg with peerless Pickett, or those unconquerable men in blue, who three long and dreadful days held these . . . heights in the face of fierce assaults. It was not Southern valor nor Northern valor. It was, thank God, American valor.

America had set another precedent with its Civil War cemeteries, too, and for Ware the common sacrifice that out of
different wars had brought Union and Confederacy and Empire
and allies closer, could perform a wider alchemy. 'I am here
to speak to you of another and stronger union,' he told his
audience in a 1930 broadcast, summoning to the cause his
own, ghostly League of Nations formed of the Empire's million
dead.

There is a strength in the League of the Dead based on
realities and finalities, that can never be equalled either in
faith or in courage by any union of living members. And
I want to tell you why our Empire, yours and mine, has
determined that those dead voices shall not be silenced, nay
that they shall be given tongues on earth for all time.

Other countries were following the Empire's example, Ware
went on: America, France, Belgium and now even Germany,
propelled by a popular desire for commemoration. 'The *one real*
common heritage of the war,' – the dead – he insisted,

is drawing the Nations together, as nothing else can;
drawing them together on no debatable ground, in no
spirit of military rivalry. Drawing the peoples together to
give constant warning to their governments; for this
standing and visible record of the cost of war is the most
potent and insistent reminder of the dread consequences
of the political conditions which obtained in the world
before 1914.

For a man of his intellect and sophistication, a man, in fact, with a good, healthy streak of cynicism running through his nature, Ware could be extraordinarily naive. He was hardly the only senior figure who refused to recognise what was coming in the 1930s, but his schooling in South Africa under Milner, dreaming with the rest of the Kindergarten of a peaceful world order firmly resting on the great 'quadrilateral' of the white Dominions, had possibly made him more desperate than most to keep faith with a dream that was dissolving in front of his eyes.

Milner had died in 1929, but his Kindergarten was still there, and through it the *religio Milneriana* still made itself felt in political circles. By the end of his life Milner had abandoned his dream of a supra-national imperial government for a looser 'moral' union, but as his disciples went their different ways, some clinging to the idea of a world government, some to a vague internationalism, some to an embryonic Commonwealth and others to die-hard imperialism, it was notable how many like Ware refused to see the danger that was emerging in Hitler's Germany.

Geoffrey Dawson, the 'appeasing' editor of *The Times* through the 1930s, Philip Kerr, now Marquess of Lothian and soon to be Britain's Ambassador to the USA, even Leo Amery, an imperial pragmatist when it came to central and eastern Europe: Ware was among old and influential friends in his stance, but it still seems remarkable that a man who saw what was happening in Germany at first hand could have kept his head in the sand as long as he did. It was partly age, perhaps; it was partly that he had lived so long with the carnage of the Great War that another must have seemed unthinkable; it was partly the optimism of an idealist and partly the blindness of the zealot, but whatever the reasons he seemed incapable of seeing that his dream of the healing role of the Imperial War Graves Commission was quite simply a dream. 'Yes, here is heard truly the voice of the Dead,' he told his listeners on the indissoluble ties binding Empire and its allies together – an address given to an audience that within little more than ten years would see those same 'old allies', Italy and Romania, siding with Hitler's Germany, Japan overrunning Britain's Empire in the East, Salazar's Portugal shamelessly profiteering with Nazi Germany, America neutral and – most unimaginable of all to the Francophile Ware – Britain and Vichy France at war in those same doubly-sacred Holy Places of the Middle East that had filled his Armistice 'Vigil' addresses: 'friends speak to friends of a peace that cannot be broken; for, so long as there is any generous impulse in the soul of man, these silent cities of our Dead make impossible any hostile contact between our Allies and the descendants of these Dead'.

I am 'tired of this gush and pretence', one old American Civil War brigadier protested against the sentimentalising fictions of 'healing' and 'reconciliation', outraged that anyone should believe that his own Union dead were the same as Rebel dead. It is uncertain if Ware ever really acknowledged the force of this kind of clear-eyed hostility. It was, in one sense, relatively easy for Britain to forgive an enemy that had never set foot on her soil, but it was asking a lot to expect a Belgium or France that had seen their country occupied, their cities reduced to rubble and their civilians murdered in their thousands, to rise to the same heights of sympathy.

It was asking even more to expect that the victors and the defeated should see their war cemeteries in the same way or hear the same message from their dead. It was all very well for Ware to invoke the authority of the Empire's fallen in his search for peace, but what did that peace mean to a German army that believed it had never been beaten in the field? What did the 'tongues' of men who fought and died so fiercely in the final weeks of 1918 say to the survivors of an army that had been humiliated by the peace forced on Germany at Versailles?

The answers were coming thick and fast in the late 1930s – the Saar and the creation of a new German air force in 1935, the reoccupation of the Rhineland in 1936, the Anschluss and Sudetenland in 1938 – but they only left Ware more convinced of the Commission's role in securing peace. In 1935 the Anglo-French Mixed Committee, set up to oversee their mutual concerns, had been extended to include Germany, and over the next four years Ware lost no opportunity, either in Britain or at conferences in Germany, to preach the doctrine of peace and the sacred trust that the dead of both sides had bequeathed to the living. 'It was like trying to turn back the tide,' the Commission's historian – seldom Ware's sternest critic – wrote of these efforts,

He did not realise that the Nazis must have taken his stress on the horror of war as an indication, like the Oxford 'Peace Vote', that Britain would not fight. He did not seem to notice that they were perverting ceremonies of remembrance into occasions for banner-waving nationalism and the glorification of German arms. In Belgium they knew better. After German ex-servicemen had laid a wreath at the Menin Gate, the ribbon with the offending swastika was stolen.

It would be absurd to single out Ware from a decade of appeasement, but if the history of war graves teaches one lesson it is that while the 'tongues of the dead' might say what they must, the living will hear what they want. It seemed entirely axiomatic to Ware that a grave – especially a Commission grave – was an irresistible argument for peace, but from the German soldiers who desecrated those same graves in Greece in the Second World War down through Eire and Palestine to the destruction of Commission cemeteries in Libya during the 'Arab Spring', the British soldier's headstone has carried a very different meaning.

Even within the Empire, too, the commemoration of the dead could be as divisive as it was healing. Within weeks of the first landings in April 1915, Gallipoli had become 'sacred ground' to Australians, but in a country split between those who had volunteered and those who had not – mainly Irish Catholics it was believed – the annual commemoration of the campaign on Anzac Day became a reminder of old sores as well as a celebration of nationhood.[19]

During the war, two plebiscites on conscription, narrowly won by the 'antis', had divided the country almost exactly down the middle and the Australian practice of recording not just the dead but the 'returned' on their war memorials at home gave a name and a face to both 'hero' and 'shirker'. It was rumoured that over ninety per cent of the Australian Imperial Force had, in fact, voted against conscription, but the stigma attached to those who

19 Australia's was the only entirely volunteer army in the war. The 1916 Easter Rising in Dublin, and the subsequent execution of its leaders, added to the antagonism of Australia's Irish communities against Britain.

had not fought effectively politicised the one day 'of any holiness' in the Australian calendar along fissure lines that would still be there when the country next went to war.[20]

Ware could hardly have been unconscious of other currents that eddied around the base of the Cenotaph – the calls in Parliament for an end to the Armistice Day commemorations, the White Poppies, the notorious Oxford debate – but nothing ever seems to have dented his faith. There is an historical gap between an imperialist and post-imperialist age that makes his kind of belief hard now to understand, and yet in the end it is not so much what he believed that distances us from him as the chasm which separates the visionary from the dull clay with which he has to work. 'His legs bestrid the ocean; his rear'd arm/ Crested the world,' Shakespeare's exultant Cleopatra says of the dead Mark Antony, metamorphosing a defeated soldier into a figure of divine majesty,

> *His voice was propertied*
> *As all the tuned spheres, and that to friends;*
> *But when he meant to quail and shake the orb,*
> *He was as rattling thunder . . . in his livery*
> *Walk'd crowns and crownets, realms and islands were*
> *As plates dropp'd from his pocket . . .*
> *Think you there was, or might be, such a man*
> *As this I dream'd of?*

20 'If they had any shame,' the Deputy Prime Minister wrote in his diary at the unveiling of the Australian National War Memorial at Villers-Bretonneux in 1938 – and his 'they' was directed specifically at Robert Menzies – 'they should not have been there, having shirked their responsibilities during the sacrifice that was now being commemorated.'

What Ware had dreamed was what Cleopatra had dreamed, and if Dolabella's answer – 'Gentle madame, no' – is the reductive answer of the man-in-the-street down the ages, it is not the *imaginative* truth anyone remembers. The same is true of Ware and his achievements. The cemeteries of the Great War might not have worked the alchemy that he hoped or sealed an Empire's unity, but as an aspiration or dream his 'Silent Cities' remain a kind of Camelot of the Dead, a mythic evocation of those human possibilities that a Dolabella or Office of Works never sees.

They remain more than that, too, because if Auden and his 'horizontal man', Sassoon and his 'sepulchre of crime', Owen and his 'old lie', will always be waiting in the wings, Ware had come as close as any man to making his vision a reality. 'He was called Legion, or nothing,' Edmund Blunden wrote of the fate of the common soldier before Ware and the Commission changed it for good,

He was merely the means by which someone else pursued the glory of a name. It has been the faith of the Commission that those who fought and died in 1914–1918 were – what we know them to have been – several and separate personalities, each in human measure 'the captain of his fate', each claiming individual comprehension. We well remember our old friends as cooperating without thought of personal advantage in the main cause. But their characteristics are clear, as various as their number; and so it is entirely laudable that the Imperial War Graves Commission has carried out its task with a vivid sense of the individual grave.

The Menin Gate . . . Villers-Bretonneux . . . the Canadian Memorial at Vimy Ridge, with its two immense pylons, symbolising Canada and France towering over the Douai Plain like a giant stone tuning-fork . . . Beaumont-Hamel and Captain Basil Gotto's bronze Caribou, high on a rock outcrop, looking out to the lone tree which marked the farthest advance of the Newfoundlanders . . . Chunuk Bair, on the Gallipoli peninsula where the New Zealanders had fought so desperately – from one end of Europe to the other the proof of Ware's success is there to see but nothing would be less true to him or to the battles he fought than to leave his story on such a note of bland affirmation. For more than thirty years he achieved what he did in the teeth of bitter opposition, and if he finally carried a country and Empire with him – so finally that we are now incapable of seeing ourselves in any other way but his – there is one grave above all others that serves as a reminder of the bruising struggle and compromises that lay behind that victory.

It is ironic, in fact, that the most imaginative and influential expression of the Imperial War Graves Commission's principles should lie in a grave that at first sight seems the denial and nega- tion of everything they had set out to do. From the early days of the war Ware had set himself against the idea of repatriation on grounds of equality, and the policy was firmly and publicly enshrined among the Commission's post-war principles when, in the August of 1920, the Reverend David Railton MC, a former Army Chaplain and now the vicar of St John the Baptist's, Margate, wrote to the Dean of Westminster with the suggestion that three months later would lead to the 'creation' of the Unknown Warrior.

The idea had come to him four years before in France when, returning from a burial service in the line, he saw a single lonely grave dug in a tiny garden near Armentières. 'At the head of the grave,' he recalled,

there stood a rough cross of white wood. On the cross was written in deep black-pencilled letters, 'An Unknown British Soldier' and in brackets beneath, 'of the Black Watch'. It was dusk and no one was near, except some officers in the billet playing cards. I remember how still it was. Even the guns seemed to be resting.

'How that grave caused me to think,' David Railton remembered, and four years later he was still thinking over that unknown soldier of the Black Watch. Towards the end of the war he had almost written to Douglas Haig proposing that the body of an unidentified soldier should be taken home to represent all the Empire's dead, but in Herbert Ryle, the Dean of Westminster, he had found an altogether more likely candidate. After a certain amount of royal and official scepticism had been overcome, Lloyd George's Cabinet unanimously agreed to set up a committee under the chairmanship of the Foreign Secretary, Lord Curzon, to supervise the ceremonial details.

The appointment of the superb Lord Curzon might seem an odd choice to oversee the burial of the 'common man' but that only reflects the ambivalence that still surrounded the idea. 'I attended a large luncheon party at around this time,' one senior Army officer remembered, 'and at it I was asked what I thought of the proposal to bring over a body. Only one person out of twenty-four agreed that it was a wonderful idea. The rest said it would never appeal to the British.'

The story has been often told – with the details, appropriately for an event of mythic transformation, different in almost every telling – but probably the most authoritative account is that left by the officer commanding the Army in France and Flanders at that time, Brigadier General Wyatt. On 7 November 1920, four small burial parties armed with shovels and sacking left the Army Headquarters at St Pol for four of the great battlefields of the Western Front, and there exhumed four – sometimes six – unidentified bodies from the earlier battles of the war and brought them back to a hut that had been turned into a temporary chapel for their reception.

The battlefields were those of Ypres, Arras, the Somme and the Aisne, the bodies, 'mere bones' beyond identification, and the burial parties who had carried out the exhumations, ignorant of what they were doing. From the start the whole operation had been marked by an odd lack of paperwork and absolute secrecy, and as each body was brought in and placed on a stretcher in the hut that secrecy was maintained, with no party overlapping another and no one able to say from which of the battlefields the bodies came.

At midnight on the same day a Colonel Gill, and Wyatt – blindfolded in the more poetic accounts – entered the chapel where in silence Wyatt placed a hand on one of the sacks of bones. The remains were placed in a plain English deal coffin, the chapel locked, and a guard placed on the door. The next day the three other bodies were taken away for reburial in a nearby cemetery and after a simple prayer returned to the obscurity from which they had been plucked; meanwhile the extraordinary metamorphosis of the fourth had already begun.

The timing was tight, the arrangements hasty, but the performance faultless. At noon a joint service was held in the hut over the body, and then the coffin, accompanied by a military escort, was carried in a 'somewhat battered' ambulance to Boulogne where a temporary chapel had been prepared in the castle library. There the body lay under guard of a company of the French 8th Infantry Battalion until the morning of the tenth when two British undertakers arrived to place it in a heavy coffin of Hampton Court oak, banded with iron work, and inscribed on the lid in an elaborate Gothic script with the text, 'A British Warrior who fell in the Great War 1914–1918 for King and Country'.

At 10.30 a.m., as all the bells of Boulogne rang out and bugles and trumpets played 'Aux Champs', the Unknown Warrior, as he now was, coffin draped in a tattered Union Flag, the military wagon on which it lay pulled by six black artillery horses and escorted by a detachment of the 6th Chasseurs of Lille, set off in a funeral cortege a mile long to the Quai Gambetta where Marshal Foch and HMS *Verdun* were waiting.

'11.17' reads the ship's log, 'Embarked coffin of "Unknown Warrior",' – the quotation marks nicely capturing the residual unfamiliarity with the phrase – and at 11.29 the *Verdun* slipped from her jetty and began her brief passage for Dover. As she left Boulogne harbour an escort of French sloops joined her in a last act of Allied respect, and then at 12.40, with a final nineteen-gun salute, fell astern to leave the *Verdun* and her six accompanying destroyers of the Royal Navy's 3rd Flotilla to mourn the Empire's dead alone.

Flags and ensigns at half-mast, another nineteen-gun salute from the castle, 'Land of Hope and Glory', a teeming quayside, a guard of Connaught Rangers – nobody had known quite what they were doing or what to expect when they took up Railton's idea but by the time that afternoon that they 'Disembarked Coffin of "Unknown Warrior"' they were beginning to see. The response of the French in Boulogne must have given them their first inkling of the scenes that lay ahead, and as the body made its way up to London in the same railway carriage that had brought home the murdered Edith Cavell and Captain Fryatt, the country prepared to receive the son and husband, brother, father, that Ware and the Commission had denied her. 'The train thundered through the dark, wet, moonless night,' wrote the *Daily Mail*,

On the platforms by which it rushed could be seen groups of women watching and silent, many dressed in deep mourning. Many an upper window was open, and against the golden square of light were silhouetted clear cut and black the head and shoulders of some faithful watcher . . . In the London suburbs there were scores of homes with back doors flung wide, light flooding out and in the garden figures of men, women and children gazing at the great lighted train rushing past.

At 9.20 the following morning – Armistice Day, 11 November 1920, the day chosen for the official dedication of the now permanent Cenotaph in Whitehall – a bearer party of Coldstream Guards entered the Cavell carriage at Victoria Station where the coffin of the Unknown Soldier had rested overnight. Drawn up outside was the gun carriage and six black horses to take him on his final journey to Westminster Abbey, and as the flag-draped coffin was lowered into position, the guns of the Royal Horse Artillery roared out their salute from Hyde Park and the armed services' twelve senior officers took their place in a great funeral cortege of service detachments, mourners and massed bands. 'Admirals Meux, Beatty, Jackson, Sturdee and Madden,' – whatever its poetic inaccuracies, Ronald Blythe's evocation of that day cannot be bettered,

Field Marshals French, Haig, Methuen, Wilson . . . Generals Horne and Byng . . . Air Marshal Trenchard. The day was gentle and fair. The soot-encrusted buildings were rimmed in the gold sunlight and late leaves rustled in the gutters. It was curiously quiet everywhere, not so much silent as hushed and muted. Although the West End pavements were packed with a vast multitude it was a subtly different crowd than the authorities had seen before. What had happened was that this most stately public show was being observed with an intense private emotion. The dead man who had set out without a name, a voice, or a face only a few hours before was being invested with a hundred thousand likenesses.

With the massed bands playing Chopin's Funeral March, and to the sound of muffled drums, the gun carriage began its slow journey towards Constitution Hill, then eastwards along the Mall and through Webb's Admiralty Arch into Trafalgar Square and Whitehall, where the King, the Royal Family and the country's leaders were waiting at Lutyens's Cenotaph.

After the dedication of the Lutyens empty tomb and a two-minutes silence – a silence that was honoured across the country, even in prison cells and in the court-room dock – the cortege continued on the last short journey to the Abbey. Inside the west door a guard of a hundred holders of the Victoria Cross flanked the nave where, at its west end, the Unknown Warrior's grave had been prepared. The service was brief and simple – 'the most beautiful, the most touching and the most impressive . . . this island has ever seen', *The Times* called it – and to the words of 'Lead, Kindly Light' the coffin, a crusader sword given by the King now resting on it, was lowered into the grave. 'The reckless destruction of young life over four mad years and the platitudes which sought to justify it were momentarily engulfed by the tenderness flooding into the tomb of this most mysterious person,' wrote Blythe. 'The formal programme broke down into a great act of compassion and love . . . The authorities had made certain that it would be dignified; they never dreamt it would be overwhelming. They had intended to honour the average soldier and instead they had produced the perfect catharsis.'

Blythe was right, it was a catharsis. Over two hundred thousand filed past the open grave that day, half a million within the month, and all superimposing their own image on this symbol of national grief. But where among all this outpouring compassion and love were Fabian Ware and the War Graves Commission, who for years had struggled with the Empire's million dead? It is extraordinary that in the official history of the Imperial – then Commonwealth – War Graves Commission there is not a single mention of the burial of the Unknown Warrior, but then on the face of it a ceremony overseen by Sir Lionel Earle and the hated

Office of Works, centred around a coffin designed by the Office of Works and holding a body exhumed against the stated trend of Commission policy, might seem the negation of everything their work stood for.

It took the egotism of a Lutyens to see it all – Chasseurs, nineteen-gun salutes, destroyers, escorts, Abbey, King – as an elaborate Church conspiracy to steal his thunder at the unveiling of the Cenotaph, though he did have a point. There was, as he said, 'some horror in Church circles' at the flagrantly pagan classicism of his austerely elegant pylon, and if the tomb of the Unknown Warrior was not the deliberately contrived 'rival shrine' that he imagined, it spoke a different language and offered different consolations to the empty tomb he had given the nation.

To the paranoid, in fact, every detail of the ceremonial trappings – the archaic Gothic script as opposed to the lucid War Graves Commission lettering, the ancient crusader sword instead of rifle and helmet, the numinous feel of the Abbey nave against the harsh, cold light of the public space, the sacred against the profane – might seem a calculated challenge and a year later the Dean himself came to add a certain substance to Lutyens's suspicions. The grave had been originally closed on 18 November with a slab of dark Tournai limestone carrying almost the same inscription as the coffin, but for the first anniversary, Dean Ryle had it replaced with a new stone of black marble, inscribed in gold with a prolix dedication that makes one pine for Kipling, and five texts chosen by the Dean himself.

If it was a deliberate provocation, he did not have long to

await the backlash. 'Very Rev. Sir', the Principal of the Liverpool Hebrew Schools wrote to him on 22 November 1922,

> At the foot of the new stone over the Unknown Warrior's grave in Westminster Abbey there is the line, 'In Christ shall all be made alive'. Beneath the stone rests the body of a British Warrior unknown by name or rank. Unknown also was the faith of the Unknown Warrior. Heavy was the toll of Jewish life on the battlefields of France. In many Jewish homes today a missing son is mourned. The line, 'In Christ shall all be made alive' does not meet the spiritual destinies of both Jew and Gentile.

Among the 'unbounded wealth' of the Bible, he insisted, it could not be hard to find a neutral text, but not even an appeal on behalf of mourners' religious sensitivities was enough to move the Dean. 'On a gravestone containing five texts,' he replied, 'it is not unreasonable that one of these should contain the Christian resurrection hope' and besides – the Church Militant in full cry, not to be denied his victory – for all Mr Levey knew, the man 'might have been a Moslem . . . or a Mormon'.

It was the old argument in miniature, the 'headstone versus cross' in caricature form, and not for the first time their opponents made the Commissioners' point for them rather better than they did themselves. The intemperance of Dean Ryle perfectly underlined the humanity and inclusiveness of the Commission's stand and for anyone who could see beyond the trappings and accidents of ceremony, the burial of the Unknown Warrior advertised the debt that Britain and her

Empire owed to the work of the Imperial War Graves Commission as nothing else could.

A war that had started with *The Times* printing casualty lists of officers only had ended with a nameless, rank-less, classless soldier enshrined 'among Kings' in the 'Empire's parish church', and for that Ware and his fellow Commissioners were largely to thank. And if Lutyens suspected sabotage Ware was astute enough to see the greater victory. Twenty-two years later, in the middle of a total war that claimed civilian and service casualties indiscriminately, he would write to another Dean of Westminster, proposing a new roll of honour for the Abbey. 'The symbolic significance,' he told the Dean, of 'the admission of these civilian dead to the adjacency and companionship with the Unknown Soldier . . . would give a right inspiration'.

'Adjacency' and 'companionship' – these are not words anyone would use of France's Unknown Warrior, exhumed from one of the nine battlefields that had taken the lives of 1,398,000 Frenchmen and buried in lonely pomp beneath the Arc de Triomphe on the same Armistice Day as Britain's – but they are right. There had been something touchingly 'domestic' about the Abbey service for the Unknown Warrior – it was essentially a 'family affair' of Empire – and from behind their simple protective walls the Commission's cemeteries exert the same emotional 'tug' of the familiar and the communal. The Unknown Warrior 'belonged', in different ways, to every person who filed past his open grave but he also 'belonged' to the country.

The same is true of every gravestone that the Commission raised. Anyone who wants to know what the Great War *did* to people, what politicians, generals and nations could consciously and deliberately do to their own people, should go to Verdun, and peer through the grime-smeared portholes of Douaumont's monstrous ossuary at the millions of fragments of shattered bones and skulls: anyone, though, who wants to know who those people *were* need only go to a British cemetery. Each headstone preserves an individuality – the 'E. W. T', the 'W. J. C', the 'A. G. V' whose memory and uniqueness Blunden yearned to rescue from the obliterating anonymity of death – but each makes a claim and recognises a debt. 'He' is the E. W. Tice who went to Christ's Hospital with Blunden, and he is also an officer in the Royal Sussex Regiment. 'He' is the Wilfred Haeffner commemorated by his family – German-speaking intellectuals, models for E. M. Forster's Schlegels, pilloried during the war for their German ancestry – in the stained glass of Hampstead's parish church but he is also Lieutenant F. W. Haeffner of the Royal Artillery, killed on the seventh day of the Somme and buried in Cerisy-Gailly Military Cemetery in France.

The 'individual' and the 'collective' – the great battleground of Ware's life, the battleground around which swirled all the arguments and the bitterness of the Commission's early years – nowhere do their rival claims come closer to being reconciled than in the grave of the Unknown Warrior. He is not the refutation of the Commission's work but the fine point and justification of it. Between Ware's Mobile Ambulance Unit and the Armistice Day service of 1920 there is as direct and unbroken a line of connection as there is between the unknown soldier of the Black Watch in the little garden near Armentières and the tomb in Westminster Abbey. He is what Ware spent his whole life fighting for.

There must have been another life – a cottage in the country, a wife, two children, the Council for the Preservation of Rural England, Gloucestershire Rural Community Council – but his wife's rather puzzled response to a request for information after his death says it all: his life was, she said, his work. Before the war he had written that for Milner work was his 'mistress' – not, as it turned out, the whole truth – but for Ware it was. It, the work of the Commission, the Canadian Prime Minister said, was all thanks to him and he was right. His methods were not always over-scrupulous, but the world needs its St Bernard as well as its St Francis. He did not achieve all he set out to do but that is no more than saying that he was a man of his time. The apostle of Empire would have hated to see a separate Canadian or an Australian Unknown Soldier diluting the imperial significance of the tomb in Westminster Abbey, but the author of *The Worker and His Country* would have seen it coming and found a way of dealing with it. For a fierce idealist and visionary, he was an unusually skilled politician; for a born autocrat, he was a smooth performer in committees; for a natural leader, he was, as he once told the New Zealand High Commissioner, a willing servant to six masters. And for an ardent patriot who had dedicated the greater part of his life to making an immense corner of a foreign field forever England, what compromise or symbolism could be more apposite than that enshrined in the tomb of the Unknown Warrior? A soldier of the Empire, resting in a coffin of English oak among England's Kings and Queens – and the soil in which he is buried? – soil from the battlefields of the Western Front. A corner of Thorney Island shall be forever Flanders.

NOTES

Abbreviations

Baker	H. Baker, *Architecture and Personalities*, London, 1944
Birkenhead	Lord Birkenhead, *Rudyard Kipling*, New York, 1978
Blomfield	R. Blomfield, *Memoirs of an Architect*, London, 1932
Blythe	R. Blythe, *The Age of Illusion*, London, 1963
CWGC	Commonwealth War Graves Commission Archives
Immortal Heritage	F. Ware, *The Immortal Heritage: An Account of the Work and Policy of the Imperial War Graves Commission during Twenty Years, 1917–1937*, London, 1937
Kenyon	F. Kenyon, *War Graves: How the Cemeteries Abroad Will Be Designed*, HMSO, London, 1918
Longworth	P. Longworth, *The Unending Vigil*, London, 1967
Lutyens Letters	ed. C. Percy and J. Ridley, *The Letters of Edwin Lutyens to his Wife Lady Emily*, London, 1985
Milner	Bodleian Library, Milner Papers
Stamp	G. Stamp, *The Memorial to the Missing of the Somme*, London, 2007

Wilson   K. M. Wilson, *A Study in the History and Politics of the Morning Post 1905–1926*, Lampeter, 1990

The Worker F. Ware, *The Worker and His Country*, London, 1912

Prologue

Ioannes Acutus . . . F. Saunders, *Hawkwood, Diabolical Englishman*, London, 2005, p. xvii

holy, haunted ground . . . Lord Byron, *Childe Harold Canto II*, London, 1812

Would it have been . . . D. A. Reid, *Memoirs of the Crimean War*, London, 1911, p. 161

Imagine them moving . . . *Immortal Heritage*, p. 27

corner of a foreign field . . . R. Brooke, *The Collected Poems of Rupert Brooke*, London, 1918, p. 148

Chapter 1

Now, God be thanked . . . Ibid., p. 144

this Rupert of the pen . . . Violet Markham, *Queen*, 28 May 1921, p. 25

dared question . . . J. R. Brooke, *Westminster Gazette*, 1911, CWGC PO1/1

My academic qualifications . . . Milner, d38 ff.36–7

pity and indignation . . . *Morning Post*, 1 February 1906

As an undergraduate . . . W. Nimocks, *Milner's Young Men: The 'Kindergarten' in Edwardian Imperial Affairs*, London, 1970, quoted, p. 13

For you your job . . . *The Worker*, p. vi

I was working late . . . Milner, d38 ff.149–50

It is magnificent . . . W. Beveridge, *Power and Influence*, London, 1953, quoted, p. 40

I told him of course . . . Ibid., p. 33

erratic but brilliant . . . J. R. Brooke, *Westminster Gazette*, 1911, CWGC PO1/1

At the time of . . . Ibid., quoted, p. 15

awake and 'miserable' . . . Ibid., quoted, p. 13

has been wanting . . . Ibid., quoted, p. 15

party hack . . . Ibid., quoted, p. 28

I am to take the views . . . Ibid., quoted, p. 20

The existence of . . . *The Worker*, pp. vii, 14–15, 276

highest attainment . . . Ibid., p. 25

third-class carriages . . . C. Carrington, *Rudyard Kipling: His Life and Work*, London 1955, quoted, p. 326

ready to perform . . . F. Ware, *Educational Foundations of Trade and Industry*, London, 1901, pp. 57–148

So long as . . . *The Worker*, p. 276

Chapter 2

The Royal Automobile Club . . . P. Longworth, *Unpublished First Draft of 'The Unending Vigil'*, CWGC

no objection . . . Ibid.

The Mobile Unit was organised . . . CWGC MU1, *Spring Report 1915*

October 29th . . . CWGC MU1, *November Report 1914*

To be fair to them . . . CWGC MU1, 26 February 1915

The strong and able . . . Ibid.

It is good work . . . Milner, d349 ff.332–33

from 'all the muddle . . . CWGC MU1, 21 December 1914

The British Red Cross . . . CWGC MU1, 21 February 1915

I shall never forget . . . L. Earle, *Turn Over the Page*, London, 1935, p. 102

when one day . . . Ibid., p. 104

The experience gained . . . CWGC MU1, *Spring Report 1915*

It was while . . . visiting . . . Ibid.

I may add . . . CWGC MU1, 6 December 1914

Another and very ingenious . . . Ibid.

the proud satisfaction . . . Ibid.

I feel sure . . . CWGC MU1, 6 December 1914

With very few exceptions . . . CWGC MU3, 10 May 1915

I was endeavouring . . . CWGC MU1, 6 December 1914

our soldiers in the shell . . . CWGC WG1298, 25 May 1916

We had one poor fellow killed . . . I. Mackay, *Tell Them of Us*, privately printed letters, 26 February 1915, ed. D. Mackay, 1994

Dear Miss F. Robertson . . . J. Robertson, *The Hair Trunk*, unpublished manuscript, p. 200

words of rough regret . . . CWGC WG548, undated press cutting

It is fully recognised . . . Longworth, quoted, p. 7

a lot of trouble over . . . CWGC SDC22, 25 September 1916

Into the old-fashioned . . . CWGC WG789, undated press cutting

At the beginning . . . CWGC SDC22, 28 September 1916

There is not, of course . . . CWGC Add4/1/3, 12 March 1915

It would be a matter . . . CWGC GRC2, 11 March 1915

neither cares nor understands . . . Milner, d350 ff.103–07

By means of this . . . CWGC GRC1, 21 August 1915

I saw the AG . . . CWGC GRC1, 31 August 1915

I am sorry . . . CWGC GRC1, 28 October 1915

to the crokers . . . I. Mackay, *Tell Them of Us*, privately printed letters, 1 October 1914, ed. D. Mackay, 1994

Chapter 3

the sole *intermediary* . . . Longworth, quoted, p. 39

The dug-outs . . . V. Brittain, *Testament of Youth*, London, 2004, p. 174

I told you . . . Milner, d350 ff.103–07

I have warned the Press . . . CWGC WG1076, 2 July 1915

In all ages . . . Ibid., *Report of the French Commission of Public Health*, Summer 1915

As regards the question . . . CWGC Add4/1/3, 27 February 1915

The noise is just like . . . Viscount Gladstone, *W. G. C. Gladstone: A Memoir*, London, 1918, quoted, p. 113

Heaven knows . . . Ibid., quoted, p. 107

We have been . . . Ibid., quoted, p. 116

I thoroughly enjoyed it . . . Ibid.

This unfinished letter . . . Ibid.

He had been warned . . . Ibid., p. 122

It was the earnest wish . . . Ibid., p. 124

I notice Gladstone's body . . . CWGC GRC1, 16 April 1915

CONFIDENTIAL . . . CWGC GRC1, 5 May 1915

detestable . . . *alien* . . . Viscount Gladstone, *W. G. C. Gladstone*, London, 1918, p. 100

Here the Germans . . . *Immortal Heritage*, quoted, pp. 20–21

I believe that you . . . CWGC GRC1, 17 July 1915

Chapter 4

Collectivist, individualist . . . *The Worker*, p. 24

To Fabian Ware . . . Violet Markham, *Queen*, 28 May 1921, p. 24

keenness of all . . . CWGC MU1, undated report of Colonel Stewart

Vitalisers are few . . . Violet Markham, *Queen*, 28 May 1921, p. 24

With such examples . . . CWGC SDC22, 7 March 1917

He had heard rumours . . . Ibid., 25 September 1916

class-bound and incompetent . . . D. Stevenson, *1914–18: The History of the First World War*, London, 2005, p. 117

I am sending you . . . CWGC WG1298, 7 July 1916

The French government . . . General Routine Orders 1104, December 1915

At the time of burial . . . CWGC GRC7, 17 April 1916

In special cases . . . Ibid.

On no account . . . CWGC Add3/1/3, 1 February 1918

We were not aware . . . J. C. Smuts, *Jan Christian Smuts*, London, 1952, p. 195

In April, 1916 . . . L. Earle, *Turn Over the Page*, London, 1935, p. 113

South Africa . . . CWGC Add3/1/3, 25 February 1919

[footnote] *It was all Australia* . . . R. Kipling, *The Five Nations*, London, 1903, p. 191

Beyond the area . . . E. Blunden, *Undertones of War*, London, 1936, p. 131

Crossing the Ancre again . . . Ibid.

the measurements and description . . . CWGC Add3/1/3, 30 June 1917

We are on the verge . . . CWGC SDC4, 29 June 1917

I am held up on my work . . . Longworth, quoted, p. 18

[footnote] *My Dear Ware* . . . CWGC SDC4, 13 December 1916

The field of Gommecourt . . . R. Holmes, *Tommy*, London, 2004, quoted, p. 46

Chapter 5

the great expansion . . . F. Ware, *General Report for the period 21ˢᵗ May 1917, to 31ˢᵗ March 1920*, II, HMSO, 1920, p. 5

It was vital . . . CWGC SDC22, 15 March 1917

old bait . . . Longworth, quoted, p. 27

In looking forward . . . CWGC SDC22, 15 March 1917

the first organisation . . . Longworth, p. 28

to keep alive . . . Ibid., quoted, p. 28

the freedom of the individual . . . H. Strachan, *The First World War*, London, 2005, quoted, p. 237

Democracy is not going . . . A. M. Gollin, *Proconsul in Politics*, New York, 1964, quoted, p. 238

When I visited . . . A. W. Hill, *Our Soldiers' Graves*, Lecture to Royal Horticultural Society, CWGC Add3/1/3, 25 February 1919

The Commission recognised . . . CWGC SDC51, 19 November 1918

There is in art . . . Stamp, quoted, p. 60

For its character . . . R. Byron, *Country Life*, January 1931

Schooled under Rhodes . . . C. Hussey, *The Life of Sir Edwin Lutyens*, London, 1950, p. 322

I realised . . . Baker, p. 88

The cemeteries, the dotted graves . . . Lutyens Letters, p. 350

I most earnestly advise . . . Stamp, quoted, p. 78

I have not had the courage . . . CWGC Add1/1/3, 3 August 1917

The first person I saw . . . Lutyens Letters, p. 357

I bearded the Archbishop . . . CWGC Add1/1/3, 7 August 1917

There must be nothing . . . Ibid., 28 August 1917

The most beautiful . . . Lutyens Letters, p. 354

Such a rush . . . Ibid., p. 351

Afterwards went and saw . . . Ibid., p. 355

Lytton said . . . CWGC Add1/1/3, 20 August 1917

I see a bell-fry . . . Ibid., 25 July 1917

Professional jealousy . . . Lutyens Letters, quoted, p. 369

You are a werry nice man . . . Ibid., p. 348

The Commission recognised . . . Kenyon, p. 2

Chapter 6

He is an interesting . . . CWGC WG517, *Chicago Tribune*, 25 January 1920

The cemeteries, carefully . . . Blomfield, p. 178

in the squalid surrounding . . . Kenyon, p. 3

I have also had . . . Ibid.

It was felt that . . . Ibid., p. 6

It is necessary . . . Ibid.

My endeavour . . . Ibid., p. 4

be marked . . . Ibid., p. 7

There is some . . . Ibid., p. 9

It would meet . . . Ibid., p. 10

That the principle . . . F. Ware, *General Report for the period 21st May 1917, to 31st March 1920, II*, HMSO, 1920, p. 6

green coverlets . . . *Immortal Heritage*, p. 10

The beauty, the serenity . . . Ibid.

Those gruesome rags . . . V. Brittain, *Testament of Youth*, London, 2004, p. 225

We see men go on . . . E. Remarque, *All Quiet on the Western Front*, trans. B. Murdoch, London, 1996, p. 46

three rather gamy Germans . . . I. Mackay, *Tell Them of Us*, privately printed letters, 20 March 1915, ed. D. Mackay, 1994

Kiss me . . . R. Holmes, *Tommy*, London, 2004, quoted, p. 569

Covered with snow . . . E. C. Vaughan, *Some Desperate Glory*, London, 1917, p. 73

Chapter 7

I have not considered . . . Kenyon, p. 21

of specifications . . . Longworth, quoted, p. 38

The resting places . . . CWGC WG237/1, Kipling Advertisement

The cemeteries were often . . . Blomfield, p. 176

The total number . . . F. Ware, *General Report for the period 21ˢᵗ May 1917, to 31ˢᵗ March 1920, II*, HMSO, 1920, p. 9

Exhumation was a routine . . . J. Summers, *Remembered: The History of the Commonwealth War Graves Commission*, London, 2007, quoted, p. 30

committee of architects . . . Kenyon, p. 21

The Principal Architects . . . Blomfield, p. 177

unspeakable tyranny . . . *The Times*, 3 May 1919

the most heartless . . . Ibid., various, 1919–1920

I know how English people dislike . . . CWGC WG219 pt 1, 8 July 1919

Nothing could put . . . *Spectator*, 1 February 1919

The last thing . . . Ibid.

when they left us . . . Ibid.

Your Royal Highness . . . CWGC Add4/2/7, *Petition to the Prince of Wales*, 1919

Lost three sons . . . Ibid.

[footnote] CWGC SDC30 various, September 1919

When the widows . . . W. Burdett-Coutts, *War Graves – Statement of Reasons in Support of the Proposal of the Imperial War Graves Commission*, London, 1920, p. 4

As I see the position now . . . CWGC WG999, 16 April 1920

as one who is strongly . . . W. Burdett-Coutts, *War Graves*, p. 2

An attack on . . . CWGC WG999, 15 April 1920

I understand that you . . . Ibid.

The Imperial War Graves Commission . . . W. Burdett-Coutts, *War Graves*, p. 10

No one could be . . . *Hansard*, 4 May 1920 [and subsequent quotations passim]

Chapter 8

The Commission itself . . . Longworth, p. 59
Life in that wilderness . . . Ibid., p. 63
It is the simplest . . . *The Times*, 2 September 1920
In France and Belgium . . . Stamp, quoted, p. 99
I, for one . . . Hansard
It is impossible . . . Ibid.
It will certainly . . . Ibid.
My own feeling . . . CWGC WG219 pt 1, 18 February 1919
Sir, my son . . . Ibid., 18 December 1919
In my recollection . . . Ibid., 4 March 1919
I may tell you . . . Ibid., 8 July 1919
Pernicious little bitch . . . Birkenhead, quoted, p. 271
Allah, for his own purposes . . . Ibid., quoted, p. 290
He was a man . . . Ibid., quoted, p. 288
One mustn't let . . . J. Flanders, *A Circle of Sisters*, London, 2001, quoted, p. 319
He looks very straight . . . Birkenhead, quoted, p. 267
Two of my men . . . Ibid.
After nearly two years' . . . CWGC WG999, 16 July 1920
There should be a granite . . . CWGC WG237/2, 18 February 1919
fragments of destroyed . . . CWGC WG237/2, 24 January 1919
The policy of the Commission . . . CWGC WG219 pt 2, 12 January 1921
During the past week . . . CWGC 219/4, 19 January 1921
Clearly . . . some compromise . . . Longworth, p. 85

Chapter 9

The design of such . . . Kenyon, p. 7
the dignity of the . . . Cabinet Papers 123, 14 November 1919

only a very few . . . CWGC WG1617 *NBMC Report*, 24 February 1921

agreed to abandon . . . H. F. Chettle, 'British Monuments on the Scenes of the Great War', *Dalhousie Review*, January 1935, p. 448

The [Naval Memorials] Committee . . . National Archives Adm116/1160

fills me with dismay . . . CWGC WG1617, 20 July 1921

great scheme of decoration . . . Longworth, quoted, p. 98

unfortunately did not understand . . . Ibid., p. 15

May I suggest something . . . CWGC WG1031, 15 March 1920

because my child . . . J. Winter, *Sites of Memory, Sites of Mourning*, Cambridge, 1996, quoted, p. 25

the temporary structure . . . Stamp, p. 42

In the autumn of 1919 . . . Blomfield, p. 186

I was in fact . . . Ibid.

I tried hard . . . Ibid., p. 188

had to find . . . Ibid., p. 187

Having regard to . . . CWGC WG1687/2, 22 November 1921

It is a memorial . . . Stamp, quoted, p. 105

For instance . . . CWGC WG219 pt 2, 10 February 1923

One only has to glance . . . Stamp, quoted, p. 123

Its high arch screams . . . Ibid., quoted, p. 184

Many preferred to look . . . Ibid., p. 158

I wanted a massive lion . . . Blomfield, p. 189

Let us pass on to . . . CWGC Add1/1/21 F, Ware Script for Armistice Broadcast, 10 November 1929

From the great wall . . . Baker, quoted, p. 92

It was laid out . . . Ibid., p. 91

[The King] expressed . . . Ibid.

It consists of . . . Ibid.

Oaks were planted . . . Ibid., p. 90

The unveiling ceremony . . . Ibid.
Teutonic spirit . . . Stamp, p. 98
What I wanted . . . Blomfield, p. 179
at eighteen . . . Birkenhead, quoted, p. 291
His loss . . . Ibid., p. 261

Chapter 10

Each stage reproduces . . . *The Worker*, p. 32
Do you think . . . CWGC WG250/1/1 pt 2, 5 February 1931
I have just returned . . . Ibid.
might ultimately be allowed . . . Longworth, quoted, p. 138
For Ware . . . CWGC Add1/1/21, Leo Amery, Memorial Service
    Address 1949
and falter in his faith . . . CWGC Add1/1/141, 10 November 1926
Can we possibly . . . Ibid., 24 April 1933
On former Novembers . . . Ibid., 10 November 1929
In the course of my pilgrimage . . . Longworth, quoted, p. 80
regenerative power of sacrifice . . . E. T. Linenthal, *Sacred Ground:*
    Americans and their Battlefields, Chicago, 1991, p. 97
Cold must be the heart . . . Ibid., quoted, p. 95
I am here to speak to you . . . CWGC Add1/1/21, 10 November 1930
The one real . . . Ibid.
Yes, here is heard . . . CWGC Add1/1/141, 10 November 1927
tired of this gush . . . E. T. Linenthal, *Sacred Ground: Americans and*
    Their Battlefields, Chicago, 1991, quoted, p. 97
It was like trying . . . Longworth, p. 159
one day 'of any holiness' . . . K. S. Inglis, J. Brazier, *Sacred*
    Places: War Memorials in the Australian Landscape, Melbourne,
    1998, quoted, p. 4
[footnote] *If they had any shame* . . . Ibid., quoted, p. 268

He was called Legion . . . *Immortal Heritage*, p. 20

At the head of the grave . . . Blythe, quoted, p. 13

I attended a large . . . B. Janes, *The Unknown Warrior and the Cavell Van*, Tenterden, nd, quoted, p. 19

'11.17' reads the ship's log . . . National Archives Adm53/869766

The train thundered through the dark . . . B. Janes, *The Unknown Warrior and the Cavell Van*, Tenterden, nd, quoted, p. 24

Admirals Meux . . . Blythe, p. 10

The reckless destruction . . . Ibid.

some horror in Church circles . . . Stamp, p. 42

Very Rev. Sir . . . Blythe, quoted, p. 12

On a gravestone . . . Ibid.

The symbolic significance . . . Longworth, quoted, p. 174

SELECT BIBLIOGRAPHY

Archives

The main source for this book is the archive of the Commonwealth War Graves Commission (CWGC) at Maidenhead. The other major archives used are the National Archives at Kew, and the Milner Papers in the Bodleian Library, Oxford

Primary and Secondary Sources

Aslet, C., *War Memorial: The Story of One Village's Sacrifice from 1914 to 2003*, London, 2012

Baker, H., *Architecture and Personalities*, London, 1944

Beveridge, Lord, *Power and Influence*, London, 1953

Birkenhead, Lord, *Rudyard Kipling*, New York, 1978

Blomfield, R., *Memoirs of an Architect*, London, 1932

Blunden, E., *Undertones of War*, London, 1928

Blythe, R., *The Age of Illusion*, London, 1963

Brittain, V., *Testament of Youth*, London, 1933

Carrington, C., *Rudyard Kipling: His Life and Work*, London, 1955

Earle, L., *Turn Over the Page*, London, 1935

Fussell, P., *The Great War and Modern Memory*, Oxford, 1975

Garfield, J., *The Fallen*, Stroud, 2008

Gibson, E., and Ward, J. K., *Courage Remembered: The Story Behind the Construction and Maintenance of the Commonwealth's Military Cemeteries and Memorials of the Wars of 1914–1918 and 1939–1945*, London, 1989

Gladstone, Viscount, *W. G. C. Gladstone: A Memoir*, London, 1918

Gollin, A. M., *Proconsul in Politics: A Study of Lord Milner in Opposition and in Power*, London, 1964

Holmes, R., *Tommy: The British Soldier on the Western Front 1914–1918*, London, 2004

———*Shots from the Front: The British Soldier 1914–1918*, London, 2008

Hurst, S., *The Silent Cities*, London, 1929

Hussey, C., *The Life of Sir Edwin Lutyens*, London, 1950

Inglis, K. S., and Brazier, J., *Sacred Places: War Memorials in the Australian Landscape*, Melbourne, 1998

Janes, B., *The Unknown Warrior and the Cavell Van*, Tenterden, no date

Karol, E., *Charles Holden Architect 1875–1960*, Donington, 2007

Kenyon, F., *War Graves: How the Cemeteries Abroad Will Be Designed*, HMSO, London, 1918

Linenthal, E. T., *Sacred Ground: Americans and Their Battlefields*, Chicago, 1991

Longworth, P., *The Unending Vigil*, London, 1967

Macready, N., *Annals of an Active Life*, London, 1924

Masefield, J., *The Old Front Line*, London, 1917

Nimocks, W., *Milner's Young Men: The 'Kindergarten' in Edwardian Imperial Affairs*, London, 1970

Percy, C., and Ridley, J., eds., *The Letters of Edwin Lutyens to his Wife Lady Emily*, London, 1985

Quinlan, M., *British War Memorials*, Hertford, 2005.

Remarque, E. M., *All Quiet on the Western Front*, translated by B. Murdoch, London, 1996

Sassoon, S., *The Complete Memoirs of George Sherston*, London, 1937

Stamp, G., *The Memorial to the Missing of the Somme*, London, 2007

Stevenson, D., *1914–1918: The History of the First World War*, London, 2004

———*With Our Backs to the Wall: Victory and Defeat in 1918*, London, 2011

Strachan, H., *The First World War*, London, 2003

Summers, J., *Remembered: The History of the Commonwealth War Graves Commission*, London, 2007

Vaughan, E., *Some Desperate Glory*, London, 1917

Ware, F., *Educational Reform*, London, 1900

———*Educational Foundations of Trade and Industry*, London, 1901

———*The Worker and His Country*, London, 1912

———*The Immortal Heritage: An Account of the Work and Policy of the Imperial War Graves Commission during Twenty Years, 1917–1937*, London, 1937

Wilson, K. M., *A Study in the History and Politics of the Morning Post 1905–1926*, Lampeter, 1990

Winter, D., *Death's Men*, London, 1978

Winter, J., *Sites of Memory, Sites of Mourning: The Great War in European Cultural History*, Cambridge, 1996

ACKNOWLEDGEMENTS

There is an immense and growing literature on every aspect of the First World War and a very distinguished one on the subject of commemoration and remembrance addressed here. The first debt of anyone writing about the Imperial War Graves Commission will always be to its original historian Philip Longworth, but I hope that the most cursory glance at the bibliography and endnotes of this book will show how much it owes to the writers who have shaped the way we see our military cemeteries and memorials. Nobody, for instance, should visit Lutyens's great memorial at Thiepval without taking along Gavin Stamp's brilliant *The Memorial to the Missing of the Somme*.

I would like to thank all those friends and family who were prepared to talk about this book, read it in manuscript, provide photographs and visit the cemeteries with me, and in particular the Schröck family for their kindness and hospitality while I was looking at German war graves in Pforzheim. My thanks, too, to the Canadian volunteers at Vimy Ridge and the Newfoundland Memorial and Park at Beaumont-Hamel, who could not have been more helpful, and to Susanna Kerr for allowing me to quote from unpublished family material. I am grateful to everyone at William Collins who has worked on this book, but especially to

Arabella Pike and Essie Cousins who suggested it in the first place, and to Kate Tolley. I have been greatly helped by the sympathetic and perceptive editing of Kate Johnson. My thanks, also, to Derek Johns.

Above all, this book would not have been possible without the kindness, patience and expertise of Roy Hemington at the Commonwealth War Graves Commission at Maidenhead. The Commission holds a vast archive covering the foundation and history of the Imperial War Graves Commission, and I could not even have begun to negotiate it without his help in answering my endless questions. I am very grateful to him and to the Commission for allowing me unstinted access to their archive, and to Peter Francis for his generous help in the latter stages of the book. I would also like to thank the Warden and Scholars of New College, Oxford, for kind permission to quote from the papers of Viscount Milner. This book, as always, is for Honor.

INDEX